The Chronicle of Marcellinus

Byzantina Australiensia

VOLUME 7

The titles published in this series are listed at *brill.com/byza*

The Chronicle of Marcellinus

A Translation with Commentary by

Brian Croke

BRILL

LEIDEN | BOSTON

This paperback was originally published as Volume 7 in the series *Byzantina Australiensia*, Australian Association for Byzantine Studies, Department of Modern Greek, University of Sydney.

Cover illustration: Fol 98v of Cod. Laur. Plut. IX.28, containing the Christian Topography of Cosmas Indicopleustes, is reproduced on the cover with the kind permission of the Biblioteca Laurenziana, Florence.

Library of Congress Control Number: 2017939650

ISSN 0725-3079
ISBN 978-09-59-36266-4 (paperback reprint, 2017)
ISBN 978-90-04-34463-1 (e-book, 2017)
ISBN 0 9593626 6 5 (paperback, 1995)

This book is printed on acid-free paper and produced in a sustainable manner.

Printed by Printforce, the Netherlands

Εἰ δὲ καὶ περὶ τῶν ἀντιπόδων ἐπεξεργαστικώτερον θελήσειέ τις ζητῆσαι, ῥᾳδίως τοὺς γραώδεις μύθους αὐτῶν ἀνακαλύψει.

Cosmas Indicopleustes, I,20.

∴

CONTENTS

PREFACE

The chronicle of Marcellinus, written in Constantinople, covers the period from 378 to 534 and there is an anonymous continuation of it which cuts out at the year 548. It constitutes an important contemporary source for the reigns of the emperors Anastasius (491–518) and Justin (518–527), as well as for the early years of Justinian (527–565). Marcellinus' work is encountered by a range of modern scholars: ancient, medieval and Byzantine political, cultural, social and economic historians, art historians, numismatists and ecclesiastical historians, as well as students of historiography. In order to facilitate understanding of any such chronicle by both the occasional and regular user a translation, preferably with some sort of annotation or commentary, is always helpful. The recent upsurge of scholarly interest and involvement in late antiquity and Byzantium throughout the English-speaking world has made the need for English translations of early Byzantine chronicles such as that of Marcellinus even more imperative. Hence the present volume.

Although intended primarily for English-speaking readers it is hoped that this translation (the first into any language) will not be entirely redundant for others. As for the commentary, it is not designed to be exhaustive but rather to be illuminating and practical. It is therefore selective and focussed on work in English except where other research is more fundamental, important or up-to-date. It attempts to explicate the information contained in the chronicle and assess both its place in the chronicler's perspective and its usefulness as historical testimony. Attention is concentrated on interpretative and chronological peculiarities in Marcellinus' work, by correcting errors or misleading information, by discussing controversial entries and by identifying the source of a particular notice. More detailed commentary is confined to places where Marcellinus' information is more crucial, controversial or complex. Yet the commentary attempts to do all this in the context of seeing the chronicle as an historiographical product of sixth-century Constantinopolitan culture, and written for a contemporary audience within a specific social, political and cultural milieu.

Finally, the text itself has been reprinted from the unsurpassed edition of Theodor Mommsen (1894), although it is now a century old. It was originally intended to provide a fresh edition of the chronicle; however, it soon became apparent that this would not be productive use of scarce research time, not least because it would be difficult to improve on Mommsen's edition. Still, a small number of new readings are proposed here. Not only was Mommsen a sound editor, but in the case of Marcellinus he had the special advantage of a manuscript (now in Oxford) written within a generation or two of the original (not that its readings are always superior). Moreover, he had himself consulted the Oxford manuscript at first hand and was not obliged to rely solely on the work of others, as he did for so many of the late Roman chronicle manuscripts; nor did he feel the need to take liberties with the chronology of the text, as he did with that of some other chronicles. Finally, the manuscripts of Marcellinus' chronicle which have come to light since Mommsen's time are late in the tradition and contribute nothing new to the reconstruction of the text. So it seemed prudent to follow the example of C.W. Jones who once set about a new edition of Bede's chronicle only to end up virtually reprinting Mommsen's edition.

Nonetheless, the problem with the presentation of annalistic chronicles in modern editions, including Mommsen's, is that the necessary apparatus of numbering and dates frequently misleads. More significantly one loses sight of what such a chronicle originally looked like with eponymous dates and multiple entries for each year; that is to say, one tends to forget the difficulties of composing such chronicles, as well as copying and comparing them over the centuries. Accordingly, in reproducing Mommsen's text here an attempt has been made to dispense with the modern dating accretions (confining them to the translation where they are of course necessary) and to present the chronicle in a format more closely reflecting the original manuscript. Anyone seeking closer study of the text itself must revert, however, to Mommsen's edition. Fuller analysis of the chronicle in its contemporary and historiographical context will be found in my forthcoming book *Count Marcellinus and his Byzantine Chronicle* (Oxford University Press).

A mutual commitment to produce and publish this book was given during a languid luncheon interlude in the course of translating the chronicle of John Malalas in the mid-1980s. It was scheduled to be available much earlier than now. That it appears at all is due to the patient cajoling and constant assistance (on matters both scholarly and practical) of Elizabeth Jeffreys, to whom I am greatly indebted. In addition, I have benefited from the helpful comments and corrections of Michael Whitby, Alanna Nobbs and Pauline Allen.

Sydney Brian Croke

ABBREVIATIONS

AASS	*Acta Sanctorum*, 71 vols. (Paris, 1863–1940)
ACO	*Acta Conciliorum Oecumenicarum* (ed. E. Schwartz, Berlin–Leipzig, 1922–84)
Add. Prosp. Haun.	*Additamenta Prosperi Hauniensis* (ed. Th. Mommsen, MGH AA IX), cited by section and page number
Adler, 1928/38	A. Adler, ed., *Suidae Lexicon*, 5 vols. (Leipzig)
Adler, 1989	W. Adler, *Time Immemorial. Archaic History and its Sources in Christian Chronography from Julius Africanus to George Syncellus* (Washington)
Agn.	Agnellus, *Liber pontificalis ecclesiae Ravennatis* (cited from Th. Mommsen, MGH AA IX by page number)
Allen, 1979	P. Allen, The 'Justinianic' Plague, *Byzantion* 49, 5–20
Allen, 1981	——, *Evagrius Scholasticus the Church Historian* (Leuven)
Amb., *de ob. Theod.*	Ambrose, *de obitu Theodosii* (ed. O. Faller, Paris, 1955)
Amm.	Ammianus Marcellinus, *Res Gestae* (ed. W. Seyfarth, Leipzig, 1978)
Ann. Rav.	*Annales Ravennatenses*, cited by page number from *Medieval Studies in Memory of A. Kingsley Porter*, vol. 1 (1939), 125–38
Anon. Val.	*Anonymus Valesianus* (ed. Th. Mommsen, MGH AA IX), cited by section and page number
Auct. Haun. ord. pr.	*Auctarium Hauniense. Ordo prior* (ed. Th. Mommsen, MGH AA IX), cited by section and page number
Auct. Haun. ord. post.	*Auctarium Hauniense. Ordo posterior* (ed. Th. Mommsen, MGH AA IX), cited by section and page number
Aug., *civ. Dei*	Augustine, *Civitas Dei* (ed. B. Dombart and A. Kalb, Leipzig, 1928–9)
Bachrach, 1973	B. Bachrach, *A History of the Alans in the West* (Minneapolis)
Bagnall et al., 1987	R. Bagnall, A.D.E. Cameron, S. Schwartz and K. Worp, *Consuls of the Later Roman Empire* (Atlanta)
Barb. Scal.	Barbarus Scaligeri (ed. Th. Mommsen, MGH AA IX), cited by section and page number
Barnes, 1981	T.D. Barnes, *Constantine and Eusebius* (Cambridge, Mass.)
Baumstark, 1922	A. Baumstark, *Geschichte der Syrischen Literatur* (Bonn)
Blackman, 1968	D. Blackman, Der Hafen von Anthedon mit Beiträgen zur Topographie und Geschichte der Stadt, *Archaeologischer Anzeiger* 83, 92

Blake, 1942	R.P. Blake, The Monetary Reform of Anastasius I and its Economic Implications, in *Studies in the History of Culture* (Menasha, Wisc.), 84–97
Blockley, 1983	R. Blockley, *The Fragmentary Classicising Historians of the Later Roman Empire*, vol. 2 (Liverpool)
Blockley, 1987	——, The Division of Armenia between the Romans and the Persians at the end of the fourth century, *Historia* 36, 222–34
Blockley, 1992	——, *East Roman Foreign Policy* (Leeds)
Bouquet, 1738	J. Bouquet, *Recueils des historiens des Gaules et de la France*, vol. 1 (Paris)
Bouquet, 1739	——, *Recueils des historiens des Gaules et de la France*, vol. 2 (Paris)
Brooks, 1893	E.W. Brooks, The Emperor Zenon and the Isaurians, *English Historical Review* 8, 209–38
Brooks, 1911	——, The East Roman Empire from Arcadius to Anastasius, *Cambridge Medieval History* , vol. 1 (Cambridge), 457–486
Burgess, 1988	R. Burgess, Quinquennial Vota and Imperial Consulship 337–511, *Numismatic Chronicle* 148, 77–96 (plates 23–28)
Burgess, 1989	——, Consuls and Consular Dating in the Later Roman Empire, *Phoenix* 43, 143–57
Burgess, 1993	——, *The Chronicle of Hydatius and the Consularia Constantinopolitana* (Oxford)
Burns, 1984	T. Burns, *A History of the Ostrogoths* (Bloomington)
Bury, 1919	Justa Grata Honoria, *JRS* 9, 1–13
Bury, 1923	J.B. Bury, *History of the Later Roman Empire*, vol. 1 (London)
Bury, 1923a	——, *History of the Later Roman Empire*, vol. 2 (London)
Call., *v. Hyp.*	Callinicus, *Vita Hypatii* (ed. C. Bartelink, Paris, 1971; SC)
Cameron, 1970	Alan Cameron, *Claudian. Poetry and Propaganda at the Court of Honorius* (Oxford)
Cameron, 1973	——, *Porphyrius the Charioteer* (Oxford)
Cameron, 1976	——, *Circus Factions* (Oxford)
Cameron, 1982	——, The Empress and the Poet: paganism and politics at the court of Theodosius II, *Yale Classical Studies* 27, 217–89
Cameron, 1982a	——, The Death of Vitalian, *ZPE* 42, 93–4
Cameron, 1985	Averil Cameron, *Procopius and the Sixth Century* (London)
Cameron, 1987	Alan Cameron, Earthquake 400, *Chiron* 17, 343–60
Cameron/Herrin, 1984	Averil Cameron and J. Herrin (eds.), *Constantinople in the Eighth Century* (Leiden)
Cameron/Long, 1993	Alan Cameron and J. Long, *Barbarians and Politics at the Court of Arcadius* (Berkeley–Los Angeles–London)
Cand.	Candidus, ed./trs R. Blockley, 1983, cited by fragment and page number
Capizzi, 1969	C. Capizzi, *L'imperatore Anastasio* (Rome)

Cass., *Var.*	Cassiodorus, *Variae* (ed. Th. Mommsen and L. Traube, MGH AA XII)
Ced.	Cedrenus (ed. I. Bekker, Bonn, 1838–9)
Charanis, 1939	P. Charanis, *Church and State in the Later Roman Empire: The Religious Policy of Anastasius 491–518* (Madison)
Chauvot, 1986	A. Chauvot, *Procope de Gaza, Priscien de Césarée. Panegyriques de l'empereur Anastase 1er* (Bonn)
Chron. ad 846	Chronicon ad AD 846 (trs. J. Chabot in CSCO, Scr. Syr. 3.4, 1903)
Chron. ad 724	Chronicon ad AD 724 (trs. J. Chabot in CSCO, Scr. Syr. 3.4, 1903)
Chron. Alex.	*Eine alexandrische Weltchronik* (ed. A. Bauer and J. Strzygowski, Vienna, 1905)
Chron. Edess.	*Chronicon Edessenum* (ed./trs. I. Guidi in CSCO, Scr. Syr. 3.4, 1903)
Chron. Gall. 452	*Chronica Gallica ad a. 452* (ed. Th. Mommsen, MGH AA IX), cited by section and page number
Chron. Gall. 511	*Chronica Gallica ad a. 511* (ed. Th. Mommsen, MGH AA IX), cited by section and page number
Chron. Pasch.	*Chronicon Paschale* (ed. L. Dindorf, Bonn, 1832), quoted by page and line number
CIG	*Corpus Inscriptionum Graecarum*
CIL	*Corpus Inscriptionum Latinarum*
CJ	*Codex Justinianus*; P. Krüger, ed., *Corpus Iuris Civilis*, vol. 2 (Berlin, 1928; reprinted 1954)
Claud., *In Eutr.*	Claudian, *In Eutropium* (ed. M. Platnauer, London–New York, 1922)
Claud., *In Ruf.*	Claudian, *In Rufinum* (ed. M. Platnauer, London–New York, 1922)
Claud., *Stil.*	Claudian, *De consolatu Stilichonis* (ed. M. Platnauer, London–New York, 1922)
Claud., *IV cons. Hon.*	Claudian, *De quarto consulatu Honorii Augusti* (ed. M. Platnauer, London–New York, 1922)
Clover, 1979	F.M. Clover, Count Gaïnas and Count Sebastian, *American Journal of Ancient History* 4, 65–76
Coll. Avell.	*Collectio Avellana* (ed. O. Günther, Vienna, 1895–8)
Cons. Const.	*Consularia Constantinopolitana* (ed. Th. Mommsen, MGH AA IX), cited by section and page number
Const. Porph., *de caer.*	Constantine Porphyrogenitus, *De Caerimoniis* (ed. J.J. Reiske, Bonn, 1829–30)
Cont.	Continuator of Marcellinus (ed. Th. Mommsen, MGH AA XI), cited by year and entry number
Cor., *Ioh.*	Corippus, *Iohannidos* (ed. J. Diggle and F.R.D. Goodyear, Cambridge, 1970)

cos	consulship
Courcelle, 1954	P. Courcelle, De la 'Regula Magistri' au corpus vivarien des chroniques, *Revue des Etudes Anciennes* 56, 425–8
Courtois, 1955	C. Courtois, *Les Vandales et l'Afrique* (Paris)
CP	Constantinople
CP	*Classical Philology*
Croke/Crow, 1983	B. Croke and J. Crow, Procopius and Dara, *JRS* 73, 143–57 (repr. in Croke, 1992, XI)
Croke, 1976	B. Croke, Arbogast and the Death of Valentinian II, *Historia* 25, 235–44
Croke, 1977	——, Evidence for the Hun Invasion of Thrace in AD 422, *GRBS* 18, 347–67 (repr. in Croke, 1992, XII)
Croke, 1978	——, Hormisdas and the Late Roman Walls of Thessalonika, *GRBS* 19, 251–58 (repr. in Croke, 1992, XV)
Croke, 1978a	——, The Date and Circumstances of Marcian's Decease, *Byzantion* 58, 1–9 (repr. in Croke, 1992, VIII)
Croke, 1980	——, Justinian's Bulgar Victory Celebration, *Byzantinoslavica* 41, 188–95 (repr. in Croke, 1992, XIX)
Croke, 1981	——, Anatolius and Nomus. Envoys to Attila, *Byzantinoslavica* 42, 159–70 (repr. in Croke, 1992, XIII)
Croke, 1981a	——, Thessalonika's Early Byzantine Palaces, *Byzantion* 51, 475–83 (repr. in Croke, 1992, XVI)
Croke, 1981b	——, Two Early Byzantine Earthquakes and their Liturgical Commemoration, *Byzantion* 51, 112–47 (repr. in Croke, 1992, IX)
Croke, 1982	——, Mundo the Gepid. From Freebooter to Roman General, *Chiron* 12, 125–35 (repr. in Croke, 1992, XVIII)
Croke, 1982a	——, The Originality of Eusebius' *Chronicle*, *American Journal of Philology* 103, 195–200 (repr. in Croke, 1992, I)
Croke, 1982b	——, The Date of the 'Anastasian Long Wall' in Thrace, *GRBS* 20, 59–78 (repr. in Croke, 1992, XVII)
Croke, 1982c	——, The Misunderstanding of Cassiodorus *Institutiones* I.17.2, *Classical Quarterly* 32, 225–6
Croke, 1983	——, The Context and Date of Priscus Fragment 6, *CP* 78, 297–308 (repr. in Croke, 1992, XIV)
Croke, 1983a	——, AD 476: The Manufacture of a Turning Point, *Chiron* 13, 81–119 (repr. in Croke, 1992, V)
Croke, 1983b	——, Basiliscus the Boy-Emperor, *GRBS* 24, 81–91 (repr. in Croke, 1992, X)
Croke, 1983c	——, The Origins of the Christian World Chronicle', in *History and Historians in Late Antiquity*, ed. B. Croke and A. M. Emmett (Sydney and Oxford), 116–31 (repr. in Croke, 1992, III)

Croke, 1984 ——, Marcellinus on Dara: A fragment of his lost *de temporum qualitatibus et positionibus locorum*, *Phoenix* 38, 77–88

Croke, 1984a ——, Dating Theodoret's *Church History* and *Commentary on the Psalms*, *Byzantion* 54, 59–74 (repr. in Croke, 1992, VII)

Croke, 1987 ——, Cassiodorus and the *Getica* of Jordanes, *CP* 82, 117–34 (repr. in Croke, 1992, VI)

Croke, 1990 ——, City Chronicles of Late Antiquity, in *Reading the Past in Late Antiquity*, ed. G. Clarke with B. Croke, R. Mortley and A. Emmett Nobbs (Sydney), 165–202 (repr. in Croke, 1992, IV)

Croke, 1992 ——, *Christian Chronicles and Byzantine History, 5th–6th Centuries* (London)

CSCO Corpus Scriptorum Christianorum Orientalium

CTh. *Codex Theodosianus* (ed. Th. Mommsen, Berlin, 1904–5)

de Halleux, 1963 A. de Halleux, *Philoxène de Mabbog: sa vie, ses écrits, sa théologie* (Louvain)

Devreesse, 1945 R. Devreesse, *Le patriarcat d'Antioche depuis la paix de l'église à la conquête arabe* (Paris)

Diehl, 1896 C. Diehl, *L'Afrique byzantine* (Paris)

Downey, 1955 G. Downey, Earthquakes at Constantinople and Vicinity AD 342–1454, *Speculum* 30, 596–600

Downey, 1961 G. Downey, *A History of Antioch in Syria* (Princeton)

Duchesne 1886 L. Duchesne, *Le Liber Pontificalis. Texte, introduction et Commentaire*, vol. 1 (Paris 1886)

Epit. *Epitome de Caesaribus* (ed. F. Pichlmayr and R. Gruendel, Leipzig, 1970)

Eun. Eunapius of Sardis, ed./trs R. Blockley, 1983, cited by fragment and page number

Evag. Evagrius, *Historia Ecclesiastica* (ed. J. Bidez and L. Parmentier, London, 1898)

Exc. Sangall. *Excerpta Sangallensia* (ed. Th. Mommsen, MGH AA IX), cited by section and page number

F. Vind. Pr. *Fasti Vindobonenses Priores* (ed. Th. Mommsen, MGH AA IX), cited by section and page number

FHG *Fragmenta Historicorum Graecorum* (ed. C. Müller, 4 vols., Paris, 1848–51)

Frend, 1972 W.H.C. Frend, *The Rise of the Monophysite Movement* (Cambridge)

GCS *Die Griechische Christliche Schriftsteller*

Genn. Gennadius, *De viris illustribus* (ed. C. Bernoulli, Fribourg, 1895)

Gibbon, 1896	E. Gibbon, *Decline and Fall of the Roman Empire* (ed. J.B. Bury, London)
GRBS	*Greek, Roman and Byzantine Studies*
Greg. Tur.	Gregory of Tours, *Historia Francorum* (ed. W. Arndt and B. Krusch, MGH Scriptores rerum Merovingicarum I)
Grierson, 1962	P. Grierson, The Tombs and Obits of the Byzantine Emperors (337–1042), *Dumbarton Oaks Papers* 16, 1–63
Grumel, 1958	P. Grumel, *La chronologie byzantine* (Paris)
Guilland, 1969	R. Guilland, *Etudes de topographie de Constantinople byzantine* (Amsterdam)
Harvey, 1991	S.A. Harvey, *Asceticism and Society in Crisis* (Berkeley–Los Angeles–London)
Heather, 1991	P. Heather, *Goths and Romans 324–489* (Oxford)
Helm	R. Helm, *Die Chronik des Hieronymus* (Berlin, 1956)
Hodgkin, 1889	T. Hodgkin, *Italy and her Invaders*, vol. 3 (Oxford)
Hohlfelder, 1977	R. Hohlfelder, Trans-Isthmian Walls in the Age of Justinian, *GRBS 18*, 173-9
Holder-Egger, 1877	O. Holder-Egger, Die Chronik des Marcellinus Comes und die oströmischen Fasten, *Neues Archiv* 2, 47–111
Holum, 1977	K. Holum, Pulcheria's Crusade and the Ideology of Imperial Victory, *GRBS* 18, 153–72
Holum, 1982	——, *Theodosian Empresses* (Berkeley–Los Angeles–London)
Honigmann, 1951	E. Honigmann, *Éveques et évêches monophysites d'Asie antérieurs au VIe siècle* (Louvain)
Honoré, 1978	T. Honoré, *Tribonian* (London–Ithaca)
Hunt, 1982	E.D. Hunt, *Holy Land Pilgrimage in the Later Roman Empire* (Oxford)
Hyd.	Hydatius, *Chronica* (ed. Th. Mommsen, MGH AA XI), cited by section and page number
Janin, 1964	R. Janin, *Constantinople Byzantine* (Paris)
Janin, 1966	R. Janin, Les processions religieuses à Byzance, *Revue des Etudes Byzantines* 24, 69–88
Jeffreys, 1990	E.M. Jeffreys, Chronological Structures in the Chronicle, in E.M. Jeffreys, with B. Croke and R. Scott (eds.), *Studies in John Malalas* (Sydney), 111–166
Jerome, *Chron.*	Jerome, *Chronicon* (ed. R. Helm; GCS) cited by page and line number
Jo. Ant.	John of Antioch; fragments in *FHG* 4, 540–622
Jo. Lyd.	John the Lydian, *de magistratibus* (ed. R. Wuensch, Leipzig, 1903)
Jo. Mal.	John Malalas, *Chronicle*, cited by book and paragaph number from E. Jeffreys, M. Jeffreys and R. Scott, *The Chronicle of*

	John Malalas (Melbourne, 1986) and by page and line number from the edition of L. Dindorf (Bonn, 1832)
Jo. Nik.	John of Nikiu; R.J. Charles, trans., *The Chronicle of John, Bishop of Nikiu* (Oxford, 1916)
Johnson, 1991	M. Johnson, On the Burial Places of the Valentinian Dynasty, *Historia* 40, 501–6
Jones, 1964	A.H.M. Jones, *The Later Roman Empire* (Oxford)
Jord., *Rom.*	Jordanes, *Romana* (ed. Th. Mommsen, MGH AA V.1)
Jord., *Get.*	Jordanes, *Getica* (ed. Th. Mommsen, MGH AA V.1)
Josh. Styl.	Joshua the Stylite; W. Wright, trans., *The Chronicle of Joshua the Stylite* (Cambridge, 1882)
JRS	*Journal of Roman Studies*
Kaegi, 1968	W.E. Kaegi, *Byzantium and the Decline of Rome* (Princeton)
Kelly, 1972	J.N.D. Kelly, *Early Christian Creeds* (London)
Kelly, 1975	——, *Jerome* (London)
Kelly, 1986	——, *The Oxford Dictionary of Popes* (Oxford)
Krüger, 1929	P. Krüger, ed., *Corpus Iuris Civilis*, vol. 1 (Berlin, 1929; reprinted 1954)
Lackner, 1970	W. Lackner, Westliche Heilige des 5. und 6. Jahrhunderts in Synaxarium Ecclesiae Constantinopolitanae, *Jahrbuch der Österreichischen Byzantinistik* 19, 182–202
Lacroix, 1965	B. Lacroix, *Orosius et ses idées* (Toronto)
Laistner, 1957	M.L.W. Laistner, *Thought and Letters in Western Europe 500–900* (2nd ed., London)
Lee, 1987	A.D. Lee, Dating a Fifth-Century Persian War in Theodoret, *Byzantion* 57, 187–90
Lib. Pont.	*Liber Pontificalis* (ed. L. Duchesne, 3 vols., Paris, 1886–1957)
Liebeschuetz, 1990	W. Liebeschuetz, *Barbarians and Bishops* (Oxford)
Lippold, 1966	A. Lippold, *Theodosius der Grosse* (Stuttgart)
M.	Marcellinus
Maas, 1992	M. Maas, *John Lydus and the Roman Past* (London)
MacCormack, 1981	S. MacCormack, *Art and Ceremony in Late Antiquity* (Berkeley–Los Angeles–London)
Maenchen-Helfen, 1973	O.J. Maenchen-Helfen, *The World of the Huns* (Berkeley–Los Angeles–London)
Malchus	Malchus of Philadelphia, ed./trs R. Blockley, 1983, cited by fragment and page number
Mango, 1959	C. Mango, *The Brazen House* (Copenhagen)
Mango, 1985	——, *Le développement urbain de Constantinople* (Paris)
Mango, 1993	——, The columns of Justinian and his successors, in *Studies on Constantinople* (London), X: 1–20
Mar. Av.	Marius of Avenches, *Chronica* (ed. Th. Mommsen, MGH AA XI), cited by section and page number

Matthews, 1975	J.F. Matthews, *Western Aristocracies and Imperial Court* (Oxford)
McCormick, 1986	M. McCormick, *Eternal Victory* (Cambridge–Paris)
Melville-Jones, 1991	J.R. Melville-Jones, Nummi Terunciani, *Proceedings of 11th International Numismatic Congress*, vol. 3 (Brussels), 9–13
Metcalf, 1969	D.M. Metcalf, *The Origins of the Anastasian Currency Reform* (Chicago)
MGH AA	*Monumenta Germaniae Historica, Auctores Antiquissimi*
Mich. Syr.	Michael the Syrian, *Chronicle* (ed. J.-B. Chabot)
Mihaescu, 1978	H. Mihaescu, *La langue latine dans le sud-est de l'Europe* (Bucharest–Paris)
Mommsen, 1894	Introduction to edition of Marcellinus (MGH AA XI, 39–59)
Mommsen, 1896/7	Th. Mommsen, Die römischen Bischöfe Liberius und Felix II, *Deutsche Zeitschrift für Geschichtswissenschaft* N.F. 1, 167–79
Mommsen, 1898	——, *Chronica Minora III* (MGH AA XIII)
Moricca, 1943	U. Moricca, *Storia della letteratura latina cristiana*, vol. 3.2 (Turin)
Mosshammer, 1979	A.A. Mosshammer, *The Chronicle of Eusebius and Greek Chronographic Tradition* (Lewisburg–London)
Müller-Wiener, 1977	W. Müller-Wiener, *Bildlexicon zur Topographie Istanbul* (Tübingen)
Nagy, 1967	T. Nagy, Reoccupation of Pannonia from the Huns in 427, *Acta Antiqua* 15, 159–86
Newton, 1972	R. Newton, *Medieval Chronicles and the Rotation of the Earth* (Baltimore)
Nic. Call.	Nicephorus Callistus Xanthopoulos, *Historia Ecclesiastica* (*Patrologia Graeca* 145–7)
Nixon, 1987	C.E.V. Nixon, *Pacatus: panegyric to the emperor Theodosius* (Liverpool)
Nov. Theod.	*Novellae Theodosii* (ed. P. Meyer, Berlin, 1904–5)
Nov. Just.	*Novellae Justiniani*; R. Schöll and W. Kroll, eds., *Corpus Iuris Civilis*, vol. 3 (Berlin, 1928, reprinted 1954)
O'Flynn, 1983	J.M. O'Flynn, *Generalissimos of the Western Roman Empire* (Edmonton)
ODB	*Oxford Dictionary of Byzantium*, 3 vols. (New York 1991)
Olymp.	Olympiodorus, ed./trs R. Blockley,1983, cited by fragment and page number
Oost, 1968	S.I. Oost, *Galla Placidia* (Chicago)
Oros.	Orosius, *Historia contra Paganos* (ed. C. Zangemeister, Leipzig, 1889)
Pac.	Pacatus, *Panegyric on Theodosius* (ed. R.A.B. Mynors, Oxford, 1964)

Pall., *Dial.*	Palladius, *Dialogus* (ed. P.R. Coleman-Norton, Cambridge, 1928)
Paras.	*Parastaseis Syntomoi Chronikai* in Cameron/Herrin, 1984
Pasch. Camp.	Paschale Campanum (ed. Th. Mommsen, MGH AA IX), cited by section and page number
Paschoud, 1979	F. Paschoud, *Zosime. Histoire Nouvelle*, vol. 2 (Paris)
Paul., *v. Amb.*	Paulinus, *vita Ambrosii* (ed. A.A.R. Bastiaensen, Milan, 1981)
Petschenig, 1899	M. Petschenig, Zu spätlateinischen Schriftstellern, *Philologus* 58, 154
Phil.	Philostorgius, *Historia Ecclesiastica* (ed. J. Bidez and F. Winkelmann, Berlin, 1981; GCS)
Pintus, 1984	M. Pintus, Eucherio di Lione nella chronologia di Gennadio e Marcellino, *Studi Medievali* 25, 795–812
PL	*Patrologia Latina*
PLRE 1	*The Prosopography of the Later Roman Empire*, vol. 1 (Cambridge, 1970)
PLRE 2	*The Prosopography of the Later Roman Empire*, vol. 2 (Cambridge, 1980)
PLRE 3	*The Prosopography of the Later Roman Empire*, vol. 3 (Cambridge, 1992)
PO	*Patrologia Orientalis*
Poss., *v. Aug.*	Possidius, *vita Augustini* (ed. A.A.R. Bastiaensen, Milan, 1981)
Preger, 1901	T. Preger, *Scriptores originum constantinopolitanarum* (Leipzig)
Priscus	Priscus of Panion, ed./trs. R. Blockley, 1983, cited by fragment and page number
Proc., *Wars*	Procopius of Caesarea, *Wars* (ed. J. Haury and G. Wirth, Leipzig, 1962–4)
Proc., *Aed.*	Procopius of Caesarea, *De aedificiis* (ed. J. Haury and G. Wirth, Leipzig. 1962–4)
Prosp.	Prosper of Aquitaine, *Chronicon* (ed. Th. Mommsen, MGH AA IX), cited by section and page number
RE	*Paulys Realencyclopädie der classischen Altertumwissenschaft*, new rev. ed., Stuttgart, 1893–
Rebenich, 1991	S. Rebenich, Zum Theodosiusobelisken in Konstantinopel, *Istanbuler Mitteilungen* 41, 447–76
Roueché, 1986	C. Roueché, Theodosius II, the cities and the date of the 'Church History' of Sozomen, *Journal of Theological Studies* 27, 130–2
s.a.	sub anno
SC	Sources Chrétiennes

Schanz/Hosius/Krüger, 1921 M. Schanz, C. Hosius and G. Krüger, *Geschichte der römischen Literatur* (Munich)

Schneider, 1941 A. Schneider, Brände in Konstantinopel, *Byzantinische Zeitschrift* 41, 382–9

Scott, 1981 R.D. Scott, Malalas and Justinian's Codification, in *Byzantine Papers*, ed. E.M. and M.J. Jeffreys and A. Moffatt (Canberra), 12–31

SEC *Synaxarium Ecclesiae Constantinopolitanae* (ed. H. Delehaye, Brussels, 1902)

Seeck, 1919 O. Seeck, *Regesten der Kaiser und Päpste* (Stuttgart)

Seeck, 1920 O. Seeck, *Geschichte des Untergangs der antiken Welt*, vol. 5 (Stuttgart)

Seeck, 1889 O. Seeck, 'cancellarii', *RE* 3

Soc. Socrates, *Historia Ecclesiastica* (ed. R. Hussey and W. Bright, Oxford, 1893)

Soz. Sozomen, *Historia Ecclesiastica* (ed. J. Bidez and G.C. Hansen, Berlin, 1960; GCS)

Stein, 1949 E. Stein, *Histoire du Bas-Empire*, vol. 1 (Paris)

Stein, 1959 E. Stein, *Histoire du Bas-Empire*, vol. 2 (Paris)

Stevenson, 1966 J. Stevenson, *Creeds, Councils and Controversies* (London)

Syme, 1971 R. Syme, *Emperors and Biography* (Oxford)

Symm., *Ep.* Symmachus, *Epistulae* (ed. O. Seeck, MGH AA VI)

Them., *Or.* Themistius, *Orations* (ed. G. Downey and A. Norman, Leipzig, 1965–74)

Theod. Theodoret of Cyrrhus, *Historia Ecclesiastica* (ed. L. Parmentier and F. Scheidweiler, Berlin, 1954; GCS)

Theod. Anag. Theodore Anagnostes, *Historia Ecclesiastica* (ed. G.C. Hansen, Berlin, 1971; GCS), cited by section and page number

Theoph. Theophanes, *Chronographia* (ed. C. De Boor, Leipzig, 1883–5), cited by *annus mundi*, page and line number

Thompson, 1948 E.A. Thompson, *A History of Attila and the Huns* (Oxford)

Tiftixoglu, 1973 V. Tiftixoglu, Die Helenianai nebst einigen anderen Besitzungen im Vorfeld des frühen Konstantinopel, in H.-G. Beck, *Studien zur Frühgeschichte Konstantinopels* (Munich), 49–120

Typ. *Typicon de la grande église* (ed. J. Mateos, 2 vols., Rome, 1962–3), cited by page and line number

Vaccari, 1958 A. Vaccari, Le antichi vite di S. Girolamo: I. La cronica di Marcellino, in *Scritti di erudizione e di filologia* (Rome), 34

van Ommeslaeghe, 1978 F. van Ommeslaeghe, La fête de S. Jean Chrysostome, *Analecta Bollandiana* 96, 338

Vasiliev, 1950 A. Vasiliev, *Justin the First* (Washington D.C.)

Vickers, 1973 M. Vickers, Observations on the Octagon at Thessaloniki, *JRS* 63, 111–20

Vict. Tonn.	Victor Tonnennensis, *Chronica* (ed. Th. Mommsen, MGH AA XI), cited by section and page number
v. Mel. Iun.	*Vita Melaniae Junioris* (ed. D. Gorce, Paris, 1962; SC)
v. Dan. Styl.	*Vita Danielis Stylites* (ed. H. Delehaye, Brussels–Paris, 1923)
v. Marcell.	*Vita Marcelli* (ed. G. Dagron, Louvain, 1968)
v. Sab.	Cyril of Scythopolis, *Vita Sabas* (ed. E. Schwartz, Leipzig, 1939)
Wattenbach/Levison, 1951	W. Wattenbach and C. Levison, *Deutschlands Geschichtsquellen im Mittelalter*, vol.1 (Weimar)
Wes, 1967	M. Wes, *Das Ende des Kaisertums im Westen de römischen Reichs* (The Hague)
Whitby, 1986	Michael Whitby, Procopius' description of Dara, in P. Freeman and D. Kennedy (eds.), *The Defence of the Roman and Byzantine East* (Oxford), 737-83
Whitby/Whitby, 1989	M. and M. Whitby, *Chronicon Paschale 284–628 AD* (Liverpool)
Wolfram, 1988	H. Wolfram, *A History of the Goths* (Berkeley–Los Angeles–London)
Zach. Rhet.	Zachariah Rhetor, *Historia Ecclesiastica* (ed./trs. E.J. Hamilton and E.W. Brooks, London, 1899)
Zon.	Zonaras (ed. L. Dindorf, Leipzig, 1868-75)
Zos.	Zosimus, *Nea Historia* (ed. F. Paschoud, Paris, 1971–86)
ZPE	*Zeitschrift für Papyrologie und Epigraphik*

Introduction

1. *Marcellinus* comes

Count Marcellinus, or Marcellinus *comes* as he is usually designated, is one of the lesser literary figures of late antiquity. He is known almost exclusively as the author of an annalistic chronicle continuing that of Jerome from AD 379 to 518, which Marcellinus himself later updated to 534.[1] He composed his chronicle in Constantinople and it was while the Roman senator Cassiodorus was there in 550/1, as a refugee from Justinian's war against the Ostrogoths, that he acquired a copy of it. If Cassiodorus did not actually meet Marcellinus then he certainly knew something about him, for in his *Institutiones*, a handbook for monks, he tells us that Marcellinus was an Illyrian:

> [Jerome] has been followed in turn by the aforesaid Marcellinus the Illyrian who is said to have acted first as *cancellarius* of the patrician Justinian, but who later, with the Lord's help upon the improvement of his employer's civil status, faithfully guided his work from the time of the emperor (Justin) to the beginning of the triumphant rule of the emperor Justinian.[2]

By 'Illyrian' Cassiodorus meant from the late Roman prefecture of Illyricum, more precisely from one of its Latin-speaking Balkan provinces. At some point (c.500) he must have migrated to the eastern imperial capital, Constantinople, as did so many of his ambitious contemporaries. At Constantinople Marcellinus was eventually able to secure a prestigious position as *cancellarius* to a fellow-Illyrian, the patrician Justinian, in the early 520s. As a *cancellarius* Marcellinus was *comes* and of senatorial status (*vir clarissimus*) — the titles he records in the preface to his chronicle. Marcellinus apparently left his court post before Justinian became emperor in 527.

In this subsequent period he probably devoted himself to literary pursuits. Marcellinus, who is generally reticent about his own life and views (not that a chronicle gave him much scope to display his individuality), tells us in the preface that his chronicle originally covered the period 379 to 518. Since it was common practice for chroniclers to update their works it is reasonable to assume that the first edition appeared in or soon after 518, that is to say, a few years before Marcellinus entered the service of Justinian. The second edition of the chronicle, the version which survives, continued the work to 534. It was arguably written as a tribute to his former employer Justinian on the occasion of the triumph over the Vandals in Africa which was celebrated at Constantinople in 534. As with other similar chronicles, that of Prosper for example, the purpose of the second edition was merely to up-date the record. Except for minor necessary changes it is unlikely that there were any substantial additions or modifications to what had been already written, for the period 379–518.

[1]In general: Mommsen, 1894, 42; Holder-Egger, 1877, 49–56; Schanz/Hosius/Krüger, 1920, 112; Moricca, 1943, 1363; *PLRE* 2: 711 s.v. 'Marcellinus 9'.

[2]*Inst.* I. 17. 2, as interpreted in Croke, 1982c.

Apart from the chronicle, Marcellinus wrote several other works which have not survived, despite the fact that Cassiodorus also recommended these in his handbook:

> Marcellinus too has traversed his journey's path in laudable fashion, completing four books on the nature of events and the locations of places with most decorous propriety; I have likewise left this work for you (*Inst*. I.17.1).
>
> Marcellinus too, concerning whom I have already spoken, should be read with equal care; he has described the city of Constantinople and the city of Jerusalem in four short books in considerable detail (*Inst*. 1.25.1)

It is deduced from this statement that there were two other works of Marcellinus (not one work described in two different ways, as sometimes suggested), both in four books, which were known to Cassiodorus: (1) a detailed work on the nature of temporal events and the location of places (*de temporum qualitatibus et positionibus locorum*) and (2) another on the topography of Constantinople and Jerusalem. The chronicle itself displays the author's interest in both Constantinople (*passim*) and the 'Holy Land' (s.a. 415, 419, 439, 443, 453, 516) and it would not be surprising if his books on Jerusalem, as well as those in the other work on the locations of places, were firmly rooted in first-hand observation — as Cassiodorus seems to imply. Moreover, it is quite possible that Marcellinus travelled as far afield as Dara on the Persian frontier on his sojourn. In any case the only surviving fragment of these works is a detailed description of Dara which appears to derive from the books 'on the locations of places'.[3]

Except for the facts that Marcellinus was Illyrian, wrote a chronicle in about 518/9, was a *cancellarius* to Justinian before 527, then retired from imperial service, updated his chronicle to 534 and was responsible for two other works now lost — except for all this, we know nothing else about the man. We have no idea when he was born or died, when he came to Constantinople, what sort of education he had and where he stood in the society of his day. Nonetheless the evidence of the chronicle itself permits a sketchy outline of his background and culture.

2. *The Chronicle's Perspective*

The predominant aspects of the chronicle are Marcellinus' treatment of events in his native area of Illyricum and of Constantinople itself, the city where he worked and wrote his chronicle. Marcellinus has a lot to say about Illyricum in his chronicle and what he does offer is generally of a distinctly precise and relatively full nature, suggesting an intimate knowledge of local personalities, local affairs and local geography. On occasion, such as for the earthquake in Dardania in 518, he may also have had direct access to official local sources.

The chronicle is an important source of information for the successive invasions of the Huns (422, 441, 442, 447, 452), Ostrogoths (478, 480) and Bulgars (499, 502, 517), and a detailed consideration of many of his entries gives rise to new discoveries on matters affecting the chronology and topography of the invasions.[4] In addition, Marcellinus frequently passes comment on the events he describes: there is unconcealed chagrin at the

[3]Croke, 1984, 77–88.
[4]Croke, 1977; 1980; 1981; 1982; 1983; 1984a.

destruction and population dislocation caused by the invasions (498, 505), and enthusiasm for the generals who are brave and successful in combatting the barbarians (479), but overall criticism at the ineffectiveness of the military response (499, 505). We have here a valuable glimpse, provided by a compatriot of Justin and Justinian, of the impact of the invasions on a single individual in the early sixth century. Even more importantly Marcellinus provides an insight into just how the imperial court and capital were affected by the invasions.

The other significant feature of Marcellinus' chronicle is the evidence it provides for the physical and social environment of Constantinople in the reigns of Justin and Justinian. Marcellinus was a long-time resident of Constantinople and very interested in it, to the extent of having written two books about the city's topography. The chronicle itself provides important and frequently unique evidence for monuments and events in the city in the early sixth century,[5] including reference to imperial constructions still standing in his day (390, 403). It contains eye-witness accounts of disturbances in 501 and 512, as well as the Nika riots in 532; he also claims to have seen in Constantinople victims of the Vandal persecution of the orthodox in Africa (484). When considered against the social, political and religious setting of the cosmopolitan imperial capital Marcellinus' information is most illuminating. It provides a carefully nuanced picture of the various Latin-speaking communities in Constantinople and of the ongoing connection between the Illyrians in Constantinople and in their homeland, as reflected in the visit of the Illyrian bishops (516). The traditional Illyrian allegiance to the bishop of Rome explains Marcellinus' attention to popes, and the grand entry of Pope John into the capital in 525/6; while the firm adherence of Illyrians to the emerging orthodoxy is strongly attested in Marcellinus' antipathy to Anastasius and his religious policies, and in his description of religious conflicts at Constantinople and elsewhere.

Above all, however, the chronicle reveals the monumental shape and intensely liturgical flavour of civic life in the city already by the early sixth century: so many entries in the chronicle derive their meaning from the fact that they were the original occurrence of a contemporary procession or other liturgical commemoration; the past is made into a living present through the annual commemoration of relic translations, natural disasters and so forth. Many of Marcellinus' apparently miscellaneous entries find their rationale in this expression of piety. As a former courtier of Justinian, Marcellinus demonstrated a strongly pro-Justinianic viewpoint which is evident in his highlighting of Justinian's consulships (521, 528), his support for the imperial policy of 'law and order' (523), the suppression of the Nika revolt (532) and the imperial defeat of the Bulgars and Persians (530), as well as the Vandals (534). It is Marcellinus' self-imposed

[5]Cisterns of Aetius (421.3) and Theodosius (407); Hagia Sophia and churches of St Anastasia (380), St Laurence (439), and St Theodore (512); Fora of Constantine, of Arcadius (421), Taurus (435, 506) and Strategius (510); imperial palace (532); senate house and hippodrome (390.3, 445, 491, 501, 507, 512, 528); columns of Eudoxia (403.2), Theodosius and Arcadius (421.2); Baths of Achilles (443.3), Theodosius (427.2) and Arcadius (394.4); public granaries (431); statue of Perdix (509.1) and Troadesian porticoes (448.2, 480); Golden Gate (514); harbour of Julian (509.2).

preoccupation with the eastern empire which dictates his limited view of the west, including the famous statement linking its fall to the deposition of Romulus in 476.[6]

3. *Sources of Information*

In writing his chronicle Marcellinus was consciously continuing the chronicle of Jerome, who had previously translated the chronicle of Eusebius of Caesarea and continued it to 378. There was an established style and format for chronicles to follow, on the model of Jerome, as well as a tradition in the type of sources utilised and how they might be employed. The basic framework of the chronicle was the list of successive indiction numbers. The indictional year ran from 1 September to 30 August and each such year was given a number in the fifteen-year cycle of indictions. Alongside the indictions Marcellinus used a consular list, recording in annual succession the names of the two chief magistrates for the year which ran from 1 January to 31 December. Marcellinus' very reliable consular list reflects the viewpoint of the eastern court in that it records the eastern consul first and normally ignores western consuls not recognised in the east.[7] Many apparent dating errors in the chronicle are to be explained by the problems caused by these two overlapping dating systems used by the chronicler; that is, Marcellinus' date is the correct indiction but the wrong consulship (e.g. 429.2, 430.3, 454.1, 465.1, 469).

For detailed information Marcellinus, like most chroniclers, relied on a strictly limited number of sources, using them to supplement information here and there:

(1) Orosius

Paulus Orosius, a native of Braga in Spain, was befriended by Augustine in Africa. It was at Augustine's request that he wrote an outline history of the world designed to provide a catalogue of all the disasters which had occurred up to the time of writing in the early fifth century. Marcellinus made extensive use of Orosius' history by generally choosing to summarise his source, but sometimes copying him verbatim. Orosius' history was used as follows:

Marcellinus	Orosius
379.2	vii.34.5
381.2	vii.34.6
382.2	vii.34.7
384.1	vii.34.8
385	vii.34.9
386.1	vii.34.9
387.2	vii.35.2
388.2	vii.34.5
391.2	vii.35.2
392.1	vii.34.11–12
394.2	vii.35.19

[6]Croke, 1983a.
[7]Bagnall et al., 1987, 56.

406.2	vii.37.4–5
406.3	vii.37.12–16
408.1	vii.38
410	vii.39.1, 15; 40.2
411.2	vii.40.4, 7
411.3	vii.42.3, 4
412.1	vii.42.5
412.2	vii.42.9
413	vii.42.16–24
414.2	vii.43.12

(2) Gennadius

Gennadius, a priest from Marseilles, wrote in c.480 a series of biographies of famous ecclesiastical writers (*de viris illustribus*) in continuation of that of Jerome. Marcellinus made use of Gennadius usually as a means of filling what would otherwise have been blank years:

Marcellinus	Gennadius
415.2	46 (Lucianus)
416.1	39 (Orosius)
416.2	52 (Atticus)
423.2	50 (Evagrius)
546.2	63 (Eucherius)
459	66 (Isaac)
463	84 (Prosper)
466	88 (Theodoret)
470	89 (Gennadius)
478	90 (Theodulus)
486	91 (John)

(3) Papal List

Marcellinus made use of a papal list which cannot be related to any other extant list.[8] It is evident that his list contained the length of each pope's reign only in years. This meant that he was always obliged to insert a new papal entry at the point dictated by the years in his list of popes, with the result that most of his entries are placed too early or too late.[9]

[8]Duchesne, 1886, xxiv.
[9]Holder-Egger, 1877, 97.

(4) Constantinopolitan chronicle source

Perhaps the source most frequently used by Marcellinus (and by the Chronicon Paschale which Mommsen reproduced for the years 395–469 in his edition of Marcellinus to illustrate their close textual similarities) was a previous chronicle which contained predominantly Constantinopolitan events. Moreover, it is likely that this chronicle was itself based on the so-called 'City Chronicle' of Constantinople (CP), or else Marcellinus used similar material himself.[10] Reflecting this source, Marcellinus devotes considerable space to eastern events of a public ceremonial nature: *Adventus* (imperial and relic arrivals),[11] Victories,[12] Imperial Accessions,[13] Deaths,[14] Births,[15] Imperial Marriages,[16] Anniversaries,[17] Portents (earthquakes, eclipses etc),[18] Building,[19] Ecclesiastical matters (popes, councils, theological writers etc)[20], Civil strife (faction and other riots),[21] Deaths of usurpers and high officials,[22] Wars in the east (Isauria and Persia),[23] Raids in the Balkans,[24] Miscellaneous.[25] Most importantly, his local CP

[10]Holder-Egger, 1877, 73–88; Mommsen, 1894, 44–46; Croke, 1990, passim; and the critical treatment by Burgess, 1993, 182–6.

[11]381.2, 382.1, 384.1, 386.2, 387.2, 389.1, 391.1, 394.1, 395.2, 401.1, 414.1, 428.2, 431.3, 436, 438.2, 438.3, 439.2, 443.2, 448.1, 448.3, 485, 496.2, 507.2, 520, 525.

[12]379.2, 382.2, 385, 386.1, 388.1, 388.2, 394.2, 394.4, 394.5, 398.4, 400, 405, 412.2, 413. 418.1, 421.4, 422.2, 422.3, 422.4, 425.1, 438.1, 439.3, 440.2, 441.1, 441.3, 445.1, 452, 469, 477, 488.1, 498.2, 530, 533, 534.

[13]379.1, 383.2, 391.3, 393, 395.3, 402.2, 411.2, 424.1, 424.2, 450.2, 455.2, 457.2, 457.1, 461.2, 467.1, 472.2, 474.1, 475.1, 475.2, 491.1, 519.1, 527.

[14]391.2, 395.1, 404.2, 408.1, 408.3, 411.3, 412.1, 424.3, 429.2, 431.1, 444.2, 444.4, 449.1, 450.1, 457.1, 461.2, 465.2, 472.2, 474.2, 474.1, 474.2, 476.1, 476.2, 480.2, 491.1, 515.6, 518.3, 527.

[15]384.2, 397, 399.2, 401.3, 403.1, 419.1, 422.1.

[16]421.1, 424.2, 437.

[17]387.1, 406.1, 411.1, 422.2, 430, 439.1, 444.1.

[18]389.2, 389.3, 390.1, 394.3, 396.3, 401.2, 402.3, 404, 408.2, 417.2, 418.2, 418.3, 419.2, 433, 442.2, 443.1, 444.3, 446.1, 447.1, 452.2, 456.1, 465.1, 460, 467, 472.1, 472.3, 480.1, 494.2, 497.1, 499, 512.1, 512.10, 518.1, 526.

[19]390.3, 394.4, 403.2, 415.1, 421.2, 421.3, 427.2, 435.1, 443.2, 447.3, 448.2, 453.5, 506, 509.2, 510.11, 528.

[20]380.1, 381.1, 382.3, 383.1, 392.2, 398.1, 398.2, 398.3, 402.1, 403.3, 415.2, 416.1, 416.2, 417.3, 419.3, 420.1, 420.3, 423.1, 426, 428.1, 430, 432.1, 440.2, 449.2, 451, 453.1–4, 456.2, 459, 461.1, 463, 466, 470, 476.2, 478, 482, 494.1, 494.3, 495, 498.1, 500.1, 510.3, 511, 512.8, 512.9, 513, 515.1, 516.2, 516.3.

[21]399.3, 409, 431.2, 445.2, 473.2, 491.2, 493.1, 501.1–3, 507.1, 509.1, 512.2–7, 523, 524, 532.

[22]396.2, 399.1, 420.2, 430.2, 432.2–3, 440.1, 449.3, 450.3, 454.2, 481.2, 490, 493.2, 497.3, 520.

[23]475.1, 484.1, 492, 497.2, 502.2, 503, 504, 515.5, 529.

[24]427.1, 434, 454.1, 464, 468, 479.1, 479.2, 481.1, 482.2, 483, 488.2, 489.1, 499.1, 502.1, 505, 512.11, 517, 530.

[25]389.4 (Temple destroyed), 390.2 (empress expelled), 392 (usurpation), 396 (exiles), 410 (sack of Rome), 414.2 (Placidia restored), 455 (Geiseric at Rome), 462 (Jacob the Doctor), 484.2 (Vandal refugees), 496.1 (donative), 498.3 (coinage reform), 500.2 (donative), 508 (Tarentum attacked), 510.2 (exile), 514 (rebellion), 515.2 (rebel defeated), 516 (Vitalian replaced), 519.2 (conspiracy), 531 (Code of Justinian).

source was also where Marcellinus found most of his information about the western empire.[26]

Other sources used by Marcellinus for specific entries include the ***Dialogus*** of Palladius for the entries on John Chrysostom (398.3, 403.3, 404.1), the ***Anonymus de inventione Capitis S. Johannis Baptistae*** for the discovery of John the Baptist's head (453), while he may possibly have used a letter of Pope Celestine (430).

4. *The Continuator of Marcellinus*

The chronicle of Marcellinus, as happened so often with such chronicles, was continued by others. Indeed Cassiodorus knew of such continuations in the early 550s. The only extant continuation of Marcellinus is that contained in the Oxford manuscript (T) which breaks off in 548. How much further it continued and by whom it was written cannot be known. At one stage it was thought that the text of Marcellinus contained in T was different from that in the Continuation so that the Continuation was added under the auspices of Cassiodorus at Vivarium.[27] While it is now apparent that both Marcellinus' text and the Continuation are the work of a single scribe and cannot be attributed to Vivarium, the manuscript is still relatively close to the autograph original. The continuation was perhaps compiled in the early 550s.

As for the Continuator himself, he was evidently writing in Constantinople for he reports much of the military activity in terms of arrivals at and departures from Constantinople, the 'royal city' (535.4, 541.1). Moreover, he reflects the perspective of the imperial court most notably in his attitudes to Italy and the ongoing war there. The Continuator tends to be religiously orthodox, pro-Belisarius (535.1, 536.8) and somewhat anti-Gothic (536.7, 542.2). His frequent mis-dating of events suggests that he was not close to the events described, nor was he always able to follow an accurate chronology.

5. *Language and style*

In writing a chronicle on the pattern established by Jerome, Marcellinus was not constrained by any conventions of literary style and was not obliged to be constantly striving for literary effect. Instead, whatever his innate stylistic and rhetorical abilities may have been,[28] the annalistic chronicle was not the vehicle for displaying them. Rather, his expression is usually straightforward, formulaic and brief. Some of his description has a certain freshness and vigour which may be a reflection of personal witness or experience. At times, however, he is content simply to copy or paraphrase his source (Orosius, Gennadius). In matters of syntax and vocabulary he demonstrates normal features of late Latin,[29] the sort of features which have traditionally been regarded as 'unclassical' and perhaps indicative of intellectual and literary limitations more broadly. Such assumptions are ill-conceived and misleading. More particularly, in a Latin-speaker in a cosmopolitan but predominantly Greek environment it is not surprising to find the

[26]Croke, 1983a.

[27]Courcelle, 1954, 425–8.

[28]Holder-Egger, 1877, 55 proposed that the chronicle shows the influence of contemporary schools of rhetoric.

[29]Fully itemised in Mommsen, 1894, 57.

occasional Grecisms such as 'Cherronesum' (400), 'Ginziricus' (439.3), 'Calchedonam' (451, 511 cf. 458), 'Eutychen' (463) and 'Denzicis' (469). Likewise, since he was a native of the Latin-speaking region of the Balkans, it is natural that traces of local Balkan Latin should also be found in the chronicle.[30]

6. *Manuscripts*[31]

The text produced by Mommsen and reproduced here is based on **T** and **S**. The full range of manuscripts is as follows:

6th cent	**T**	Codex Tilianus: Oxford, Bodleian Library, Auct. T. II. 26
11th cent.	**S**	Codex Sanctomerensis: St. Omer, Public Library 697
	U	Udine, Episcopal Library 14
12th cent.		Brussels, Lat. 6439–6451
14th cent.	**R**	Paris, Bibliothèque Nationale, Lat. 4870
15th cent.		Vienna, Nationalbibliothek 138
		Venice, Biblioteca Marciana Lat. VI.135
		Oxford, Bodleian Library, Canon. script. eccl. 193
		Oxford, Bodleian Library, Canon. script. eccl. 96
		Vatican, Urb. Lat. 382
		Vatican, Palat. Lat. 818
		Florence, Biblioteca Mediceae-laurenziana 58
		Milan, Bibliotheca Ambrosiana C. 290
		Toulouse, Bibliothèque Municipale 468 (excerpts only)[32]
		Canterbury, St Augustine's Abbey 379[33]
16th cent.		Berlin, Lat. 118

7. *Editions*[34]

Mommsen's edition (1894) superseded all others. It was the first critical one to be based on a full collation of all available manuscripts and, as has been observed, 'a more comprehensive edition of [M.'s] chronicle is not likely'.[35] The editions of the chronicle are as follows:

[30]Mihaescu, 1978, 9–10.

[31]I omit the three manuscripts which Mommsen (1894, 52) was unable to trace and which have never appeared subsequently.

[32]Manuscript not known to Mommsen, 1894.

[33]Manuscript not known to Mommsen, 1894.

[34]For editions of extracts only see Bouquet, 1738, 640 and 1739, 19–20, and Mommsen, 1898, 'Additamenta ad vol. II, p. 53'.

[35]Wattenbach/Levison, 1951, 54 n.50.

1546	A. Schonhovius, *Chronicon Marcellini Comitis ... quod rerum orientalium historiam Eusebii & divi Hieronymi usque ad Iustiniani tempora prosequitur, nunc primum in lucem editum* (Paris) [based on S]
1552	J. Cuspinianus in *De Consulibus Romanorum Commentarii* (Basel), 513–72 [based on Vienna, Nationalbibliothek 138]
1558	O. Panvinius in *Fastorum libri V a Romulo rege usque ad Imp. Caesarem Carolum V Austrium Augustum* (Venice), 58–78 [conflation of Schonhovius and Cuspinian]
1606	J. Scaliger in *Thesaurus Temporum* (Leiden), 22–43 [based on Panvinius, 1558]
1618	reprint of Schonhovius, 1546 in M. de la Bigne, *Magna Bibliotheca Veterum Patrum* (Cologne), vol. 6, 362–9
1619	J. Sirmond, *M.V.C. Comitis Illyriciani Chronicon emendatius et auctius* (Paris) [an improved Scaliger, 1606, based on **T**]
1654	reprint of Schonhovius, 1546 in M. de la Bigne, *Magna Bibliotheca Veterum Patrum* (Cologne), vol. 15, 712–22
1658	reprint of Sirmond, 1619 in J. Scaliger, *Thesaurus Temporum* (2nd edition, ed. A. Morus; Amsterdam), 33–57
1677	reprint of Sirmond 1619 in M. de la Bigne, *Maxima Bibliotheca Veterum Patrum* (Lyons), vol. 9, 517–23
1696	J. de la Baune's revision of Sirmond, 1619, in *J. Sirmondi Opera* (Paris), vol. 2, 349–88 [utilising **R**]
1774	reprint of de la Baune's Sirmond, 1696 in A. Galland, *Bibliotheca Veterum Patrum* (Venice), vol. 10, 343–56
1787	Th. Roncalli [from de la Baune's Sirmond, 1696 and others], *Vetustiora Latinorum Scriptorum Chronica* (Padua), vol 2, 265–336
1846	J.P. Migne [reprint of de la Baune's Sirmond, 1774] in *PL* 51, 913–48
1894	Th. Mommsen, *MGH AA*. XI, 39–108 [based on **T** and S].

Text

and

Translation

PRAEFATIO[1]

Post mirandum opus, quod a mundi fabrica usque in Constantinum principem Eusebius Caesariensis, huius saeculi originem tempora annos regna virtutesque mortalium et variarum artium repertores omniumque paene provinciarum monumenta commemorans, Graeco edidit stilo, noster Hieronymus cuncta transtulit in Latinum et usque in Valentem Caesarem Romano adiecit eloquio. igitur uterque huius operis auctor quinque milium et quingentorum septuaginta novem annorum hunc mundum tunc fore miro computavit ingenio. ego vero vir clarissimus Marcellinus comes simplici dumtaxat computatione, Orientale tantum secutus imperium, per indictiones perque consules infra scriptos centum quadraginta annos, a septima videlicet indictione et a consulatu Ausonii et Olybrii, quibus etiam consulibus Theodosius Magnus creatus est imperator, enumerans et usque in consulatu Magni indictione undecima colligens, eorundem auctorum operi subrogavi.

Itemque alios sedecim annos a consulatu Iustini Augusti primo usque in consulatum Iustiniani Augusti quartum suffeci, id sunt simul anni centum quinquaginta sex, et meum rusticum opus subposui.

VII INDICTIONE CONSVLATV AVSONII ET OLYBRII

Theodosius Hispanus Italicae divi Traiani civitatis a Gratiano Augusto apud Sirmium tricensimus nonus post Valentis interitum imperator creatus est XIIII kalendas Februarias, Orientalem dumtaxat rem publicam recturus, vir admodum religiosus et catholicae ecclesiae propagator omnibusque Orientalibus principibus praeponendus, nisi quod Marcianum tertium post se principem imitatorem habuerit.

[1]Since it was copied as an appendix to the chronicle of Jerome no manuscript of Marcellinus contains an authentic title for his work (cf. Mommsen, 1894, 43), just an indication of the transition to a new author by the heading *praefatio Marcellini* (T) or *chronica Marcellini comitis: praefatio* (S).

PREFACE

After the marvellous work from the creation of the world down to the emperor Constantine, which Eusebius of Caesarea composed in Greek – recording the beginnings of this present era, its timespan, years, kingdoms and the good qualities of men as well as the inventors of the various arts and also the monuments from almost all regions — our Jerome translated the whole work into Latin and continued it in the Roman language down to Valens Caesar. Consequently, both authors of this work calculated with astonishing ingenuity that this world would at that time have been five thousand five hundred and seventy-nine years old. So I, Marcellinus, a count and man with the rank 'Most Distinguished', have continued the work of these same authors (following only the Eastern empire) with simple straightforward calculation, counting by means of the indictions and consuls written below, for one hundred and forty years — namely from the seventh indiction and the consulship of Ausonius and Olybrius during which Theodosius the Great was also appointed emperor, summarising down to the consulship of Magnus in the eleventh indiction.

Further, I have added another sixteen years from the first consulship of Justin Augustus to the fourth of Justinian Augustus (there being one hundred and fifty-six years altogether), and have attached this to my own unpretentious work.

1 Sept. 378– 31 Aug. 379 7th indiction, consulship of Ausonius and Olybrius *379*

1. After the death of Valens, the Spaniard Theodosius from Italica, the town of the deified Trajan, was made thirty-ninth emperor by Gratian Augustus at Sirmium on 19 January, to rule over the Eastern empire only. He was a singularly religious man and propagator of the Catholic church, surpassing all the Eastern emperors except for his emulator, Marcian, the third emperor after him.

Halanos, Hunnos, Gothos, gentes Scythicas magnis multisque proeliis vicit.

VIII GRATIANI AVGVSTI V ET THEODOSII AVGVSTI

Gregorius Nazianzenus facundissimus Christi sacerdos et Hieronymi nostri praeceptor ecclesia nostra aput Byzantium ab Arrianis capta plebem catholicam in beatae Anastasiae oratorio catholico cottidiana adlocutione continuit. saepe namque pravorum conviciis insectatus est: sed gratia Christi praeditus usque ad id tempus, quo eadem ecclesia sui praesentia nostris est reddita, perfidiis obstitit Arrianis. nam his consulibus Theodosius Magnus postquam de Scythicis gentibus triumphavit, expulsis continuo de orthodoxorum ecclesia Arrianis, qui eam per quadraginta ferme annos sub Arrianis imperatoribus tenuerant, nostris catholicis orthodoxus restituit imperator mense Decembrio.

VIIII EVCHERII ET SVAGRII

Sanctis centum quinquaginta patribus urbe Augusta congregatis adversus Macedonium in sanctum spiritum naufragantem ab iisdem episcopis sancta synodus confirmata est: Damaso videlicet sedem beati Petri tenente, Constantinopoli vero per Timotheum Alexandrinum perque Meletium Antiochenum et Cyrillum Hierosolymitanum episcopos Nectario ex pagano protinus baptizato et in praefata synodo pontifice ordinato.

Athanaricus rex Gothorum, cum quo Theodosius imperator foedus pepigerat, Constantinopolim mense Ianuario venit eodemque mense morbo periit.

X ANTONII ET SYAGRII

Divi Valentiniani magni cadavere Theodosius princeps ab Italia reportato apud comitatum regio in sepulchro recondidit.

Eodem anno universa gens Gothorum Athanarico rege suo defuncto Romano sese imperio dedit mense Octobrio.

2. He [Theodosius] conquered the Scythian tribes of the Alans, Huns, and Goths in many great battles.

1 Sept. 379– 8th indiction, consulship of Gratian Augustus (5th) and
31 Aug. 380 Theodosius Augustus *380*

When our church at Byzantium had been taken over by the Arians Gregory of Nazianzus, the most eloquent priest of Christ and teacher of our Jerome, united the Catholic people by preaching daily in the Catholic chapel of blessed Anastasia. Indeed he was often assaulted by the insults of heretics but, endowed with the grace of Christ, he fought the Arian falsehoods right up to the time when our church was restored to us in his presence. For in the month of December in this year, after Theodosius the Great had triumphed over the Scythian tribes and had immediately driven out from the church of the orthodox the Arians who had held it for almost forty years under Arian emperors, he, the orthodox emperor, restored the church to us Catholics.

1 Sept. 380– 9th indiction, consulship of Eucherius and Syagrius
31 Aug. 381 *381*

1. After one hundred and fifty holy fathers had assembled in the imperial city a sacred synod was instituted by these very bishops against Macedonius, who was blaspheming against the Holy Spirit. This was when Damasus was in the chair of St. Peter; at Constantinople Nectarius was baptized instantly out of paganism and ordained bishop in the aforementioned synod by the bishops Timothy of Alexandria, Meletius of Antioch and Cyril of Jerusalem.

2. Athanaric, the king of the Goths, with whom the emperor Theodosius had made a treaty, came to Constantinople in the month of January and died through disease in the same month.

1 Sept. 381– 10th indiction, consulship of Antonius and Syagrius
31Aug. 382 *382*

1. In the presence of the imperial court, the emperor Theodosius interred in the royal tomb the body of the deified Valentinian the Great which had been brought from Italy.

2. In the same year in the month of October, following the death of their king Athanaric, the whole tribe of the Goths

Damasus Romanae ecclesiae exceptis Liberio et Felice tricensimus quintus episcopus anno pontificatus sui octavo decimo in domino requievit.

XI MEROBAVDIS II ET SATVRNINI

Romanae ecclesiae Siricius tricensimus sextus antistes factus vixit annos quindecim.
Arcadius patri suo Theodosio Augusto consors imperii septimo ab urbe miliario coronatus est.
Gratianus imperator Maximi tyranni dolo apud Lugdunum occisus est VIII kal. Septembris.

XII RICHEMERIS ET CLEARCHI

Legati Persarum Constantinopolim advenerunt pacem Theodosii principis postulantes.
Eodem tempore Honorius alter Theodosio natus est filius mense Septembrio.

XIII ARCADII ET BAVTONIS

Theodosius imperator aliquantas eoas nationes per legatos suos suo utpote imperio subdidit.

XIV HONORII CAESARIS ET EVODII

Invasam princeps Theodosius ab hostibus Thraciam vindicavit victorque cum Arcadio filio suo urbem ingressus est.

Galla Theodosii regis altera uxor his consulibus Constantinopolim venit.

XV VALENTINIANI III ET EVTROPII

Arcadius Caesar cum patre suo Theodosio sua quinquennalia celebravit.
Theodosius Magnus Italiam contra Maximum tyrannum pugnaturus accessit.

submitted themselves to Roman authority.
3. Damasus, the thirty-fifth bishop of the Roman church, excluding Liberius and Felix, fell asleep in the Lord in the eighteenth year of his pontificate.

1 Sept. 382– 31 Aug. 383 11th indiction, consulship of Merobaudes (2nd) and Saturninus *383*

1. Siricius was made thirty-sixth bishop of the Roman church and lived for fifteen years.
2. Arcadius was crowned as his father Theodosius' co-emperor at the seventh milestone from the city.
3. The emperor Gratian was killed on 25 August at Lyons through the treachery of the usurper Maximus.

1 Sept. 383– 31 Aug. 384 12th indiction, consulship of Richomer and Clearchus *384*

1. Persian ambassadors came to Constantinople requesting peace from the emperor Theodosius.
2. At the same time Theodosius' second son, Honorius, was born in the month of September.

1 Sept. 384– 31 Aug. 385 13th indiction, consulship of Arcadius and Bauto *385*

The emperor Theodosius subjected several Eastern nations to his own empire through his ambassadors.

1 Sept. 385– 31 Aug. 386 14th indiction, consulship of Honorius Caesar and Evodius *386*

1. The emperor Theodosius won back Thrace, which had been invaded by the enemy, and entered the city in victory together with his son Arcadius.
2. Galla, the second wife of the emperor Theodosius, came to Constantinople during this consulship.

1 Sept. 386– 31 Aug. 387 15th indiction, consulship of Valentinian (3rd) and Eutropius *387*

1. Arcadius Caesar celebrated his fifth anniversary with his father Theodosius.
2. Theodosius the Great came to Italy to fight against the usurper Maximus.

I THEODOSII AVGVSTI II ET CYNEGII

Valentinianus Gratiani frater et Theodosius imperatores Maximum tyrannum et Victorem filium eius apud Aquileiam rebellantem vicerunt.
Andragathius comes morte Maximi cognita praecipitem sese e navi in undas dedit ac suffocatus est.

II TIMASII ET PROMOTI

Theodosius imperator cum Honorio filio suo Romam mense Iunio introivit, congiarium Romano populo tribuit urbeque egressus est kal. Septembris.
Per idem tempus grando crepitans per biduum continuum pro pluvia cecidit, pecudum arborumque pernicies.
Stella a septentrione gallicinio surgens et in modum luciferi ardens potius quam splendens apparuit, vicensimo sexto die esse desiit.
Templum Serapis apud Alexandriam Theodosii imperatoris edicto solutum est.

III VALENTINIANI AVG. IIII ET NEOTERII

Signum in caelo quasi columna pendens ardensque per dies triginta apparuit.
Galla Theodosii uxor ab Arcadio privigno suo eiecta est.

Oboliscum in circo positum est: columna haut longe ab ecclesia constituta est, quae argenteam Theodosii Magni statuam ferens hactenus contemplatur.

IIII TATIANI ET SYMMACHI

Theodosius imperator Italia decedens Constantinopolim remeavit.

Valentinianus imperator apud Viennam dolo Arbogasti strangulatus interiit idibus Martiis.
Eugenius Arbogasti favore confisus imperium sibimet usurpavit.

1 Sept. 387– 1st indiction, consulship of Theodosius (2nd) and Cynegius
31 Aug. 388 *388*

1. The emperors Valentinian, the brother of Gratian, and Theodosius conquered the usurper Maximus and his son Victor, who was in revolt at Aquileia.
2. When Count Andragathius learnt of Maximus' death he threw himself headlong from his ship into the sea and was drowned.

1 Sept. 388– 2nd indiction, consulship of Timasius and Promotus
31 Aug. 389 *389*

1. The emperor Theodosius entered Rome in the month of June with his son Honorius, distributed a donation to the Roman people and left the city on 1 September.
2. During that same time for two continuous days clattering hail, rather than rain, fell – a disaster for cattle and trees.
3. A star appeared, rising from the north at dawn and blazing like the morning star [Venus], instead of glittering. On the twenty-sixth day it disappeared.
4. The temple of Serapis at Alexandria was destroyed by an edict of the emperor Theodosius.

1 Sept. 389– 3rd indiction, consulship of Valentinian Augustus (4th) and
31 Aug. 390 Neoterius *390*

1. A sign, in the shape of a suspended blazing column, appeared in the sky for thirty days.
2. Galla, the wife of Theodosius, was banished by her stepson Arcadius.
3. An obelisk was placed in the hippodrome. A column supporting a silver statue of Theodosius the Great was erected not far from the church, and can still be seen.

1 Sept. 390– 4th indiction, consulship of Tatian and Symmachus
31 Aug. 391 *391*

1. The emperor Theodosius left Italy and returned to Constantinople.
2. The emperor Valentinian, who was strangled at Vienne through the treachery of Arbogast, died on the Ides of March.
3. Eugenius, relying on the goodwill of Arbogast, usurped the empire for himself.

V ARCADII II ET RUFINI

Arbogastes Valentiniano imperatore extincto et Eugenio Caesare facto innumeras invictasque copias undique in Gallias contraxit, Occidentale sibi imperium utpote vindicaturus.

Hieronymus noster litteris Graecis ac Latinis Romae adprime eruditus, presbyter quoque ibidem ordinatus est. porro ad Bethleem oppidum iuvenis advenit, ubi prudens animal ad praesepe domini se mox optulit permansurum. inter cetera studiorum suorum opuscula usque ad hunc Theodosii quartum decimum imperii annum a beato Petro sumens exordium usque in semet ipsum de viris inlustribus scribit. innumeris praeterea libris apostolorum prophetarumque constructionibus editis immobilem catholicae turrem ecclesiae contra perfidorum iacula consummavit, litteris quoque Hebraicis atque Chaldaicis ita edoctus, ut omnes veteris testamenti libros ex Hebraeorum scilicet codicibus verteret in Latinum, Danihelem quoque prophetam Chaldaeico stilo locutum et Iob iustum Arabico in Romanam linguam utrumque auctorem perfecta interpretatione mutaverit. Matthaei nihilominus euangelium ex Hebraeo fecit esse Romanum. namque mentis corporisque virginitatem et delictorum paenitentiam praedicans atque custodiens solus omnium Romanorum omnes sedecim prophetarum commentatus est libros iunctis praeterea librorum suorum prologis. ita se luculentissimum interpretem et immensa epistularum suarum volumina nervosum catholicis exhibuit lectoribus, ut nec perfidis quandoque pepercisse nec invidis cessisse videatur. nonagenarius ferme, ut perhibent, postea in domino requievit. quem Stridon oppidum genuit, Roma inclita erudivit, Bethlem alma tenet.

VI THEODOSII III ET ABVNDANTII

Honorium pater suus Theodosius in eodem loco quo fratrem eius Arcadium Caesarem fecit, id est septimo ab urbe regia miliario. tunc quippe hora diei tertia tenebrae factae sunt.

1 Sept. 391– 5th indiction, consulship of Arcadius (2nd) and Rufinus
31 Aug 392 *392*

1. After the emperor Valentinian had been done away with and Eugenius had been made Caesar, Arbogast assembled in Gaul countless unconquered forces from all areas so as to acquire the Western empire for himself.

2. Our Jerome, the most skilled of all at Rome in Greek and Latin literature, was also ordained a priest there. Next, while a young man, he came to the town of Bethlehem where, being a creature of foresight, he soon decided to remain at the Lord's manger. Among the other short products of his studies he wrote about famous men, beginning with Blessed Peter, down to himself in this the fourteenth year of the reign of Theodosius. Moreover, by publishing his innumerable books on the apostles and his interpretations of the prophets, he made the tower of the Catholic church impregnable to the darts of heretics. He was also so learned in Hebrew and Chaldaean literature that he turned into Latin (from Hebrew manuscripts evidently) all the books of the Old Testament and translated into the Roman language with perfect understanding both the prophet Daniel, who spoke Chaldaean, and Job the Just, who spoke Arabic. Furthermore, he turned the Gospel of Matthew from Hebrew into Latin. For, while he was both preaching and defending virginity of mind and body and repentance for sins, he alone of all Romans commented on all sixteen books of the prophets, adding to them as well the prologues of his own books. He showed himself to his Catholic readers as so lucid an interpreter and so prolific by the immense volumes of his letters that he seemed at no time to spare the treacherous or yield to the envious. He was almost ninety, so they say, when he fell asleep in the Lord. He whom the town of Stridon begot, and glorious Rome educated, kind Bethlehem holds.

1 Sept. 392– 6th indiction, consulship of Theodosius (3rd) and Abund-
31 Aug. 393 antius *393*

Honorius' father Theodosius made him a Caesar in the same place as his brother Arcadius, that is, at the seventh milestone from the royal city. Then there was in fact an eclipse at the third hour of the day.

VII ARCADII III ET HONORII II

Theodosius Augustus adsumpto Honorio Caesare eodemque filio contra Arbogasten, qui Eugenium tyrannum imperatorem facere ausus est, iterum properavit.
Bello commisso Eugenius victus atque captus interfectus est. Arbogastes sua se manu perculit.
Terrae motu a mense Septembrio in Novembrium continuo inminente aliquantae Europae regiones quassatae sunt.
Thermae Arcadianae ex conditoris sui nomine nomen acceperunt.

VIII OLYBRII ET PROBINI

Theodosius Magnus apud Mediolanum vita decessit. imperavit annos decem et septem.
Corpus eius eodem anno Constantinopolim adlatum atque sepultum.
Arcadius et Honorius germani utrumque imperium divisis tantum sedibus tenere coeperunt.
Rufinus patricius Arcadio principi insidias tendens Alaricum Gothorum regem missis clam pecuniis infestum rei publicae fecit et in Graeciam misit.
Porro detectus dolo suo Rufinus ab Italicis militibus cum Gaina comite Arcadio missis ante portas urbis merito trucidatus est. caput eius manusque dextra per totam Constantinopolim demonstrata.

VIIII ARCADII IIII ET HONORII III

Rufini uxor et filia exulata.
Eutropius sacri palatii cubicularius omnes opes abripuit avaritiamque transgressus est.
Terrae motus per dies plurimos fuit caelumque ardere visum est.

X CAESARII ET ATTICI

His consulibus Flaccilla Arcadio nata est filia.

1 Sept. 393– 7th indiction, consulship of Arcadius (3rd) and Honorius
31 Aug. 394 (2nd) *394*

1. Theodosius Augustus, taking Honorius his son and Caesar with him, set out once more against Arbogast, who had dared to make the usurper Eugenius an emperor.
2. When battle had been joined Eugenius was conquered, captured and killed. Arbogast perished by his own hand.
3. Several areas of Europe were shaken by a continuous and menacing earthquake from September to November.
4. The Arcadian Baths were named after their founder.

1 Sept. 394– 8th indiction, consulship of Olybrius and Probinus
31 Aug. 395 *395*

1. Theodosius the Great departed this life in Milan. He ruled for seventeen years.
2. In the same year his body was brought to Constantinople and buried.
3. As the regions of the empire were divided, the brothers Arcadius and Honorius began to rule each part.
4. The patrician Rufinus, devising treachery against the emperor Arcadius, made the Gothic King Alaric a threat to the state by secretly bribing him and sent him into Greece.
5. Next, when his treachery had been discovered Rufinus was deservedly cut down in front of the city gates by the Italian soldiers who had been sent to Arcadius, together with Gaïnas the count. His head and right hand were displayed throughout Constantinople.

1 Sept. 395– 9th indiction, consulship of Arcadius (4th) and Honorius
31 Aug. 396 (3rd) *396*

1. The wife and daughter of Rufinus were exiled.
2. Eutropius, a bedchamberlain of the sacred palace, robbed everyone of their wealth and surpassed all avarice.
3. There was an earthquake for many days and the sky appeared to glow.

1 Sept. 396– 10th indiction, consulship of Caesarius and Atticus
31 Aug. 397 *397*

In this year Flaccilla, the daughter of Arcadius, was born.

XI HONORII IIII ET EVTYCHIANI

Romanae ecclesiae Anastasius tricensimus septimus episcopus ordinatus vixit annos quattuor.
Ambrosius Mediolanensis, virtutum episcopus, arx fidei, orator catholicus, ad Christum dominum commigravit.
Iohannes Antiochiae natus ibique a Meletio eiusdem civitatis episcopo eodemque confessore lector ecclesiae ordinatus per singulos officii gradus ascendit. ubi per quinquennium continuum diaconus multos divinosque edidit libros: presbyter quoque factus per duodecim annos pluriores confecit. tanta dehinc opinione ubique merito propagatus Constantinopolim in locum Nectarii pontifex suffectus est: ubi plurima dulciaque divinarum scripturarum volumina suo operi catholico addidit, hosque episcopos habuit inimicos: Theofilum Alexandrinum, Epiphanium Cyprium, Acacium Beroensem, Antiochum Ptolomensem, Severianum Gabaliensem et Severum Calchedonensem.

Gildo comes idemque paganus, qui mortuo Theodosio principe Africae praeerat, dum Arcadio et Honorio adhuc pueris regnantibus invidet Africamque nititur optinere, frater eius Mascezel cognita eius vesania relictisque duobus aput Africam filiis in Italiam remeat. Gildo utrumque fratris filium dolo trucidat. Mascezel fratris scelere cognito, cum quinque milibus suorum contra Gildonem cum septuaginta milibus armatorum sibimet obviantem infestus accedit Gildonemque parricidam ieiuniis et orationibus, immo beati Ambrosii in somnis ammonitu auxiliantibus fugavit. Gildo fugiens propria se manu strangulavit: sicque Mascezel sine bello victoriam meruit ac sine caede vindictam.

XII THEODORI ET EVTROPII EVNVCHI

Hic Eutropius omnium spadonum primus adque ultimus consul fuit: de quo Claudianus poeta ait:

> Omnia cesserunt eunucho consule monstra.

Pulcheria Arcadio altera filia nata est.
Gaina comes apud Constantinopolim ad praeparandum civile bellum barbaros suos occulte ammonet: ipse valitudinem simulans

1 Sept. 397– 31 Aug. 398 11th indiction, consulship of Honorius (4th) and Eutychianus 398

1. Anastasius was ordained thirty-seventh bishop of the Roman Church and lived for four years.
2. Ambrose of Milan, a virtuous bishop, citadel of the faith and Catholic orator, departed to Christ the Lord.
3. John, born at Antioch and ordained a reader of the church there by Meletius, a confessor and bishop of the same city, ascended through each grade of the office. As a deacon there for five successive years he published many religious books, and when made a priest he compiled many more over twelve years. After that, since he was deservedly advanced by such a widespread reputation, he was chosen bishop of Constantinople in place of Nectarius. There he added very many delightful volumes of divine writings to his catholic work, and had these bishops as his enemies: Theophilus of Alexandria, Epiphanius of Cyprus, Acacius of Beroea, Antiochus of Ptolemais, Severianus of Gabala and Severus of Chalcedon.
4. The pagan count Gildo, who at the death of the emperor Theodosius was in charge of Africa, attempted to take Africa since he envied the rulers Honorius and Arcadius who were still children. When Gildo's brother, Mascezel, learnt of his madness he left his two sons in Africa and went back to Italy. Gildo treacherously cut down both his brother's sons. Mascezel learnt of his brother's wickedness and, with five thousand of his own men, made a threatening advance against Gildo who came to meet him with seventy thousand armed men; he put the murderer Gildo to flight with the aid of prayers and fasting and indeed the advice of Blessed Ambrose in a dream. Gildo strangled himself in his flight with his very own hand. So Mascezel achieved a victory without war and a bloodless vengeance.

1 Sept. 398– 31 Aug. 399 12th indiction, consulship of Theodorus and Eutropius the Eunuch 399

1. This Eutropius was the first and the last eunuch to be consul. The poet Claudian says of him:

> 'All portents pale before our eunuch consul'.

2. Pulcheria, Arcadius' second daughter, was born.
3. The count Gaïnas secretly incited his barbarians to make preparations for civil war at Constantinople while he himself,

urbe digreditur. coepto adversum Byzantios proelio plurimi hostium cadunt, ceteri fugientes ecclesiae nostrae succedunt ibique detecto ecclesiae culmine iactisque desuper lapidibus obruuntur.

XIII STILICHONIS ET AVRELIANI

Bellum navale contra Gainam tyrannum inter Cherronesum et Hellespontum gestum est: multa milia Gothorum caesa vel demersa sunt. Gaina comes de hoc bello fugiens evasit: ipso tamen anno occisus est mense Februario.

XIIII VINCENTII ET FRAVITAE

Caput Gainae hastili praefixum Constantinopolim allatum est.

Maris Pontici superficies ita gelu frenata est, ut per triginta dies soluta tandem glacies instar montium per Propontidem superne portata decurreret.
Theodosius iunior patre Arcadio natus est IIII idus Apriles.

XV ARCADII V ET HONORII V

Romanae ecclesiae Innocentius tricensimus octavus creatus antistes vixit annis quindecim.
Theodosius iunior in loco quo pater patruusque suus Caesar creatus est.
Constantinopolim ingens terrae motus fuit.

I THEODOSII IVNIORIS ET RVMORIDI

Marina patre Arcadio nata III idus Febr.
Eudoxiae Arcadii uxoris super porfyreticam columnam argentea statua iuxta ecclesiam posita hactenus sistit.

Iohannem Constantinopolitanae civitatis episcopum, cui supradicti sex antistites incassum aemuli fuere aliosque triginta sibimet episcopos conscivere, nolente Arcadio principe in Cuccusum Armeniae oppidum exulem miserunt eumque post annum in

feigning ill-health, departed from the city. When battle against the Byzantines had commenced, most of the enemy fell, while others fled to our church, and there they were overwhelmed by stones thrown from above when the roof was dismantled.

1 Sept. 399– 13th indiction, consulship of Stilicho and Aurelian
31 Aug. 400 *400*

A naval battle was fought between the Chersonese and the Hellespont against the tyrant Gaïnas. Many thousands of Goths were killed or drowned. Count Gaïnas fled from this battle and escaped. Nevertheless he was killed in the month of February in this very year.

1 Sept. 400– 14th indiction, consulship of Vincentius and Fravitta
31 Aug. 401 *401*

1. The head of Gaïnas was fixed on a pole and brought to Constantinople.
2. The surface of the Pontic sea was so frozen over that, when it finally broke up, for thirty days ice the size of mountains was carried from above and surged down the Propontis.
3. The younger Theodosius, son of Arcadius, was born on 10 April.

1 Sept. 401– 15th indiction, consulship of Arcadius (5th) and Honorius
31 Aug. 402 (5th) *402*

1. Innocent was made thirty-eighth bishop of the Roman church and lived for fifteen years.
2. Theodosius the younger was made Caesar in the same place as his father and his uncle.
3. There was a huge earthquake at Constantinople.

1 Sept. 402 1st indiction, consulship of Theodosius the younger and
31 Aug. 403 Rumoridus *403*

1. Marina, daughter of Arcadius, was born on 11 February.
2. A silver statue of Eudoxia, the wife of Arcadius, was placed on a porphyry column beside the church. It is still standing.
3. The six bishops mentioned above were unsuccessful rivals of John, the bishop of the city of Constantinople, and they were in league with another thirty bishops. Against the will of the emperor Arcadius, they sent him into exile to the town of

villam, quae Comana in regione Pontica dicitur, de exilio in exilium relegarunt. hunc ibidem mortuum religiosa orthodoxorum plebs in atrio Basilisci episcopi idemque martyris ab eodem martyre in somnis ammonita in novum moxque repertum sepulchrum recondidit.

II HONORII VI ET ARISTAENETIS

Ecclesiam Constantinopolitanam flamma ignis, quae de beati Iohannis throno quondam episcopi nata fuit, subito conflagravit vicinamque ecclesiae urbis faciem serpens nihilo minus exussit.

Eudoxia uxor Arcadii diem obiit.

III STLICHONIS II ET ANTHEMII

Isauri per montem Tauri discursantes ingens dispendium rei publicae inportarunt: quibus Narbazaicus legatus maius continuo rependit incommodum.

IIII ARCADII VI ET PROBI

Theodosius iunior quinquennalia dedit.
Radagaisus paganus et Scytha cum ducentis milibus suorum totam Italiam inundavit.
Huldin et Sarus Hunnorum Gothorumque reges Radagaisum continuo devicerunt, ipsius capite amputato, captivos eius singulis aureis distrahentes.

V HONORII VII ET THEODOSII IVN. II

Cisterna maxima iuxta porfyreticam Constantini imperatoris columnam in foro eius sub plateae transitum constructa est.

VI BASSI ET PHILIPPI

Stilico comes, cuius duae filiae Maria et Thermantia singulae uxores Honorii principis fuere, utraque tamen virgo defuncta, spreto Honorio regnumque eius inhians, Halanorum, Suevorum,

Cuccusus in Armenia, and after a year relegated him from one exile to another, at a villa called Comana in the Pontic region. When he died there the religious people from among the orthodox buried him in the new and recently discovered tomb in the church of the bishop and martyr Basiliscus, after being directed in dreams by the martyr.

1 Sept. 403– 2nd indiction, consulship of Honorius (6th) and Aristaenetus
31 Aug. 404 *404*

1. A fire which originated in the throne of Blessed John the former bishop suddenly enveloped the church at Constantinople, and spreading gradually to the nearby facade of the city's church nevertheless consumed it.
2. Eudoxia, the wife of Arcadius, died.

1 Sept. 404– 3rd indiction, consulship of Stilicho (2nd) and Anthemius
31 Aug. 405 *405*

The Isaurians invaded through the Taurus mountains and caused huge loss to the empire, but the legate Narbazaicus immediately inflicted greater harm on them.

1 Sept. 405– 4th indiction, consulship of Arcadius (6th) and Probus
31 Aug. 406 *406*

1. Theodosius the Younger celebrated his fifth anniversary.
2. Radagaisus, a pagan and Scythian, overwhelmed the whole of Italy with two thousand of his men.
3. Uldin and Sarus, kings of the Huns and the Goths, defeated Radagaisus immediately; they cut off his head and sold his prisoners for a gold piece each.

1 Sept. 406– 5th indiction, consulship of Honorius (7th) and Theodosius
31 Aug. 407 the Younger (2nd) *407*

A very large reservoir was constructed beside the porphyry column of the emperor Constantine under the street-crossing in his forum.

1 Sept. 407– 6th indiction, consulship of Bassus and Philippus
31 Aug. 408 *408*

1. Count Stilicho, whose two daughters Maria and Thermantia were each wives of the Emperor Honorius (both of whom died virgins, however), despised Honorius and coveted

Vandalorum gentes donis pecuniisque inlectas contra regnum Honorii excitavit, Eucherium filium suum paganum et adversus Christianos insidias molientem cupiens Caesarem ordinare; qui cum eodem Eucherio dolo suo detecto occisus est.

Romae in foro Pacis per dies septem terra mugitum dedit.

Arcadius imperator vitae finem fecit: regnavit post obitum patris sui Theodosii annos tredecim.

VII HONORII VIII ET THEODOSII IVN. III

Aput Constantinopolim magna populi exarsit seditio, panis videlicet penuria sibimet ingruente.

VIII VARANAE SOLIVS

Halaricus trepidam urbem Romam invasit partemque eius cremavit incendio, sextoque die quam ingressus fuerat depraedata urbe egressus est, Placidia Honorii principis sorore abducta, quam postea Athaulfo propinquo suo tradidit uxorem.

IX HONORII VIIII ET THEODOSII IIII

Theodosius iunior decennalia, Honorius Romae vicennalia dedit.

Constantinus apud Gallias invasit imperium filiumque suum ex monacho Caesarem fecit.
Ipse apud Arelatum civitatem occiditur, Constans filius apud Viennam capite plectitur.

X THEODOSII IMP. V SOLIVS

Iovinus ac Sebastianus in Galliis tyrannidem molientes occisi sunt.

Attalus in mari captus atque Honorio exhibitus truncata manu vitae relictus est.

his kingdom. He enticed with gifts and money the tribes of the Alans, Suevi and Vandals, stirred them up against Honorius' kingdom and wished to make Caesar his son Eucherius, a pagan who was plotting treachery against the Christians. When his deceit was discovered he, together with Eucherius, was put to death.

2. The earth rumbled for seven days in the Forum of Peace at Rome.

3. The emperor Arcadius' life came to an end. He ruled for thirteen years after his father Theodosius.

1 Sept. 408– 7th indiction, consulship of Honorius (8th) and Theodosius
31 Aug. 409 the Younger (3rd) *409*

A great revolt of the people broke out at Constantinople, precipitated by a bread shortage.

1 Sept. 409– 8th indiction, consulship of Varanes alone
31 Aug. 410 *410*

Alaric invaded the fear-struck city of Rome and fired part of it in a conflagration. On the sixth day after he had entered he left the plundered city, having abducted Placidia, the sister of the emperor Honorius, whom he afterwards gave in marriage to his kinsman Athaulf.

1 Sept. 410– 9th indiction, consulship of Honorius (9th) and Theodosius
31 Aug. 411 (4th) *411*

1. Theodosius the Younger celebrated his tenth anniversary, Honorius his twentieth at Rome.

2. Constantine usurped power in Gaul and made Caesar his son, who had been a monk.

3. He himself was killed at the town of Arles, while his son Constans was put to death at Vienne.

1 Sept. 411– 10th indiction, consulship of Theodosius the Emperor (5th)
31 Aug. 412 alone *412*

1. Jovinus and Sebastianus were killed while plotting an usurpation in Gaul.

2. Attalus was captured at sea and brought before Honorius. His hand was cut cut off but his life was spared.

XI LVCII SOLIVS

Heraclianus Africae comes cum septingentis et tribus milibus nauium mox ad urbem Romam egressus est. occursu Marini comitis territus et in fugam versus adrepta nave solus Carthaginem rediit ibique ilico interfectus est.

XII CONSTANTII ET CONSTANTIS

Pulcheria Theodosii soror Augusta appellata est.

Valia rex Gothorum facta cum Honorio principe pace Placidiam sororem eius eidem viduam reddidit.

XIII HONORII X ET THEODOSII VI

Ecclesia Constantinopolitana dudum igne cremata his consulibus restaurata dedicataque est Attico episcopo eandem regente ecclesiam.

Lucianus presbyter vir sanctus, cui revelavit deus his consulibus locum sepulchri et reliquiarum corporis sancti Stephani primi martyris, scripsit ipsam relationem Graeco sermone ad omnium ecclesiarum personam.

XIIII THEODOSII AVG. VII ET PALLADII

Orosius presbyter Hispani generis septem libros historiarum descripsit. missus ab Augustino episcopo idem Orosius pro discenda animae ratione ad Hieronymum presbyterum reliquias beati Stephani tunc nuper inventas rediens primus intulit Occidenti.
Atticus Constantinopolitanus episcopus scripsit ad reginas Arcadii imperatoris filias de fide et virginitate librum valde egregium, in quo praeveniens Nestorianum dogma inpugnat.

XV HONORII XI ET CONSTANTII II

Tenebrae in die factae sunt.

1 Sept. 412– 11th indiction, consulship of Lucius alone
31 Aug. 413 *413*

Heraclian, a count of Africa, suddenly advanced towards the city of Rome with three thousand seven hundred ships. Frightened by the opposition of Count Marinus and put to flight, he returned to Carthage alone, having taken ship, and was immediately killed there.

1 Sept. 413– 12th indiction, consulship of Constantius and Constans
31 Aug. 414 *414*

1. Pulcheria, the sister of Theodosius, was designated Augusta.
2. Vallia, king of the Goths, made peace with the emperor Honorius and returned his widowed sister Placidia to him.

1 Sept. 414– 13th indiction, consulship of Honorius (10th) and Theodosius
31 Aug. 415 (6th) *415*

1. The church at Constantinople, which had been destroyed in a blaze long ago, was restored and dedicated in this consulship when Atticus was the bishop in charge of the church.
2. The priest Lucianus, a holy man to whom God revealed in this consulship the location of the tomb and the bodily remains of St. Stephen the first martyr, wrote the account itself in Greek to all the churches.

1 Sept. 415– 14th indiction, consulship of Theodosius (7th) and Palladius
31 Aug. 416 *416*

1. Orosius, a priest of the Spanish nation, compiled a seven-book history. This same Orosius, sent by the bishop Augustine to the priest Jerome to find out about the essence of the soul, was on his return the first to obtain for the West the then recently found relics of the Blessed Stephen.
2. Atticus, bishop of Constantinople, wrote to the royal daughters of the emperor Arcadius a quite excellent book 'On Faith and Virginity' in which he attacked the Nestorian dogma in advance.

1 Sept. 416– 15th indiction, consulship of Honorius (11th) and Constantius
31 Aug. 417 (2nd) *417*

1. There was darkness during the day.

Cibyra Asiae civitas aliquantaque praedia terrae motu demersa.

Romanae ecclesiae Zosimus XXXVIIII episcopus ordinatus vixit annos tres.

I HONORII XII ET THEODOSII VIII

Plinta comes idemque rebellio aput Palaestinam provinciam deletus est.
Solis defectio facta est.
Stella ab oriente per septem menses surgens ardensque apparuit.

II MONAXII ET PLINTAE

Valentinianus iunior apud Ravennam patre Constantio et Placidia matre V nonas Iulias natus est.
Multae Palaestinae civitates villaeque terrae motu conlapsae.

Dominus noster Iesus Christus semper ubique praesens et super montem oliveti Hierosolymae vicinum sese de nube manifestavit. multae tunc utriusque sexus vicinarum gentium nationes tam visu quam auditu perterritae atque credulae sacro Christi fonte ablutae sunt omniumque baptizatorum in tunicis crux salvatoris divinitatis nutu extemplo inpressa refulsit.

III THEODOSIO VIIII ET CONSTANTII III

Romanae ecclesiae Bonifatius quadragensimus episcopus ordinatus vixit annos tres.
In Oriente tumultum milites excitarunt ductoremque suum Maximinum nomine extinxerunt.
In Persida Christianis persecutio desaeviit.

IIII EUSTATHII ET AGRICOLAE

Theodosius imperator Eudociam Achivam duxit uxorem.

2. Cibyra, a town of Asia, and several estates were destroyed in an earthquake.
3. Zosimus was ordained thirty-ninth bishop of the Roman Church and lived for three years.

1 Sept. 417–31 Aug. 418 1st indiction, consulship of Honorius (12th) and Theodosius (8th) *418*
1. Plinta was made a count and at the same time the rebellion in the province of Palestine was squashed.
2. An eclipse of the sun occurred.
3. A star appeared from the East, rising and shining for seven months.

1 Sept. 418–31 Aug. 419 2nd indiction, consulship of Monaxius and Plinta *419*
1. Valentinian the Younger was born at Ravenna on 3 July. Constantius was his father and Placidia his mother.
2. Many cities and villages of Palestine collapsed in an earthquake.
3. Our Lord Jesus Christ, who is always and everywhere present, appeared from a cloud above the Mount of Olives near Jerusalem. At that time both male and female of many tribes of the neighbouring races were awe-struck, not so much by what they saw as what they heard, and believed. They were cleansed in the sacred fountain of Christ and there shone out the Saviour's cross which, through divine command, was immediately impressed on the tunics of all those baptized.

1 Sept. 419–31 Aug. 420 3rd indiction, consulship of Theodosius (9th) and Constantius (3rd) *420*
1. Boniface was ordained fortieth bishop of the Roman church and lived for three years.
2. In the East the soldiers raised a tumult and killed their general, named Maximinus.
3. In Persia persection raged violently against the Christians.

1 Sept. 420–31 Aug. 421 4th indiction, consulship of Eustathius and Agricola *421*
1. The emperor Theodosius married his wife, Eudocia the Greek.

Patri suo Arcadio in foro eius super inmanem columnam ingentem statuam idem Theodosius dedicavit.
Cisterna Aetii constructa est.
Romani cum Persis conflixere.

V HONORII XIII ET THEODOSII X

Theodosius imperator Eudoxiam filiam genuit.

In tricennalia Honorii Maximus tyrannus et Iovinus ferro vincti de Hispanias adducti atque interfecti sunt.

Hunni Thraciam vastaverunt.
Persae cum Romanis pacem pepigere.

VI ASCLEPIODOTI ET MARINIANI

Caelestinus Romanae ecclesiae quadragensimus primus antistes creatus vixit annos novem.
Euagrius scripsit altercationem Iudaei Simonis et Theofili Christiani, quae paene omnibus nota est.

Terrae motus multis in locis fuit et frugum inedia subsecuta.

Philippus et Sallustius philosophi morbo perierunt.

Stella saepe ardente crinita Honorius imperator fatale munus implevit.

VII VICTORIS ET CASTINI

Placidia mater Valentiniani Augusta nuncupata est.

Valentinianus Caesar creatus Theodosii imperatoris Eudoxiam filiam sibimet desponsavit.
Iohannes regnum Occidentale Honorio defuncto invasit.

VIII THEODOSII XI ET VALENTINIANI CAESARIS

Suprafatus Iohannes dolo potius Ardaburis et Asparis magis quam virtute occiditur.

2. Theodosius dedicated a huge statue on an enormous column to his father Arcadius, in his forum.

3. The reservoir of Aetius was built.

4. The Romans fought with the Persians.

1 Sept. 421– 5th indiction, consulship of Honorius (13th) and Theodosius
31 Aug. 422 (10th) *422*

1. Eudoxia, the daughter of the emperor Theodosius, was born.

2. On the thirtieth anniversary of Honorius, Maximus the usurper and Jovinus who had been conquered in battle were brought from Spain and put to death.

3. The Huns devastated Thrace.

4. The Persians made peace with the Romans.

1 Sept. 422– 6th indiction, consulship of Asclepiodotus and Marinianus
31 Aug. 423 *423*

1. Celestine was made forty-first bishop of the Roman church and lived for nine years.

2. Evagrius wrote the 'Confrontation of Simon the Jew and Theophilus the Christian', which is known to almost everybody.

3. There were earthquakes in many places and a food shortage followed.

4. The philosophers Philippus and Sallust perished through disease.

5. After a comet had glowed on and off, the emperor Honorius met his appointed fate.

1 Sept. 423– 7th indiction, consulship of Victor and Castinus
31 Aug. 424 *424*

1. Placidia, the mother of Valentinian was proclaimed Augusta.

2. Valentinian was made a Caesar and betrothed to Eudoxia, the daughter of the emperor Theodosius.

3. John usurped the Western empire on Honorius' death.

1 Sept. 424– 8th indiction, consulship of Theodosius (11th) and
31 Aug. 425 Valentinian Caesar *425*

1. The above mentioned John was killed by the treachery, rather than the manliness, of Ardaburius and Aspar.

Valentinianus iunior apud Ravennam factus est imperator.

VIIII THEODOSII XII ET VALENTINIANI II

Sisinnius vir sanctae simplicitatis et simplicis sanctitatis Constantinopolitanus episcopus factus est.

X HIERII ET ARDABVRIS

Pannoniae, quae per quinquaginta annos ab Hunnis retinebantur, a Romanis receptae sunt.
Thermae Theodosianae dedicatae.

XI FELICIS ET TAVRI

Nestorius Antiochia natus, vir satis quidem eloquentiae, sapientiae vero parum, Constantinopolitanis ammodum adnitentibus ex presbytero episcopus ordinatus est.

Beatissimi Iohannis episcopi, dudum malorum episcoporum invidia exsulati, apud comitatum coepit memoria celebrari mense Septembrio die XXVI.

XII FLORENTII ET DIONYSII

Orthodoxi nostri Macedonianorum ecclesiam extra muros urbis positam abstulerunt, quoniam iidem Macedoniani Antoninum Germis catholicum episcopum interfecerunt.

Beatissimus Augustinus Hipponiensis ecclesiae elegantissimus Christi sacerdos doctorque praecipuus placida morte quievit.

XIII THEODOSII XIII ET VALENTINIANI III

Theodosius imperator tricennalia gessit.

Felix apud Ravennam occiditur.
Caelestinus Romanae arcis pontifex Nestorio pravitatis episcopo per epistulam suam datis eidem decem dierum indutiis vel paenitenti veniam vel dissentienti damnationem denuntiat. idem

2. Valentinian the Younger was made emperor at Ravenna.

1 Sept. 425– 9th indiction, consulship of Theodosius (12th) and
31 Aug. 426 Valentinian (2nd) *426*
Sisinnius, a man of holy simplicity and simple holiness, was made bishop of Constantinople.

1 Sept. 426– 10th indiction, consulship of Hierius and Ardaburius
31 Aug. 427 *427*
1. The Pannonian provinces which had been retained for fifty years by the Huns were retaken by the Romans.
2. The Theodosian baths were dedicated.

1 Sept. 427– 11th indiction, consulship of Felix and Taurus
31 Aug. 428 *428*
1. The Antiochene-born Nestorius, a man of quite some eloquence but of insufficient wisdom, was ordained bishop, after being a priest, with the support of the people of Constantinople.
2. The memory of Blessed John the bishop, long ago exiled by the envy of evil bishops, began to be celebrated among the imperial court on the twenty-sixth day of September.

1 Sept. 428– 12th indiction, consulship of Florentinus and Dionysius
31 Aug. 429 *429*
1. Our orthodox believers took possession of the church of the Macedonians situated outside the walls of the city since the same Macedonians had killed Antonius, the catholic bishop of Germae.
2. The most Blessed Augustine of the church of Hippo, a most wonderful priest of Christ and an outstanding teacher, died a peaceful death.

1 Sept. 429– 13th indiction, consulship of Theodosius (13th) and
31 Aug. 430 Valentinian (3rd) *430*
1. The emperor Theodosius celebrated his thirtieth anniversary.
2. Felix was killed at Ravenna.
3. Celestine, the bishop of the Roman see, in a letter to the heretic bishop Nestorius, gave him a ten-day respite and promised forgiveness if he repented or condemnation if he

Nestorius ecclesiae Constantinopolitanae perfidus antistes, a quo et Nestoriana perfidia pullulavit, apud Ephesum ducentorum sanctorum patrum sententia in synodo condemnatus est, Caelestino Cyrillum Alexandriae civitatis episcopum pro tempore vicarium denuntiante. in locum Nestorii Maximianus episcopus subrogatus.

XIIII ANTIOCHI ET BASSI

Flaccilla Theodosii Augusti filia extremum spiritum fudit.

Barbari urbe augusta enutriti ad ecclesiam nostram hostili ritu confluunt: ignem in ecclesiam ad comburendum altare dum infesti iaciunt, invicem sese resistente deo trucidant.

Hoc tempore dum ad horrea publica Theodosius processum celebrat, tritici in plebem ingruente penuria imperator ab esuriente populo lapidibus inpetitur.

XV VALERII ET AETII

Romanae ecclesiae Xystus quadragensimus secundus episcopus ordinatus vixit annos octo.
Placidiae matris Valentiniani imperatoris instinctu ingens bellum inter Bonifatium et Aetium patricios gestum est.

Aetius longiore Bonifatii telo pridie sibimet praeparato Bonifatium congredientem vulneravit inlaesus, tertioque mense Bonifatius vulnere quo sauciatus fuerat emoritur, Pelagiam uxorem suam valde locupletem nulli alteri nisi Aetio nupturam fore exhortans.

I THEODOSII AVG. XIIII ET MAXIMI

Maxima urbis regiae pars septentrionalis per tres dies continuos incensa conlapsaque est mense Augusto.

refused. This Nestorius, a faithless bishop of the church of Constantinople and from whom the Nestorian heresy sprang, was condemned by a decree of two hundred holy fathers in a synod at Ephesus. Celestine proclaimed that Cyril, bishop of the city of Alexandria, was to be his replacement for the time being. Maximian was summoned as bishop in place of Nestorius.

1 Sept. 430– 4th indiction, consulship of Antiochus and Bassus
31 Aug. 431 *431*

1. Flaccilla, the daughter of Theodosius Augustus, breathed her last.
2. The barbarians who were being sheltered by the imperial city converged on our church in a threatening manner. When in their hostility they hurled fire into the church in order to burn the altar, they killed each other because God was against them.
3. At this time, while the emperor Theodosius was in procession to the public granaries, he was pelted with stones by a hungry populace because of the severe grain shortage among the people.

1 Sept. 431– 15th indiction, consulship of Valerius and Aetius
31 Aug. 432 *432*

1. Sixtus was ordained forty-second bishop of the Roman church, and lived for eight years.
2. On the instigation of Placidia, the mother of the emperor Valentinian, a great battle was waged between the patricians Boniface and Aetius.
3. Aetius engaged Boniface and wounded him, with a longer sword than that of Boniface, which had been made for him the previous day. He himself was unscathed. Three months later Boniface died from the injury he had incurred, imploring his very wealthy wife Pelagia to marry no one other than Aetius.

1 Sept. 432– 1st indiction, consulship of Theodosius Augustus (14th) and
31 Aug. 433 Maximus *433*

In the month of August, most of the northern part of the imperial city was ablaze for three successive days and collapsed to the ground.

II AREOBINDI ET ASPARIS

Honoria Valentiniani imperatoris soror ab Eugenio procuratore suo stuprata concepit, palatioque expulsa Theodosio principi de Italia transmissa Attilanem contra Occidentalem rem publicam concitabat.

III THEODOSII XV ET VALENTINIANI IIII

Forum Theodosii imperatoris in loco qui Heliane dicitur aedificatum est.
Sebastianus Bonifatii quondam patricii gener urbe augusta fugit atque in Africa interemptus est.

IIII ISIDORI ET SENATORIS

Theodosius imperator Cyzicum civitatem navibus petiit multaque eidem civitati munificentia praestita urbem augustam renavigavit.

V AETII II ET SIGISVVLDI

Valentinianus imperator Roma digressus ad copulandam sibi in matrimonium Eudoxiam Theodosii principis filiam, quam dudum desponsaverat, Constantinopolim advenit eaque sibi nupta aput Thessalonicam Italiam repetens hiemavit.

VI THEODOSII XVI ET FAVSTI

Contradis praedo cum piratis suisque comitibus captus interfectusque est.
Reliquiae beatissimi Iohannis augustae urbis quondam episcopi eidem redditae civitati ibique sepultae mense Ianuario die vicensimo octavo.
Valentinianus imperator cum Eudoxia uxore Ravennam ingressus.

1 Sept. 433– 2nd indiction, consulship of Areobindus and Aspar
31 Aug. 434 *434*

Honoria, the sister of the emperor Valentinian, was defiled by her procurator Eugenius and conceived. She was expelled from the palace and sent off from Italy to the emperor Theodosius, and incited Attila against the Western empire.

1 Sept. 434– 3rd indiction, consulship of Theodosius (15th) and
31 Aug. 435 Valentinian (4th) *435*

1. The forum of the emperor Theodosius was built in the place called Heliane.
2. Sebastian, the son-in-law of the former patrician Boniface, fled from the imperial city and was killed in Africa.

1 Sept. 435– 4th indiction, consulship of Isidore and Senator
31 Aug. 436 *436*

The emperor Theodosius set out with his fleet for the city of Cyzicus and, when he had demonstrated considerable generosity towards that city, he sailed back to the imperial city.

1 Sept. 436– 5th indiction, consulship of Aetius (2nd) and Sigisvult
31 Aug. 437 *437*

The emperor Valentinian set out from Rome to secure his marriage to Eudoxia the daughter of the emperor Theodosius, to whom he had been betrothed for a considerable time, and arrived at Constantinople. After the marriage, he spent the winter at Thessalonike on his way back to Italy.

1 Sept. 437– 6th indiction, consulship of Theodosius (16th) and Faustus
31 Aug. 438 *438*

1. The brigand Contradis, along with his pirates and companions, was captured and killed.
2. The relics of the most blessed John, formerly bishop of the imperial city, were given back to that city and were buried there on the twenty-eighth day of the month of January.
3. The emperor Valentinian entered Ravenna together with his wife Eudoxia.

VII THEODOSII XVII ET FESTI

Theodosius imperator octava quinquennalia edidit.

Eudocia uxor Theodosii principis ab Hierosolymis urbem regiam remeavit, beatissimi Stephani primi martyris reliquias, quae in basilica sancti Laurentii positae venerantur, secum deferens.

Hoc tempore Ginsiricus rex Vandalorum Africae civitates Carthaginemque metropolim cum suis satellitibus occupavit X kalendas Novembris.

VIII VALENTINIANI V ET ANATOLII

Paulinus magister officiorum in Caesarea Cappadociae iubente Theodosio principe interemptus est.
Romanae Ecclesiae Leo quadragensimus tertius papa creatus vixit annos viginti unum.

VIIII CYRI SOLIVS

Persae, Saraceni, Tzanni, Isauri, Hunni finibus suis egressi Romanorum sola vastaverunt. missi sunt contra hos Anatolius et Aspar magistri militiae pacemque cum his unius anni fecerunt.

Iohannes natione Vandalus magisterque militiae Arnigiscli fraude in Thracia interemptus est.
Hunnorum reges numerosis suorum cum milibus Illyricum irruerunt: Naisum, Singidunum aliasque civitates oppidaque Illyrici plurima exciderunt.

X EVDOXII ET DIOSCORI

Stella quae crinita dicitur per plurimum tempus ardens apparuit.

Bleda et Attila fratres multarumque gentium reges Illyricum Thraciamque depopulati sunt.

1 Sept. 438– 7th indiction, consulship of Theodosius (17th) and Festus
31 Aug. 439 *439*

1. Theodosius the emperor held his eighth quinquennial celebration.
2. Eudocia, the wife of the emperor Theodosius, returned from Jerusalem to the imperial city, bringing with her the relics of most blessed Stephen, the first martyr, which were placed in the basilica of St. Laurence where they are venerated.
3. At this time Geiseric the king of the Vandals occupied the cities of Africa and, together with his allies, the capital Carthage on 23 October.

1 Sept. 439– 8th indiction, consulship of Valentinian (5th) and Anatolius
31 Aug. 440 *440*

1. Paulinus, the Master of the Offices, was killed at Caesarea in Cappadocia on the order of the emperor Theodosius.
2. Leo was made forty-third Pope of the Roman church and lived for twenty-one years.

1 Sept. 440– 9th indiction, consulship of Cyrus alone
31 Aug. 441 *441*

1. The Persians, Saracens, Tzanni, Isaurians and Huns left their own territories and plundered the land of the Romans. Anatolius and Aspar, Masters of the Soldiery, were sent against them, and made peace with them for one year.
2. John, a Vandal and Master of the Soldiery, was killed in Thrace through the treachery of Arnigisclus.
3. The Hun kings, with countless thousands of their men, invaded Illyricum; they destroyed Naissus, Singidunum and very many other cities and towns of Illyricum.

1 Sept. 441– 10th indiction, consulship of Eudoxius and Dioscorus
31 Aug. 442 *442*

1. There appeared a star called a comet which glowed for some considerable time.
2. Bleda and Attila, who were brothers and kings of many tribes, ravaged Illyricum and Thrace.

XI MAXIMI ET PATERII

His consulibus tanta nix cecidit, ut per sex menses vix liquesci potuerit: multa hominum et animalium milia frigoris rigore confecta perierunt.

Theodosius imperator ex Asiana expeditione urbem rediit.

Thermarum quae Achilleae dicuntur encaeniae factae.

XII THEODOSII XVIII ET ALBINI

Theodosius princeps nona quinquennalia dedit.

Arcadia soror Theodosii vivendi finem fecit.
Aliquanta Bithyniae oppida atque praedia continuarum pluviarum et fluviorum inundatione crescentium sublabsa dissolutaque perierunt.
Severum presbyterum et Iohannem diaconum Eudociae reginae apud Aeliam urbem ministrantes missus ab imperatore Theodosio Saturninus comes domesticorum occidit. Eudocia nescio quo excita dolore Saturninum protinus obtruncavit, statimque mariti imperatoris nutu, regiis spolitata ministris, apud Aeliam civitatem moritura remansit.

101

XIII VALENTINIANI VI ET NOMI

Bleda rex Hunnorum Attilae fratris sui insidiis interimitur.

Aput Byzantium populari orta in circo seditione multi sese invicem occiderunt multaque intrinsecus hominum pecudumque morbo corpora perierunt.

XIV VALENTINIANI VII ET AETII III

His consulibus magna fames Constantinopolim invasit, pestisque ilico subsecuta.
Templum regiae civitatis igne crematum.

1 Sept. 442– 11th indiction, consulship of Maximus and Paterius
31 Aug. 443 *443*

1. In this consulship so much snow fell that for six months scarcely anything melted. Many thousands of men and animals were weakened by the severity of the cold and perished.
2. The emperor Theodosius returned to the city from his Asian expedition.
3. The dedication of the so-called Baths of Achilles was held.

1 Sept. 443– 12th indiction, consulship of Theodosius (18th) and Albinus
31 Aug. 444 *444*

1. The emperor Theodosius held his ninth quinquennial celebration.
2. Arcadia, the sister of Theodosius, ended her life.
3. Several towns and estates of Bithynia, which were levelled and washed away by the inundation of continual rain and rising rivers, were destroyed.
4. Saturninus, the Count of the Domestics sent by the emperor Theodosius, killed the priest Severus and the deacon John who were ministering to the empress Eudocia in the city of Jerusalem. Eudocia, spurred on by some grief or other, murdered Saturninus forthwith. On the command of her husband the emperor she was immediately stripped of her royal attendants and remained in the city of Jerusalem until her death.

1 Sept. 444– 13th indiction, consulship of Valentinian (6th) and Nomus
31 Aug. 445 *445*

1. Bleda, the king of the Huns, was killed through the plots of his brother Attila.
2. A popular insurrection arose in the Hippodrome at Byzantium and many slaughtered each other. Many bodies of men and beasts inside the city also perished through disease.

1 Sept. 445– 14th indiction, consulship of Valentinian (7th) and Aetius
31 Aug. 446 (3rd) *446*

1. In this consulship a great famine arose at Constantinople and a plague immediately followed.
2. The church of the imperial city was burnt in a fire.

XV ARDABVRIS ET CALEPII

Ingenti terrae motu per loca varia inminente plurimi urbis augustae muri recenti adhuc reaedificatione constructi cum quinquaginta septem turribus corruerunt. saxa quoque ingentia in foro Tauri dudum super sese in aedificio posita statuaeque plurimae sine ullius videlicet laesione conlapsae sunt, plurimis nihilominus civitatibus conlapsis: fames et aerum pestifer odor multa milia hominum iumentorumque delevit.

Ingens bellum et priore maius per Attilam regem nostris inflictum paene totam Europam excisis invasisque civitatibus atque castellis conrasit.
Eodem anno urbis augustae muri olim terrae motu conlapsi intra tres menses Constantino praefecto praetorio operam dante reaedificati sunt.

Attila rex usque ad Thermopolim infestus advenit.
Arnigisclus magister militiae in ripense Dacia iuxta Utum amnem ab Attila rege viriliter pugnans plurimis hostium interemptis occisus est.

I ZENONIS ET POSTVMIANI

Provincia India Theodosio principi tigrim domitam pro munere misit.
Utramque porticum Troadensem turresque portarum utrasque ignis subitus exussit: qua ruina continuo repurgata Antiochus praefectus praetorio in pristinam erexit speciem:

legatis Attilae a Theodosio depectas olim pecunias flagitantibus.

II PROTOGENIS ET ASTVRII

Marina Theodosii regis soror fati munus implevit.

Flavianus episcopus in secunda aput Ephesum synodo vi Dioscori Alexandriae episcopi et Saturnini spadonis in Epipam exulatus est.

1 Sept. 446– 15th indiction, consulship of Ardabur and Calepius
31 Aug. 447 *447*

1. A great earthquake shook various places and most of the walls of the imperial city, which had only recently been rebuilt, collapsed along with fifty-seven towers. Also huge stone blocks, long since positioned on each other in a building in the Forum of Taurus, as well as very many statues all collapsed without any apparent damage, but very many cities were levelled. Hunger and plague-bearing air destroyed many thousands of men and beasts.
2. A mighty war, greater than the previous one, was brought upon us by king Attila. It devastated almost the whole of Europe and cities and forts were invaded and pillaged.
3. In the same year, the walls of the imperial city, which had recently been destroyed in an earthquake, were rebuilt inside three months with Constantine the Praetorian Prefect in charge of the work.
4. King Attila advanced menacingly as far as Thermopylae.
5. Arnigisclus, the Master of the Soldiery, fought bravely in Dacia Ripensis alongside the Utum river and was killed by king Attila, when most of the enemy had been destroyed.

1 Sept. 447– 1st indiction, consulship of Zeno and Postumianus
31 Aug. 448 *448*

1. The province of India sent a domesticated tiger as a gift to the emperor Theodosius.
2. A sudden fire engulfed each Troad portico and both towers of the gates. The ruin was immediately cleared away and the Praetorian Prefect Antiochus restored it to its former appearance:
3. while an embassy of Attila was demanding from Theodosius the subsidies which had been agreed on.

1 Sept. 448– 2nd indiction, consulship of Protogenes and Asturius
31 Aug. 449 *449*

1. Marina, the sister of the emperor Theodosius, fulfilled her due fate.
2. In the second synod at Ephesus bishop Flavian was forcibly exiled to Epipa by Dioscorus the bishop of Alexandria and Saturninus the eunuch.

Ariobinda et Taurus patricii communi vita defuncti sunt.

III VALENTINIANI VII ET AVIENI

Theodosius imperator vivendi finem fecit: regnavit post mortem Arcadii patris sui annos XLII.

Loco eius Marcianus imperium adeptus est.
Chrysafius eunuchus Pulcheriae Theodosii sororis nutu sua cum avaritia interemptus est.

IIII MARCIANI AVGVSTI ET ADELFII

Leone pontifice sedem beati Petri regente sexcentorum triginta patrum sancta et universalis synodus contra Eutychetem nefandissimorum praesulem monachorum apud Calchedonam in basilica sanctae Eufemiae firmata est: solus Dioscorus Alexandrinae ecclesiae episcopus dissensit statimque ab iisdem catholicis patribus sacerdotio abdicatus est.

V SPORACII ET HERCVLANII

Marcianus Augustus suis statuit decretis, ut hi qui consules fieri cupiebant nihil aeris in populum spargerent, sed statutam pecuniam ad reparandum urbis aquae ductum dependerent.

Hoc tempore tres magni lapides e caelo in Thracia ceciderunt.
Aquileia civitas ab Attila Hunnorum rege excisa est.

VI VINCOMALI ET OPILIONIS

Iohannes praecursor domini et baptista caput suum, quod olim Herodias impia nefandaque postulatione ab umeris amputatum et in disco positum accepit proculque a truncato eius corpore sepelivit, duobus Orientalibus monachis ob adorandam apud Hierosolymam Christi domini resurrectionem introeuntibus revelavit, ut ad Herodis quondam regis habitaculum accedentes

3. The patricians Ariobindus and Taurus completed this common life.

1 Sept. 449– 31 Aug. 450 3rd indiction, consulship of Valentinian (7th) and Avienus *450*

1. The emperor Theodosius reached the end of his life. He ruled for forty-two years after the death of his father Arcadius.
2. Marcian took command of the empire in his place.
3. The eunuch Chrysaphius, along with his avarice, was eliminated on the command of Pulcheria the sister of Theodosius.

1 Sept. 450– 31 Aug. 451 4th indiction, consulship of Marcian Augustus and Adelphius *451*

While Leo was ruling as pontiff in the see of Blessed Peter a holy and universal synod of six hundred and thirty fathers was declared in the basilica of Saint Euphemia in Chalcedon against Eutyches, leader of the most impious monks. Only Dioscorus, bishop of Alexandria, disagreed and he was immediately removed from the priesthood by these same catholic fathers.

1 Sept. 451– 31 Aug. 452 5th indiction, consulship of Sporacius and Herculanus *452*

1. Marcian Augustus declared by his decrees that those who wished to become consuls should disburse no money among the people but spend the prescribed sum on repairing the city's aqueduct.
2. At this time three huge rocks fell from the sky in Thrace.
3. The city of Aquileia was destroyed by Attila king of the Huns.

1 Sept. 452– 31 Aug. 453 6th indiction, consulship of Vincomalus and Opilio *453*

John, the herald of the Lord and his baptizer, revealed his head which, at an unspeakably horrible demand, Herodias had once accepted after it had been cut from his shoulders and placed on a dish, and buried far from his headless body; he revealed his head to two eastern monks entering Jerusalem to celebrate the resurrection of Christ the Lord, so that when they ammoniti requirerent fideliter humo extollerent. hoc ergo caput fide repertum suaque hispida in mantica conditum dum ad propria remeantes habitacula pervehunt quidam Emetzenae figulus civitatis diutinam imminentemque sibi fugiens paupertatem sese his exhibuit comitem: quique dum nescius peram sibi creditam cum sacro capite portat, ab eo cuius caput vehebat noctu ammonitus utrumque comitem fugiens dereliquit, statimque Emetzenam urbem cum sancto levique onere introgressus est, ibique dum advixit, praecursoris Christi veneratus est caput moriensque sorori suae rerum nesciae signatum in vasculo tradidit recolendum. illa vero successori suo repositum signatumque ut erat dereliquit. porro Eustochius quidam occultus Arrianae fidei presbyter talem tantumque thesaurum indignus optinuit gratiamque quam Christus dominus per Iohannem Baptistam infirmo populo tribuebat, is eam ac si suam dumtaxat in vulgo disseminabat. hinc pravitate sua detectus Emetzana civitate expulsus est. hoc deinde antrum, in quo beatissimi Iohannis caput in urnam missum sub terraque reconditum erat, quidam monachi pro habitaculo habere coeperunt. Marcellus demum presbyter totiusque monasterii praesul dum in eodem specu vita inreprehensibili habitat, idem beatus Iohannes Christi praecursor sese eidem suumque ostendit caput, ibidemque sepultum multis praefulgens virtutibus patefecit. hoc igitur venerabile caput sub Uranio memoratae episcopo civitatis per Marcellum praefatum presbyterum constat inventum Vincomalo et Opilione consulibus mense Februario die vicensimo quarto media ieiuniorum paschalium septimana, imperatoribus vero Valentiniano et Marciano regnantibus.

Pulcheria Augusta Marciani principis uxor beati Laurentii atrium inimitabili opere consummavit beatumque vivendi finem fecit.

VII AETII ET STVDII

Attila rex Hunnorum Europae orbator provinciae noctu mulieris manu cultroque confoditur. quidam vero sanguinis reiectione

reached the place where the former king Herod lived they were advised to search around and dig the ground up faithfully. So while they were journeying back to their own places, carrying in their rough saddle-bag the head they had discovered by faith, a certain potter from the city of Emesa, fleeing from the poverty which threatened him daily, showed himself to them as a companion. While, in ignorance, he was carrying the sack entrusted to him with the sacred head, he was admonished in the night by him whose head he was carrying, and fleeing both his companions he made off. He entered the city of Emesa immediately with his holy and light burden, and as long as he lived there he venerated the head of Christ's herald. At his death, he handed it over in a jar to his sister, who was ignorant of the matter. She in fact left it to her heir, put away and sealed just as it was. Next a certain Eustochius, who was secretly a priest of the Arian faith, unworthily obtained this great treasure and dispensed to the rabble, as if it were purely his own, the grace which Christ the Lord bestows on his inconstant people through John the Baptist. When his wickedness was detected he was driven out of the city of Emesa. Afterwards this cave, in which the head of the most blessed John was set in an urn and reburied underground, became the abode of certain monks. Finally, while the priest and head of the monastery, Marcellus, was living a faultless life in that cave, blessed John, the herald of Christ, revealed himself and his head to Marcellus and showed that it was buried here, conspicuous by its many miracles. It is agreed therefore that this venerable head was found by the foresaid priest Marcellus while Uranius was bishop of the city mentioned. This was on the twenty-fourth day of February in the consulship of Vincomalus and Opilio, in the middle week of Lent, and the ruling emperors were in fact Valentinian and Marcian.

2. Pulcheria Augusta, wife of the emperor Marcian, completed the church of Blessed Laurence with exquisite workmanship and ended her life in sanctity.

1 Sept. 453– 7th indiction, consulship of Aetius and Studius

31 Aug. 454 *454*

1. Attila, king of the Huns, ravager of the province of Europe, was stabbed at night with a knife brandished by his

necatum perhibent.

Aetius magna Occidentalis rei publicae salus et regi Attilae terror a Valentiniano imperatore cum Boethio amico in palatio trucidatur, atque cum ipso Hesperium cecidit regnum nec hactenus valuit relevari.

VIII VALENTINIANI VIII ET ANTHEMII

Valentinianus princeps dolo Maximi patricii, cuius etiam fraude Aetius perierat, in campo Martio per Optilam et Thraustilam Aetii satellites iam percusso Heraclio spadone truncatus est.

Idem Maximus invasit imperium tertioque tyrannidis suae mense membratim Romae a Romanis discerptus est.

Gizericus rex Vandalorum, ab Eudoxia Valentiniani uxore epistulis invitatus ex Africa Romam ingressus est eaque urbe rebus omnibus spoliata eandem Eudoxiam cum duabus filiabus secum rediens abduxit.

IX VARANAE ET IOHANNIS

His consulibus innumera lucustarum agmina fructum Phrygiae vastaverunt.
Eucherius Lugdunensis ecclesiae pontifex multa scripsit tam ecclesiasticis quam monasticis studiis necessaria.

X CONSTANTINI ET RVFI

Marcianus imperator bonis principibus conparandus vitae spiritum amisit: imperavit annos sex menses sex. Leo eidem defuncto successit.
Cuius voluntate Maiorianus aput Ravennam Caesar est ordinatus.

wife. Some people in fact relate that he was killed by coughing up blood.
2. Aetius, the main salvation of the Western empire and a scourge to king Attila, was cut down in the palace together with his friend Boethius by the emperor Valentinian, and with him fell the Western Kingdom and it has not as yet been able to be restored.

1 Sept. 454– 8th indiction, consulship of Valentinian (8th) and Anthemius
31 Aug. 455 *455*

1. Through the treachery of the patrician Maximus, by whose deceit Aetius too had perished, the emperor Valentinian was cut down in the Campus Martius by means of Optila and Thraustila, accomplices of Aetius, after they had already killed Heraclius the eunuch.
2. The same Maximus usurped power and in the third month of his usurpation was torn limb from limb by the Romans in Rome.
3. Geiseric, king of the Vandals, was invited in a letter by Eudoxia, the wife of Valentinian, and entered Rome from Africa; after despoiling the city of everything he abducted the same Eudoxia and her two daughters, taking them back with him.

1 Sept. 455– 9th indiction, consulship of Varanes and John
31 Aug. 456 *456*

1. In this consulship countless swarms of locusts destroyed the crops of Phrygia.
2. Eucherius, a priest of the church of Lyons, wrote many things necessary for both church and monastic studies.

1 Sept. 456– 10th indiction, consulship of Constantine and Rufus
31 Aug. 457 *457*

1. The emperor Marcian, who must be numbered among the good emperors, breathed his last. He ruled for six years and six months. Leo succeeded him on his death.
2. By the will of Leo Majorian was proclaimed Caesar at Ravenna.

XI LEONIS AVG. ET MAIORIANI

Leo imperator pro tomo Calchedonense per universum orbem singulis orthodoxorum episcopis singulas consonantesque misit epistulas, quo sibi quid de eodem tomo sentirent cuncti suis rescriptionibus indicarent. horum omnium episcoporum ita conspirantes suscepit epistulas, ut eas putares uno tempore uniusque viri eloquio fuisse dictatas.

XII PATRICII ET RICIMERIS

Isaac Antiochenae ecclesiae presbyter scripsit Syro sermone multa praecipuaque adversus Nestorianos et Eutychianos. ruinam etiam Antiochiae elego carmine planxit, quemammodum Ephrem diaconus Nicomediae lapsum.

XIII APOLLONII ET MAGNI

Cyzicus civitas terrae motu concussa murorumque suorum ambitu interrupto sese suosque diu deplanxit.

XIIII DAGALAIFI ET SEVERINI

Romanae ecclesiae Hilarus quadragensimus quartus pontifex factus vixit annos sex.
Maiorianus Caesar apud Dertonam iuxta fluvium, qui Hira dicitur, interemptus. locum eius Severus invasit.

XV LEONIS AVG. II SOLIVS

Iacobus natione Achivus, religione paganus, medicinae artis peritia tam ingenio quam litteratura perclaruit. hic ob medendum Leonem Augustum febre defetigatum sacrum palatii cubiculum vocatus intravit statimque in sella iuxta torum imperialem posita sine ullo Augusti nutu consedit, sicque medicas adhibuit manus. porro meridie ad eundem sacrum pulvinar reversus sublatum sui propter solium, in quo matutinus resederat, protinus intellexit spondamque tori regiam intrepidus supersedit, veterumque studii

1 Sept. 457–31 Aug. 458 11th indiction, consulship of Leo Augustus and Majorian *458*

The emperor Leo sent to each of the orthodox bishops throughout the entire world individual and identical letters in support of the Chalcedonian Tome, so that they could all indicate in their replies what they felt about this Tome. He received such identical replies from all these bishops that you would think they had been dictated at the same time from the speech of a single man.

1 Sept. 458–31 Aug. 459 12th indiction, consulship of Patricius and Ricimer *459*

Isaac, a priest of the church of Antioch, wrote many outstanding things in Syriac against the Nestorians and Eutychians. He also lamented the ruin of Antioch in an elegiac poem, as the deacon Ephrem had treated the fall of Nicomedia.

1 Sept. 459–31 Aug. 460 13th indiction, consulship of Apollonius and Magnus *460*

The town of Cyzicus was shaken by an earthquake and since its surrounding walls had crumbled it mourned for itself and its people for a long time.

1 Sept. 460–31 Aug. 461 14th indiction, consulship of Dagalaifus and Severinus *461*

1. Hilary was made forty-fourth bishop of the Roman church and lived for six years.
2. Majorian Caesar was slaughtered at Dertona beside the river which is called Hira. Severus usurped his position.

1 Sept. 461–31 Aug. 462 15th indiction, consulship of Leo Augustus (2nd) alone *462*

Jacob, a Greek by nationality and pagan in religion, was famous for his medical skills as much as for his character and his writings. When he was called to the sacred bedchamber of the palace to cure Leo Augustus, who was stricken by a fever, he came in and immediately sat down in the chair placed beside the imperial bed without any signal from the emperor, and so he applied his healing hands. When he next returned at noon to the same sacred couch elevated near the seat where he

sui repertorum praeceptionibus monitum id sese gessisse, non temere praesumpsisse aegrotantem docuit principem.

I VIVIANI ET FELICIS

Prosper homo Aquitanicae regionis sermone scholasticus et adsertionibus nervosus multa composuisse dicitur. epistulae quoque papae Leonis adversus Eutychem de vera Christi incarnatione ad diversos datae ab isto dictatae creduntur.

II RVSTICI ET OLYBRII

Beorgor rex Halanorum a Ricimere rege occiditur.

III BASILISCI ET ARMENARICI

Constantinopolis magno invasa incendio facieque foedata deplanxit.
Severus, qui Occidentis arripuit principatum, Romae interiit.

IIII LEONIS AVG. III SOLIVS

Theodoritus episcopus Cyri civitatis scripsit de incarnatione domini adversus Eutychem presbyterum et Dioscorum Alexandriae episcopum, qui humanam in Christo carnem fuisse denegant.

V PVSAEI ET IOHANNIS

Leo imperator Anthemium patricium Romam misit imperatoremque constituit.
Romanae ecclesiae Simplicius quadragensimus quintus pontifex creatus vixit annos quindecim.
Ravennam civitatem terrae motus deterruit.

had sat in the morning he immediately understood and, undaunted, he seated himself above the royal bedstead. He explained to the ailing emperor that he had not acted arrogantly but had done this in accordance with the practices of the ancient founders of his discipline.

1 Sept. 462–31 Aug. 463 1st indiction, consulship of Vivianus and Felix *463*

Prosper, a man from the region of Aquitania, rhetorical in his language and vigorous in his declarations, is said to have composed many things. In addition it is believed that the letters of Pope Leo against Eutyches, concerning the true incarnation of Christ, which were sent to various people were dictated by this same man.

1 Sept. 463–31 Aug. 464 2nd indiction, consulship of Rusticius and Olybrius *464*

Beorgor, king of the Alans, was killed by king Ricimer.

1 Sept. 464–31 Aug. 465 3rd indiction, consulship of Basilicus and Hermenericus *465*

1. Constantinople was enveloped by a great blaze and disfigured in appearance, and it mourned.
2. Severus, who had seized the Western empire, died at Rome.

1 Sept. 465–31 Aug. 466 4th indiction, consulship of Leo Augustus (3rd) alone *466*

Theodoret, bishop of the town of Cyrrhus wrote about the incarnation of the Lord, against Eutyches the priest and Dioscorus the bishop of Alexandria, who deny that there was human flesh in Christ.

1 Sept. 466–31 Aug. 467 5th indiction, consulship of Pusaeus and John *467*

1. The emperor Leo sent the patrician Anthemius to Rome and made him emperor.
2. Simplicius was made forty-fifth bishop of the Roman church and lived for fifteen years.
3. An earthquake destroyed the city of Ravenna.

VI ANTHEMII AVG. II SOLIVS

Marcellinus Occidentis patricius idemque paganus dum Romanis contra Vandalos apud Carthaginem pugnantibus opem auxiliumque fert, ab iisdem dolo confoditur, pro quibus palam venerat pugnaturus.

VII ZENONIS ET MARCIANI

His consulibus caput Denzicis Hunnorum regis Attilae filii Constantinopolim adlatum est.

VIII IORDANIS ET SEVERI

Gennadius Constantinopolitanae ecclesiae pontifex Danihelem prophetam ex integro ad verbum commentatus est et homilias multas composuit.

VIIII LEONIS AVG. IIII ET PROBIANI

Aspar primus patriciorum cum Ardabure et Patriciolo filiis, illo quidem olim patricio, hoc autem Caesare generoque Leonis principis appellato, Arrianus cum Arriana prole spadonum ensibus in palatio vulneratus interiit.

X MARCIANI ET FESTI

Vesuvius mons Campaniae torridus intestinis ignibus aestuans exusta evomuit viscera nocturnisque in die tenebris incumbentibus omnem Europae faciem minuto contexit pulvere. huius metuendi memoriam cineris Byzantii annue celebrant VIII idus Novemb.

Anthemius imperator Romae a Recimero genero suo occiditur. loco eius Olybrius substitutus septimo mense imperii sui vita defunctus est.
In Asia aliquantae civitates vel oppida terrae motu conlapsa sunt.

1 Sept. 467– 6th indiction, consulship of Anthemius Augustus (2nd) alone
31 Aug. 468 *468*

Marcellinus, patrician of the West and a pagan, brought money and military support to the Romans who were fighting against the Vandals at Carthage. He was stabbed treacherously by the very persons on whose behalf he had openly come to fight.

1 Sept. 468– 7th indiction, consulship of Zeno and Marcian
31 Aug. 469 *469*

In this consulship the head of Denzic, son of Attila, king of the Huns, was brought to Constantinople.

1 Sept. 469– 8th indiction, consulship of Jordanes and Severus
31 Aug. 470 *470*

Gennadius, a priest of the church of Constantinople, wrote a new word-by-word commentary on the prophet Daniel and composed many sermons.

1 Sept. 470– 9th indiction, consulship of Leo Augustus (4th) and Probianus
31 Aug. 471 *471*

Aspar, chief of the patricians, with his sons Ardabur and Patriciolus (the former, on the one hand, was once a patrician and the latter, on the other, was designated Caesar and son-in-law of prince Leo) — an Arian, together with his Arian family — was wounded in the palace by the eunuchs' swords and perished.

1 Sept. 471– 10th indiction, consulship of Marcian and Festus
31 Aug. 472 *472*

1. Vesuvius, the volcanic mountain of Campania, roared with internal fires as it spat out boiling debris and nocturnal darkness overshadowed the day, and it showered the whole surface of Europe with fine particles of dust. The Byzantines celebrate the memory of this fearful ash on 6 November each year.
2. The emperor Anthemius was killed at Rome by his son-in-law Ricimer. Olybrius filled in his place and died in the seventh month of his reign.
3. In Asia several cities and towns were levelled in an earthquake.

XI LEONIS AVG. V SOLIVS

Glycerius apud Ravennam plus praesumptione quam electione Caesar factus est.
Constantinopoli seditione in circo orta multi Isaurorum a populo interempti sunt.

XII LEONIS IVNIORIS SOLIVS

Leo senior imperator Leone iuniore a se iam Caesare constituto morbo periit, tam sui imperii annis quam huius Leonis regni mensibus computatis annis decem et septem mensibus sex. Zenonem Leo iunior imperator idemque filius principem regni constituit.

Glycerius Caesar Romae imperium tenens a Nepote Marcellini quondam patricii sororis filio imperio expulsus in Portu urbis Romae ex Caesare episcopus ordinatus est et obiit.

XIII ZENONIS AVGVSTI II SOLIVS

Zeno imperator Verinae socrus suae et Basilisci fratris eius insidiis circumventus cum Ariagne uxore sua profugus in Isauriam tetendit. regnum Zenonis Basiliscus tyrannus invasit.

Nepos, qui Glycerium regno pepulerat, Romae elevatus est imperator. Nepote Orestes protinus effugato Augustulum filium suum in imperium conlocavit.

XIIII BASILISCI ET ARMATI

Basiliscus tyrannus Marco filio suo Caesare facto, dum contra fidem catholicam Nestoriana perfidia intumescens conatur adsurgere, ante inflatus crepuit quam paenitens stare potuerit. Basiliscus cum filio suo et cum Zenonida uxore sua, iam Zenone pristinum ad imperium remeante, in exilium missus est atque in oppidulo, quod Limnis in provincia Cappadociae dicitur, trusus fame extabuit.
Odoacar rex Gothorum Romam optinuit. Orestem Odoacer ilico trucidavit. Augustulum filium Orestis Odoacer in Lucullano

1 Sept. 472– 31 Aug. 473 11th indiction, consulship of Leo Augustus alone (5th) *473*

1. Glycerius was made Caesar at Ravenna more by presumption than election.
2. A sedition arose in the hippodrome at Constantinople and many Isaurians were killed by the people.

1 Sept. 473– 31 Aug. 474 12th indiction, consulship of Leo the Younger alone *474*

1. The emperor Leo the Elder died of a disease, after he had already made Leo the Younger a Caesar. Counting not only the years of his own rule but also the months of Leo the Younger, it comes to seventeen years and six months. Zeno was made emperor of the kingdom by his son and emperor Leo the Younger.
2. While holding power at Rome Glycerius Caesar was expelled from the empire by Nepos, the son of the sister of the former patrician Marcellinus; he was made a bishop instead of Caesar at the harbour of the city of Rome and died.

1 Sept. 474– 31 Aug. 475 13th indiction, consulship of Zeno Augustus (2nd) alone *475*

1. The emperor Zeno was surrounded by the plots of Verina his mother-in-law and her brother Basiliscus, fled with his wife Ariadne, and headed towards Isauria. Basiliscus the usurper seized the kingdom of Zeno.
2. Nepos, who had driven Glycerius from the kingdom, was elevated as emperor at Rome. After Nepos had fled, Orestes immediately put his son Augustulus into power.

1 Sept. 475– 31 Aug. 476 14th indiction, consulship of Basiliscus and Armatus *476*

1. The usurper Basiliscus made Marcus his son Caesar, but while swelling with the Nestorian heresy he tried to rise up against the catholic faith, he boasted loudly before he could stand repentant. When Zeno was restored to his former empire Basiliscus was sent into exile with his son and his wife Zenonis, and in a village called Limnis in Cappadocia he wasted away with hunger and died.
2. Odovacer, king of the Goths, took Rome. Odovacer cut down Orestes on the spot. Odovacer condemned Augustulus,

Campaniae castello exilii poena damnavit. Hesperium Romanae gentis imperium, quod septingentesimo nono urbis conditae anno primus Augustorum Octavianus Augustus tenere coepit, cum hoc Augustulo periit, anno decessorum regni imperatorum quingentesimo vigesimo secundo, Gothorum dehinc regibus Romam tenentibus.

XV SINE CONSVLIBVS

Bracilam comitem Odoacer rex apud Ravennam occidit.

I ILLI SOLIVS

Theodolus presbyter in Coelesyria multa conscripsit clarusque habetur.

II ZENONIS AVG. III

Sabinianus Magnus Illyricianae utriusque militiae ductor creatus curiam fragilem conlapsumque iustum rei publicae censum vel praepaventem fovit vel dependentem tutatus est. disciplinae praeterea militaris ita optimus institutor coercitorque fuit, ut priscis Romanorum ductoribus conparetur.

Theodoricum idem Sabinianus regem aput Graeciam debacchantem ingenio magis quam virtute deterruit.

III BASILII SOLIVS

Urbs regia per quadraginta continuos dies adsiduo terrae motu quassata magnopere sese adflicta deplanxit. ambae Troadenses porticus conruerunt: aliquantae ecclesiae vel scissae sunt vel conlapsae: statua Theodosii magni in foro Tauri super cochlidem columnam posita conruit duobus fornicibus eiusdem conlapsis. hunc formidolosum diem Byzantii celebrant VIII kal. Octobris.

His consulibus Nepos, quem dudum Orestes imperio abdicaverat, Viatoris et Ovidae comitum suorum insidiis haut longe a Salonis

the son of Orestes, with the punishment of exile in Lucullanum, a fort in Campania. With this Augustulus perished the Western empire of the Roman people, which the first Augustus, Octavian, began to rule in the seven hundred and ninth year from the foundation of the city. This occurred in the five hundred and twenty-second year of the kingdom of the departed emperors, with Gothic kings thereafter holding Rome.

1 Sept. 476– 15th indiction, no consuls
31 Aug. 477 *477*

Odovacer the king killed count Brachila at Ravenna.

1 Sept. 477– 1st indiction, consulship of Illus alone
31 Aug. 478 *478*

Theodolus, a priest in Coelesyria, wrote many things and was regarded as famous.

1 Sept. 478– 2nd indiction, consulship of Zeno Augustus (3rd)
31 Aug. 479 *479*

1. Sabinianus Magnus was appointed commander of both the Illyrian services; he either bolstered the frail senate when panic-stricken and the just imperial census that had collapsed, or supported them when vulnerable. He was so much the best administrator and disciplinarian in military affairs that he can be compared to the Romans' former commanders.
2. The same Sabinianus warded off king Theodoric, who was ranting madly in Greece, by shrewdness rather than manliness.

1 Sept. 479– 3rd indiction, consulship of Basil alone
31 Aug. 480 *480*

1. The imperial city, which was continuously shaken by an earthquake for forty successive days, greatly mourned its afflictions. Both Troad porticoes collapsed, several churches were either damaged or fell to the ground. The statue of Theodosius the Great, which had been placed in the forum of Taurus above the spiral column, collapsed after two of its supports had given way. The Byzantines celebrate this terrible day on 24 September.
2. In this consulship Nepos, whom Orestes had previously dismissed from the empire, was killed in his villa not far from

sua in villa occisus est.

IIII PLACIDI SOLIVS

Theodoricus Triari filius rex Gothorum adscitis suis usque ad Anaplum quarto urbis miliario armatus advenit: nulli tamen Romanorum noxius continuo reversus. porro in Illyricum properans dum inter suorum moventia plaustra progreditur, iacentis super carpentum teli acumine et pavescentis equi sui inpulsione fixus transverberatusque interiit.

Sabinianum Magnum mors, quae huic peccanti mundo merito imminet, ante ademit quam integrum defetigatae rei publicae subsidium ferret.

V TROCONDI ET SEVERINI

Romanae ecclesiae Felix quadragensimus sextus episcopus ordinatus vixit annos duodecim.
Theodoricus cognomento Valamer utramque Macedoniam Thessaliamque depopulatus est, Larissam quoque metropolim depraedatus.

VI FAVSTI SOLIVS

Idem Theodoricus rex Gothorum Zenonis Augusti munificentiis paene pacatus magisterque praesentis militiae factus, consul quoque designatus creditam sibi Ripensis Daciae partem Moesiaeque inferioris cum suis satellitibus pro tempore tenuit.

VII THEODORICI ET VENANTII

Illus natione Isaurus, dignitate magister officiorum, amputata apud comitatum auricula Orientem Zenoni infestus invasit. porro cum Leontio tyrannidem arripuit.

Totam namque per Africam crudelis Hunerici Vandalorum regis in nostros catholicos persecutio inportata est. nam exulatis diffugatisque plus quam trecentis triginta quattuor orthodoxorum episcopis ecclesiisque eorum clausis plebs fidelium variis subacta

Salona through the treachery of counts Viator and Ovida.

1 Sept. 480– 4th indiction, consulship of Placidus alone
31 Aug. 481 *481*

1. Theodoric, son of Triarius king of the Goths, together with his recruits, advanced in arms to Anaplous four miles from the city. However, he returned immediately without harming any of the Romans. Next, while hastening into Illyricum, as he proceeded among his own moving wagons he was run through and transfixed by the point of a weapon set above his carriage and by the weight of his fearstruck horse, and died.
2. Death, which deservedly threatens this sinful world, carried off Sabinianus Magnus before he could bring fresh help to the exhausted empire.

1 Sept. 481– 5th indiction, consulship of Trocundes and Severinus
31 Aug. 482 *482*

1. Felix was consecrated forty-sixth bishop of the Roman church and lived for twelve years.
2. Theodoric, called Valamer, devastated both Macedonias and Thessaly in addition to plundering the capital Larissa.

1 Sept. 482– 6th indiction, consulship of Faustus alone
31 Aug. 483 *483*

The same Theodoric, king of the Goths, was almost pacified through the bounties of Zeno Augustus and made Master of the Soldiers in the Imperial Presence, as well as consul-designate. Together with his allies he held in his trust for a while part of Dacia Ripensis and Lower Moesia.

1 Sept. 483– 7th indiction, consulship of Theodoric and Venantius
31 Aug. 484 *484*

1. Illus, an Isaurian by race, Master of the Offices by rank, had an ear cut off in the imperial court and invaded the East, posing a threat to Zeno. He, together with Leontius, then seized power.
2. Now the persecution of the cruel Huneric, king of the Vandals, was visited upon our catholic people throughout the whole of Africa. For when more than three hundred and thirty four orthodox bishops were banished and dispersed and their

suppliciis beatum consummavit agonem. nempe tunc idem rex Hunericus unius catholici adulescentis vitam a nativitate sua sine ullo sermone ducentis linguam praecepit excidi, idemque mutus, quod sine humano auditu Christo credens fidem didicerat, mox praecisa sibi lingua locutus est gloriamque deo in primo vocis suae exordio dedit. denique ex hoc fidelium contubernio aliquantos ego religiosissimos viros praecisis linguis manibus truncatis apud Byzantium integra voce conspexi loquentes. haec Arrianorum crudelitas in religiosos Christi cultores supra scriptis consulibus mense Februario coepit infligi.

VIII SYMMACHI SOLIVS

Longinus Zenonis frater Augusti post decennalem custodiam, quam eidem Illus apud Isauriam inflixerat, ad germanum suum Constantinopolim advenit.

IX LONGINI SOLIVS

Iohannes Antiochenae paroeciae ex grammatico presbyter scripsit adversum eos, qui in una tantum substantia adorandum adserunt Christum nec adquiescunt duas in Christo confitendas naturas.

X BOETHII SOLIVS

Theodoricus rex Gothorum Zenonis Augusti numquam beneficiis satiatus cum magna suorum manu usque ad regiam civitatem et Melentiadam oppidum infestus accessit plurimaque loca igne cremata ad Novensem Moesiae civitatem, unde advenerat, remeavit.

XI DYNAMII ET SIFIDII

Leontius interrex et Illus tyrannus in Papyrio Isauriae castello capti decollatique sunt. capita eorum Constantinopolim adlata praefixa hastilibus tabuere.

churches closed, the faithful people, hard-pressed by a variety of torments, completed their blessed struggle. At that time the same king Huneric had indeed ordered that the tongue of a Catholic youth who had lived without the gift of speech from his birth be cut out, and that same dumb man, because he had learnt the faith believing in Christ without any human hearing, suddenly began to speak after his tongue was cut out and, with his first words, gave glory to God. Afterwards, from this band of the faithful I myself saw several very religious men, with their tongues cut out and their hands chopped off, speaking at Byzantium in their normal voice. This Arian cruelty began to be inflicted on the devoted worshippers of Christ in the month of February in the consulship listed above.

1 Sept. 484–31 Aug. 485 8th indiction, consulship of Symmachus alone *485*

Longinus, the brother of Zeno Augustus, came to his kinsman in Constantinople after the ten-year imprisonment which Illus had inflicted on him in Isauria.

1 Sept. 485–31 Aug. 486 9th indiction, consulship of Longinus alone *486*

John a priest of the parish of Antioch, formerly a grammarian, wrote against those who assert that Christ must be worshipped in only one substance and who do not agree that the two natures in Christ must be acknowledged.

1 Sept. 486–31 Aug. 487 10th indiction, consulship of Boethius alone *487*

Theodoric, king of the Goths, was never satisfied by the favours of Zeno Augustus and made a hostile advance with a large force of his own as far as the royal city and the town of Melantias. When most places had been engulfed by fire he went back to Novae, the city in Moesia whence he had come.

1 Sept. 487–31 Aug. 488 11th indiction, consulship of Dynamius and Sividius *488*

1. The regent Leontius and the usurper Illus were captured and beheaded in the Isaurian fort of Papyrium. Their heads were fixed on spears and were brought to Constantinople where they rotted away.

Eodem anno Theodoricus rex omnium suorum multitudine adsumpta Gothorum in Italiam tetendit.

XII EVSEBII ET PROBINI

Idem Theodoricus rex Gothorum optatam occupavit Italiam. Odoacer itidem rex Gothorum metu Theodorici perterritus Ravennam est clausus. porro ab eodem Theodorico periuriis inlectus interfectusque est.

XIII LONGINI II ET FAVSTI

Zenon imperator Pelagii gulam in insula quae Panormum dicitur laqueo frangi praecepit.

XIIII OLYBRII SOLIVS

Zenon Augustus vita decessit tam sui imperii annis quam Basilisci tyrannidis mensibus conputatis anno XVII mense sexto. Anastasius ex silentiario imperator creatus est.

Bellum plebeium inter Byzantios ortum parsque urbis plurima atque circi igne combusta.

XV ANASTASII AVG. ET RVFI

Dum bellum paratur Isauricum dumque iidem Isauri imperium sibi vindicare nituntur, in Frygia iuxta Cottiaium civitatem undique confluunt, ibique Lilingis, segnis quidem pede, sed eques in bello acerrimus a Romanis primus in proelio trucidatur, omnesque simul Isauri fugae dediti per montana asperaque loca Isauriam repetunt. hoc bellum Isauricum per sex annos tractum est.

I EVSEBII II ET ALBINI

Bella civilia adversus Anastasii regnum apud Constantinopolim gesta sunt: statuae regis reginaequae funibus ligatae atque per urbem tractae.

2. In the same year, king Theodoric reached Italy with a crowd of his own Goths.

1 Sept. 488– 12th indiction, consulship of Eusebius and Probinus
31 Aug. 489 *489*

This Theodoric, king of the Goths, occupied Italy as he desired. Odovacer, king of the Goths at the same time, was paralysed with fear of Theodoric and was shut up in Ravenna. He was later misled by the lies of this Theodoric and put to death.

1 Sept. 489– 13th indiction, consulship of Longinus (2nd) and Faustus
31 Aug. 490 *490*

The emperor Zeno ordered that the neck of Pelagius be broken by a rope, on the island called Panormus.

1 Sept. 490– 14th indiction, consulship of Olybrius alone
31 Aug. 491 *491*

1. Zeno Augustus departed this life after ruling for seventeen years and six months, counting both the years of his own rule and the months of the usurpation of Basiliscus. Anastasius, formerly a silentiary, was made emperor.
2. Civil strife arose among the Byzantines and most of the city and the hippodrome was engulfed by a blaze.

1 Sept. 491– 15th indiction, consulship of Anastasius Augustus and Rufus
31 Aug. 492 *492*

While the Isaurian war was being prepared and while the same Isaurians were aiming to acquire the empire for themselves, they came from everywhere to Phrygia, near the city of Cotiaium. There Lilingis, who was slow on foot but the keenest horseman in war, was the first to be cut down by the Romans in the battle. All the Isaurians took flight at the same time and made for Isauria through the mountains and the difficult terrain. This Isaurian war lasted for six years.

1 Sept. 492– 1st indiction, consulship of Eusebius (2nd) and Albinus
31 Aug. 493 *493*

1. Civil strife occurred at Constantinople against the rule of Anastasius. Statues of the emperor and empress were bound with ropes and dragged through the city.

Iulianus magister militiae nocturno proelio pugnans Scythico ferro in Thracia confossus interiit.

II ASTERII ET PRAESIDII

Anastasius imperator contra orthodoxorum fidei maiestatem intestina coepit proelia commovere: piaculi sui perfidiam prius in Eufemium urbis episcopum sibi pro orthodoxorum fide viriliter resultantem profano manifestavit ingenio.

Laudicia, Hierapolis et Tripolis atque Agathicum uno tempore unoque terrae motu conlapsae sunt.
Romanae ecclesiae quadragensimus septimus Gelasius episcopus ordinatus vixit annos quattuor.

III VIATORIS SOLIVS

Eufemius augustae civitatis antistes, de quo superius fecimus mentionem, falso ab Anastasio principe accusatus atque damnatus in exilium ductus est. locum Eufemii Macedonius tenuit.

IIII PAVLI SOLIVS

Augustatico suo dudum Anastasius militibus praestito donativum quoque hoc fratre consule tribuit.
India Anastasio principi elephantum, quem Plautus poeta noster lucabum nomine dicit, duasque camelopardalas pro munere misit.

V ANASTASII AVG. II SOLIVS

Solis defectus apparuit.
Bellumque Isauricum hoc sexto anno sedatum.
Athenodorus Isaurorum primus in Isauria captus decollatusque est: caput eius Tarsum civitatem adlatum pro portis hastili fixum extabuit.

VI IOHANNIS SCYTHAE ET PAVLINI

Romanae ecclesiae quadragensimus octavus Anastasius pontifex ordinatus vixit annos II.

2. Julian, the Master of the Soldiery, was struck by a Scythian sword while fighting in a night battle in Thrace, and died.

1 Sept. 493– 2nd indiction, consulship of Asterius and Praesidius
31 Aug. 494 *494*

1. The emperor Anastasius began to declare civil war on the dignity of those of the orthodox faith. With evil scheming he first demonstrated the cruelty of his punishment against Euphemius, the bishop of the city, who was resisting the emperor manfully on behalf of the faith of the orthodox.
2. Laodicea, Hierapolis and Tripolis as well as Agathicum were destroyed by the same earthquake at the same time.
3. Gelasius was ordained forty-seventh bishop of the Roman church, and lived for four years.

1 Sept. 494– 3rd indiction, consulship of Viator alone
31 Aug. 495 *495*

The bishop of the imperial city, Euphemius, about whom we made mention above, was wrongly accused by the emperor Anastasius, condemned and led into exile. Macedonius took the place of Euphemius.

1 Sept. 495– 4th indiction, consulship of Paulus alone
31 Aug. 496 *496*

1. Along with his usual anniversary contributions Anastasius granted a donation to the soldiers at his brother's consulship.
2. India sent as a gift to the emperor Anastasius an elephant, which the poet Plautus calls a Lucanian cow, and two giraffes.

1 Sept. 496– 5th indiction, consulship of Augustus (2nd) alone
31 Aug. 497 *497*

1. An eclipse occurred.
2. The Isaurian war was ended in this its sixth year.
3. Athenodorus, the Isaurian chief, was captured and beheaded in Isauria. His head was taken to the city of Tarsus where it was fixed on a spear in front of the gates and rotted away.

1 Sept. 497– 6th indiction, consulship of John the Scythian and Paulinus
31 Aug. 498 *498*

1. Anastasius was ordained forty-eighth bishop of the Roman church and lived two years.

Longinus Isaurus cognomento Selinunteus apud Antiochiam Isauriae civitatem a comite Prisco captus Constantinopolim missus est catenatusque per agentem circumductus Anastasio principi et populo ingens spectaculum fuit, variisque deinde cruciatibus apud Nicaeam Bithyniae civitatem expensus est.
Nummis, quos Romani teruncianos[2] vocant, Graeci follares, Anastasius princeps suo nomine figuratis placibilem plebi commutationem distraxit.

VII IOHANNIS GIBBI SOLIVS

Aristus Illyricianae ductor militiae cum quindecim milibus armatorum et cum quingentis viginti plaustris armis ad proeliandum necessariis oneratis contra Bulgares Thraciam devastantes profectus est. bellum iuxta Tzurtam fluvium consertum, ubi plus quam quattuor milia nostrorum aut in fuga aut in praecipitio ripae fluminis interempta sunt. ibique Illyriciana virtus militum periit, Nicostrato, Innocentio, Tanco et Aquilino comitibus interfectis.

Hoc anno ingens terrae motus Ponticam concussit provinciam.

VIII PATRICII ET HYPATII

Romanae ecclesiae quadragensimus nonus Symmachus episcopus factus vixit annos quindecim.
Anastasius imperator donativum Illyriis militibus per Paulum tribunum notariorum misit.

IX POMPEI ET AVIENI

Constantio praefecto urbis ludos theatrales meridiano tempore spectante pars in eodem spectaculo cerealis parti adversae caeruleae occultas praeparavit insidias. nam enses saxaque in vasis inclusa fictilibus eademque arma diversis pomis desuper cumulata sub theatri porticu ritu vendentium statuit.

[2]Mommsen prints 'Terentianos' (the reading of T, U and R), assuming a reference to a proper name, in preference to the 'teruncianos' of previous editions. Yet 'teruncianos' makes better textual and numismatic sense (Melville-Jones, 1991).

2. Longinus the Isaurian, nick-named Selinunteus, was captured by count Priscus at Antioch, a city in Isauria, and sent to Constantinople. He was bound and led by an official to the emperor Anastasius and provided a great spectacle for the people. Afterwards he died under various tortures at Nicaea, a city of Bithynia.

3. By striking, in his own name, the coins which the Romans call 'terunciani' and the Greeks 'follares' the emperor Anastasius brought a peaceful change to the people.

1 Sept. 498– 7th indiction, consulship of John the Hunchback
31 Aug. 499 *499*

1. The Master of the Illyrian Soldiery, Aristus, with fifteen thousand armed men and five hundred and twenty wagons, weighed down with the arms necessary for fighting, set out against the Bulgars who were invading Thrace. They engaged in battle beside the river Tzurta where more than four thousand of our men were killed, either in flight or in the collapse of the river's bank. There perished the soldiery's Illyrian gallantry with the deaths of counts Nicostratus, Innocent, Tancus and Aquilinus.

2. In this year an immense earthquake shook the province of Pontica.

1 Sept. 499– 8th indiction, consulship of Patricius and Hypatius
31 Aug. 500 *500*

1. Symmachus was made forty-ninth bishop of the Roman church and lived for fifteen years.

2. The emperor Anastasius sent a donative to the Illyrian soldiers through Paulus, his Tribune of the Notaries.

1 Sept. 500– 9th indiction, consulship of Pompeius and Avienus
31 Aug. 501 *501*

1. While the Prefect of the City Constantius was watching the theatrical games in the middle of the day, the Greens prepared secret ambushes against the opposing Blues in the theatre itself. For they had swords and stones hidden in earthenware jars, and similar weapons concealed by various fruits under the portico of the theatre in the manner of the vendors.

dum residente Constantio ex more civium concrepant voces, ante visa quam audita arma excutiuntur saxaque in incautos cives instar imbrium iaciuntur ensesque vibrantes in amicorum inque vicinorum sanguine obliti suis cum percussoribus debacchantur: nutat et congemescit theatri cavea et refugientium huc atque illuc suorum pedibus conculcata occisorumque foedata cruore deplangit.

plus enim quam tria milia civium saxis gladiisque conpressionibus et aquis proscaenii amissos urbs augusta deflevit.

X PROBI ET AVIENI

Consueta gens Bulgarorum depraedatam saepe Thraciam, nullo Romanorum milite resistente, iterum devastata est.

Amidam opulentissimam civitatem monachorum eius astu proditam Choadis rex Persarum quinto mense, quam expugnare eam coeperat, inrupit, proditoresque eius monachos obtruncavit.

XI DEXICRATIS ET VOLVSIANI

Tres Romanorum ductores Patricius, Hypatius et Areobindas qui cum quindecim milibus armatorum olim in Persas missi fuerant pugnaturi, iuxta Syficum castellum cum iisdem Persis sine audacia conflixerunt, multis tunc militum ductoribus de proelio fugientibus caesis. inmenso dehinc auri pondere hostibus dato captam rebusque vacuam Amidam civitatem iidem nostri redemere ductores, iam Celere magistro officiorum sibi cum duobus milibus bellatorum in subsidium destinato.

XII CETHEGI SOLIVS

Interea Celer magister officiorum per Callinicum Mesopotamiae civitatem armatum ducens militem ad devastanda Persarum rura discurrit, plurimos agrestes rusticis intentos laboribus more

2. While Constantius was sitting down as was customary, the voices of the citizens grew louder; weapons were being thrown and being heard before being seen, stones were pelted like showers onto unwary citizens and swords, glistening heedlessly with the blood of friends and neighbours, raged together with those wielding them. The seating of the theatre tottered and creaked; it groaned as it was trampled by the feet of those fleeing this way and that and was polluted with the blood of the slain.
3. For the imperial city wept for more than three thousand citizens lost to stones and swords, to the crush of spectators and the waters of the stage.

1 Sept. 501– 31 Aug. 502 10th indiction, consulship of Probus and Avienus *502*

1. The familiar race of the Bulgars again devastated the oft-ravaged Thrace as there was no Roman solidery to resist them.
2. In the fifth month after commencing his attack on the very rich city of Amida, Choades, the king of the Persians, broke into it after it had been betrayed with the connivance of its monks, and killed its monastic traitors.

1 Sept. 502– 31 Aug. 503 11th indiction, consulship of Dexicrates and Volusianus *503*

Three Roman generals, Patricius, Hypatius and Areobindus, who had previously been sent into Persia with fifteen thousand armed men in order to fight, engaged the Persians without distinction near the fort of Siphrios. Many generals were killed at that time while fleeing from the battle. Thereupon when a large amount of gold had been given to the enemy, these same generals of ours ransomed the city of Amida, which had been captured and stripped of its contents, after Celer, the Master of the Offices, had already been sent to them with two thousand armed men as reinforcements.

1 Sept. 503– 31 Aug. 504 12th indiction, consulship of Cethegus alone *504*

Meanwhile Celer, the Master of the Offices, while leading his armed soldiery through Callinicum, a city of Mesopotamia,, diverted to ravage Persian farms. He killed like cattle, very many farmers engaged in their rural labours, led off the

pecudum trucidat, pastores diversorum pecorum cum numerosa iumenta abducit, castella latere lutoque constructa invadit, usque ad pontem Ferreum sic nomine dictum cuncta vastando progreditur, omnique praeda potitus ad communia castra ditato milite remeat. aliquanta dehinc ob percutiendum foedus cum Persis deliberat, misso ad se pro pepigendo foedere Armonio a secretis.

XIII SABINIANI ET THEODORI

Idem Sabinianus Sabiniani Magni filius ductorque militiae delegatus contra Mundonem Getam arma construxit. decem milia armatorum sibimet adscitorum plaustraque armis atque conmeatibus secum trahens pugnaturus accessit. commissoque ad Horreo Margo proelio multis suorum militibus in hoc conflictu perditis et in Margo flumine enecatis, amissis praeterea plaustris in castellum, quod Nato dicitur, cum paucis fugit. tanta in hoc lamentabile bello spes militum cecidit, ut quantum apud mortales nequaquam potuerit reparari.

XIIII AREOBINDAE ET MESSALAE

His consulibus Anastasii principis statua in eodem loco, quo dudum Theodosii magni steterat, super inmanem columnam in foro Tauri statuta est.

XV ANASTASII AVG. III

Seditio popularis in circo facta est: miles ei armatus obstitit.

Gradus circi septentrionalis sua cum fornice incensi conlapsique sunt Anastasio Caesare in processibus commorante.

I CELERIS ET VENANTII

Romanus comes domesticorum et Rusticus comes scholariorum cum centum armatis navibus totidemque dromonibus octo milia

shepherds of diverse flocks with their numerous herds, invaded a fort constructed of brick and mud and advanced as far as the so-called Ironbridge by laying waste everywhere. After taking possession of all the booty and enriching the soldiery, he returned to the common camp. Some time after, he resolved to conclude a treaty with the Persians when Armonius, secretary *a secretis*, had been sent to him to draft the treaty.

1 Sept. 504– 13th indiction, consulship of Sabinianus and Theodorus
31 Aug. 505 *505*

Sabinianus, the son of Sabinianus Magnus, was appointed Master of the Soldiery and gathered arms against Mundo the Goth. He set out to fight taking with him ten thousand armed recruits and wagons of arms and provisions. When battle had begun at Horreum Margi and many thousands of his men were lost in this conflict and drowned in the Margus river, and especially as the wagons had been lost at the fort called Nato, Sabinianus fled with a few men. So much of the soldiers' hope was destroyed in this unfortunate war that mortal men could never hope to make it up.

1 Sept. 505– 14th indiction, consulship of Areobindus and Messala
31 Aug. 506 *506*

In this consulship a statue of the emperor Anastasius was set up on the top of a lofty column in the Forum of Taurus in the same place where that of Theodosius the Great had once stood.

1 Sept. 506– 15th indiction, consulship of Anastasius Augustus (3rd)
31 Aug. 507 *507*

1. A popular uprising broke out in the hippodrome. The armed soldiery thwarted it.
2. While Anastasius was waiting in the procession the northern tier of the hippodrome, together with its arch, caught fire and collapsed.

1 Sept. 507– 1st indiction, consulship of Celer and Venantius
31 Aug. 508 *508*

Romanus, the count of Domestics, and Rusticus, the count of the scholae, with one hundred armed boats and the same

militum armatorum secum ferentibus ad devastanda Italiae litora processerunt et usque ad Tarentum antiquissimam civitatem adgressi sunt, remensoque mari inhonestam victoriam, quam piratico ausu Romani ex Romanis rapuerunt, Anastasio Caesari reportarunt.

II OPPORTVNI SOLIVS

Orto augusta urbe incendio utramque porticum a foro Constantini usque ad Perdicae tenuissimam statuam ignis in pulverem redegit.

Portus Iuliani undis suis rotalibus machinis prius exhaustus caenoque effoso purgatus est.

III BOETHII SOLIVS

Simulacrum aeneum in foro Strategii super fornicem residens et cornu copiae Fortunae retinens incendio proflammatum est conbustumque amisit brachium, quod tamen statuarii continuo solidarunt.
Appius patricius exulatus est.
Constantinus olim magister militiae episcopus Laodiciae ordinatus.

IIII SECVNDINI ET FELICIS

Macedonius augustae urbis episcopus, licet olim Anastasii imperatoris dolis fallaciisque circumventus pravorumque testimoniis eidem Caesari accusatus, quoniam tomum sanctorum patrum apud Calchedonam sancta dudum subscriptione roboratum eidem principi dare distulit, ab eodem Euchaita in exilium deputatus. locum Macedonii Timotheus meridiano tempore ab Anastasio Caesare episcopus ordinatus invasit.

V PAVLI ET MVSCIANI

Saepe caelum a septentrionali plaga ardere visum est.

number of fast naval vessels with eight thousand armed soldiers on board, set out to ravage the coasts of Italy and advanced as far as the ancient city of Tarentum. When they had crossed the sea they won for Anastasius Caesar a shameful victory, which Romans snatched from Romans with piratical daring.

1 Sept. 508– 2nd indiction, consulship of Opportunus alone
31 Aug. 509 *509*

1. A conflagration broke out in the imperial city and the fire reduced to dust both porticoes, from the Forum of Constantine as far as the very delicate statue of Perdix.
2. The harbour of Julian was first drained of its waters by wheeled machines and cleaned by excavating the mud.

1 Sept. 509– 3rd indiction, consulship of Boethius alone
31 Aug. 510 *510*

1. A copper image standing in the forum of Strategius above an arch and holding a horn of Fortune's plenty caught alight in a fire and was burnt. It lost an arm which, however, the sculptors refashioned immediately.
2. The patrician Appion was exiled.
3. Constantine, formerly Master of the Soldiery, was ordained bishop of Laodicea.

1 Sept. 510– 4th indiction, consulship of Secundinus and Felix
31 Aug. 511 *511*

Macedonius, the bishop of the imperial city, was at one stage surrounded by the treachery and lies of the emperor Anastasius and was denounced to that Caesar by the testimony of the heretics, because he refrained from handing over to the emperor the record of the holy Fathers at Chalcedon, previously reinforced by the list of holy names. He was sent into exile at Euchaita by Anastasius. The position of Macedonius was usurped by Timothy, who was ordained bishop by Anastasius Caesar in the middle of the day.

1 Sept. 511– 5th indiction, consulship of Paulus and Moschianus
31 Aug. 512 *512*

1. Frequently the sky appeared to glow in the northern region.

Die dominicorum, dum iubente Anastasio Caesare per Marinum perque Platonem in ecclesiae pulpito consistentes in hymnum trinitatis deipassianorum quaternitas additur, multi orthodoxorum pristina voce psallentes perfidosque praecones clamoribus obiurgantes in eiusdem ecclesiae gremio caesi sunt ductique in carceres perierunt.

altera nihilominus die in atrio sancti Theodori maiore caede catholici pro fide unica perculsi sunt. quapropter commota orthodoxorum agmina die sequenti, id est VIII idus Novemb., in quo die memoria cineris dudum totam Europam tegentis apud Byzantios celebratur, in foro Constantini undique confluunt.

quorum alii quidem, ceteris die noctuque hymnum trinitatis Christo deo psallentibus, totam peragrant civitatem et Anastasii Caesaris monastico habitu adsectatores[3] ferro flammisque interimunt: alii claves portarum omniumque signa militaria ad forum quo religionis castra metati fuerant, deferunt ibique Anastasio Caesare in processibus degente Areobindam sibi imperatorem fieri clamitant.

imaginibus deinde statuisque Anastasii in terram deiectis Celerem et Patricium senatores ad se supplicandi sibi vel satisfaciendi gratia missos iactis pluviae instar lapidibus reppulerunt domibus Marini et Pompei succensis.

in circum ad Anastasium ante suum solium consistentes hymnum trinitatis iuxta morem catholicum concinentes coruscansque evangelium crucemque Christi ferentes e foro plurimi convenerunt, Marinum Platonemque pravitatis eius auctores feris subici conclamantes.

hos cives idem Anastasius Caesar solitis periuriis simulatisque vocibus, sese facturum cuncta promittens, tertio die quam in forum advenerant sine ullo rerum effectu ad sua fecit habitacula repedare.

Porro redintegrata Anastasius pravitate infamem et inridendam

[3]Mommsen prints 'adsentatores' where 'adsectatores' (Petschenig, 1889, 154) is preferable.

2. On a Sunday, while on the order of Anastasius Caesar the fourth verse of the 'Theopaschites' was being added to the hymn of the Trinity by Marinus and Plato standing in the pulpit of the church, many of the orthodox, singing in the original version and loudly rebuking the objectionable proclamations, were cut down in the nave of that church and perished after being led away to prison.

3. Nevertheless, on the next day in the church of St. Theodore the catholics were killed on behalf of the one faith in a greater slaughter. As a result of this the distressed ranks of the orthodox on the following day gathered from everywhere in the forum of Constantine. That was on 6 November, the day on which the memory of the ash which once covered the whole of Europe is celebrated among the Byzantines.

4. Indeed, while the rest of them day and night sang the hymn of the Trinity to Christ their God, some of the people traversed the whole city and killed by fire and sword the supporters of Anastasius Caesar who were dressed in monastic garb. Others brought the keys of all the gates and the military standards to the forum where they had measured out a religious camp and there, while Anastasius was passing in procession, they shouted for Areobindus to be made emperor.

5. Afterwards, when statues and images of Anastasius had been hurled on the ground, they drove back with a storm of stones the senators Celer and Patricius, who had been sent to placate and satisfy them. The homes of Pompeius and Marinus were burnt.

6. Very many came from the forum into the hippodrome to Anastasius and they assembled in front of his throne, singing together the hymn of the Trinity in the catholic version, carrying a gospel book and a glittering cross of Christ, shouting for the instigators of the heresy, Marinus and Plato, to be thrown to the wild beasts.

7. But Anastasius Caesar, with his usual lies and empty words, promised that he would do everything and sent them back to their homes without any result on the third day after they had entered the forum.

8. Next, when the heresy had broken out again, Anastasius ordered a notorious and laughable synod to be held at the city

synodum apud Sidonem civitatem, cuius de nomine in ridiculis nomina praeponuntur, octoginta ferme perfidorum episcopis congregatis adversum orthodoxorum episcopos fieri imperavit. Flavianus Antiochiae catholicus patriarcha et Iohannes Paltensium oppidi pontifex, quoniam hunc coetum sacrilegum refellerant, in castellum quod Petra dicitur exules missi sunt. ibi Flavianus confessor Christi in domino requievit, Iohannem Iustinus Augustus, mox imperator factus est, revocavit.

His fere temporibus solis defectus contigit.
Gens Herulorum in terras atque civitates Romanorum iussu Anastasii Caesaris introducta.

VI CLEMENTINI ET PROBI

Severus Eutychetis perfidiae cultor Anastasio Caesare volente sedem Flaviani antistitis ex monacho factus episcopus occupavit.
Dorotheus Ancyrae civitatis venerandus antistes Anastasio principi propter unicam orthodoxorum fidem iugiter adversarius finem vivendi, quem sibimet misso contra se a Caesare magistriano ipse praedixerat, in dicto tempore fecit.

VII SENATORIS SOLIVS

Vitalianus Scytha, adsumpta Romanorum equitum peditumque plus quam sexaginta milia armatorum in triduo congregatorum, in locum qui Septimus dicitur advenit ibique castra metatus est, dispositisque a mari in mare suorum ordinibus ipse ad usque portam, quae aurea dicitur, sine ullius accessit dispendio, scilicet pro orthodoxorum se fide proque Macedonio urbis episcopo incassum ab Anastasio principe exulato Constantinopolim accessisse asserens. porro Anastasii simulationibus atque periuriis per Theodorum internuntium inlectus atque inlusus octavo die quam urbem accesserat remeavit.

Hinc Odyssum Moesiae civitatem Vitalianus pernoctans astu ingressus est.
Cyrillum lenocinantem magis quam strenuum militiae ductorem inter duas paelices Vitalianus repperit dormientem, eumque

of Sidon (whose name surpasses all others in stupidity), with about eighty heretic bishops assembling there in opposition to the orthodox bishop.

9. Flavianus, the catholic patriarch of Antioch, and John, the bishop of the town of Paltos, although they refuted the sacrilegious assembly, were sent as exiles to the fort called Petra. There Flavianus, a confessor of Christ, fell asleep in the Lord. Justin Augustus, who was made emperor soon after, recalled John.

10. At about this time an eclipse occurred.

11. The tribe of the Heruli was introduced into the territories and cities of the Romans by order of Anastasius Caesar.

1 Sept. 512– 31 Aug. 513 6th indiction, consulship of Clementinus and Probus *513*

Severus, an adherent of the Eutychian heresy, was made a bishop after being formerly a monk, and occupied the see of Flavianus in accordance with the will of Anastasius Caesar. Dorotheus, the venerable bishop of the city of Ancyra, who consistently opposed the emperor Anastasius on behalf of the one faith of the orthodox, came to the end of his life at this time, as he had foretold to the official sent to him by Caesar.

1 Sept. 513– 31 Aug. 514 7th indiction, consulship of Senator alone *514*

1. Vitalian, a Scythian, took more than sixty thousand Roman cavalry and infantry collected in three days and went to the place called the Hebdomon and pitched camp there. After arranging his contingents from one sea across to the other he himself advanced up to the Golden Gate (as it is called) without losing a single man, while maintaining ostensibly that he had approached Constantinople on behalf of Macedonius the bishop of the city, exiled without reason by the emperor Anastasius. Next, misled and deluded by the pretences and lies of Anastasius through his intermediary Theodorus, he departed on the eighth day after reaching the city.

2. Vitalian came cunningly by night to the city of Odyssus in Moesia.

3. Vitalian found Cyril, a soft rather than a hardy Master of the Soldiery, sleeping between two concubines and, when he

abstractum mox cultro Getico iugulavit hostemque se Anastasio Caesari palam aperteque exhibuit.

VIII ANTHEMII ET FLORENTII

Romanae ecclesiae quinquagensimus Hormisda episcopus ordinatus vixit annos novem.
Idem Vitalianus eidem Anastasio imperatori immanior factus est inimicus: praemissis quippe suorum equitibus armatisque naviculis sinistro sibi litore decurrentibus ipse peditum armis stipatus Systhenense praedium ingressus est totiusque loci palatium habuit mansionem.

missi sunt ad Vitalianum a Caesare senatores, qui pacis cum eo leges componerent: nongenta pondo auri, exceptis regalibus muneribus, pro pretio tunc accepit Hypatii, iam mille centum auri libris cum Uranio captivo sibi a suis in Sozopoli oblatis.

magister militum Vitalianus per Thracias factus Hypatium, quem captivum catenatumque apud Acres castellum tenebat, reversus suo remisit avunculo.
Ea tempestate Hunni Armenia transmissa totam Cappadociam devastantes usque Lycaoniam perrexerunt.

Ariagne Augusta sexaginta annis in palatio exactis vita decessit.

IX PETRI SOLIVS

Mutata fide Anastasius imperator Vitaliano succedit eidemque Rufinum destinat successorem.
Helias Hierosolymitanae urbis episcopus in villa quae Haila dicitur ab eodem principe relegatus emoritur.
Laurentium praeterea Lychnidensem, Domnionem Serdicensem, Alcissum Nicopolitanum, Gaianum Naisitanum et Euangelum Pautaliensem, catholicos Illyrici sacerdotes, suis Anastasius praesentari iussit obtutibus. Alcissus et Gaianus episcopi apud Byzantium vita defuncti sunt unoque sepulchro reconditi. Domnione et Euangelo ad sedes proprias ob metu Illyriciani

had extricated him, he slaughtered him with a Gothic knife and he revealed himself both publicly and openly as an enemy to Anastasius Caesar.

1 Sept. 514– 31 Aug. 515 8th indiction, consulship of Anthemius and Florentius *515*

1. Hormisdas was ordained fiftieth bishop of the Roman church and lived nine years.
2. This same Vitalian became a more ruthless enemy of the emperor Anastasius, for when his cavalry had been sent ahead and his armed boats had been put off from the left shore he himself entered the estate of Sosthenium, surrounded by his armed infantry, and took over the palace of the whole area as his own station.
3. Senators were sent to Vitalian from Caesar to draw up terms of peace with him. At that time he accepted nine hundred pounds of gold, not counting the royal levies, as the price for Hypatius — one thousand one hundred pounds having already been offered to him by his own men, together with Uranius, who had been taken prisoner in Sozopolis.
4. Vitalian was made Master of the Soldiery for Thrace and on his return sent Hypatius, whom he was holding captive and in chains, at the fort of Acrae, back to his uncle.
5. At that time the Huns, after crossing Armenia, were laying waste the whole of Cappadocia and reached as far as Lycaonia.
6. Ariadne Augusta died in the palace, after completing sixty years.

1 Sept. 515– 31 Aug. 516 9th indiction, consulship of Peter alone *516*

1. The emperor Anastasius went back on his word, relieved Vitalian and nominated Rufinus as his successor.
2. Elias, bishop of the city of Jerusalem, was exiled by the same emperor to a village called Aila and died.
3. Anastasius ordered some catholic priests of Illyricum to be presented to his sight, especially Laurence of Lychnidos, Domnio of Serdica, Alcissus of Nicopolis, Gaianus of Naissus and Evangelus of Pautalia. The bishops Alcissus and Gaianus died at Byzantium and were buried in one tomb. Since Domnio and Evangelus had suddenly been sent back to their

catholici militis extemplo remissis solus Laurentius Anastasium imperatorem in palatio pro fide catholica saepe convincens apud comitatum ac si in exilio relegatus retentusque est, mobiliorque deinde corpore, quam Constantinopolim advenerat, effectus. nam septimo infirmitatis suae anno idem Laurentius fide sua et Christi gratia in atrio Cosmae et Damiani sanatus est pedibusque sistere propriis gressìbusque meruit confirmari suaeque dein patriae incolumis reddi, ibique maior octogenario requiescit.

X ANASTASII ET AGAPITI

Olla illa, quae in Hieremia vate ab aquilone adversum nos nostraque delicta saepe succenditur, tela ignita fabricavit maximamque partem Illyrici iisdem iaculis vulneravit. duae tunc Macedoniae Thessaliaque vastatae et usque Thermopylas veteremque Epirum Getae equites depraedati sunt. mille tunc librarum auri denarios per Paulum Anastasius imperator pro redimendis Romanorum captivis Iohanni praefecto Illyrici misit: deficiente pretio vel inclusi suis cum domunculis captivi Romani incensi sunt vel pro muris clausarum urbium trucidati.

XI MAGNI SOLIVS

In provincia Dardania adsiduo terrae motu viginti quattuor castella uno momento conlapsa sunt: quorum duo suis cum habitatoribus demersa, quattuor dimidia aedificiorum suorum hominumque amissa parte destructa, undecim tertia domorum totidemque populi clade deiecta, septem quarta tectorum suorum totaque plebis parte depressa, vicina vero metu ruinarum despecta sunt. Scupus namque metropolis, licet sine civium suorum hostem fugientium clade, funditus tamen corruit. plurimi totius provinciae montes hoc terrae motu scissi sunt saxaque suis evulsa conpagibus devolutaque arborum crepido. per triginta passuum milia patens et in duodecim pedum latitudinem dehiscens profundam aliquantis

own sees through fear of the catholic Illyrian soldiery, only Laurence was retained as if he had been exiled, while frequently arguing about the catholic faith with the emperor in the palace in the presence of the imperial court. He afterwards proved more agile in body than when he had come to Constantinople for, in the seventh year of his infirmity, this very Laurence was healed by his faith and by the grace of Christ in the church of Cosmas and Damian, and he won the reward of standing firm on his feet and being strengthened in his gait. Afterwards he returned safely to his country where he died aged more than eighty.

1 Sept. 516– 31 Aug. 517 10th indiction, consulship of Anastasius and Agapitus *517*

That famous woman, who in the prophet Jeremiah is often enkindled by the north wind against us and our sins, forged weapons of fire and with the same weapons damaged a very great part of Illyricum. At that time both Macedonias and Thessaly were ravaged and the Gothic cavalry plundered as far as Thermopylae and Epirus Vetus. Through Paul the emperor Anastasius sent one thousand pounds of gold denarii to John, the prefect of Illyricum, to ransom the Romans' prisoners. Because that was not enough the Roman prisoners were either burnt while shut in their dwellings or killed in front of the walls of the enclosed cities.

1 Sept. 517– 31 Aug. 518 11th indiction, consulship of Magnus alone *518*

1. In the province of Dardania twenty-four forts collapsed at the same time in a violent earthquake. Of these, two were buried completely along with their inhabitants, four lost half their buildings and inhabitants in a partial destruction, eleven had one-third of their homes and the same number of people lost, seven had one-quarter of their houses along with all their inhabitants demolished. Finally, the neighbouring places were abandoned in fear of destruction. For the metropolis of Scupi was completely ruined, although it lost none of its citizens who had been fleeing from their enemy. Most of the mountains of this entire province were split by this earthquake, stones torn from their outcrops and trees uprooted. Through a deep chasm thirty miles long and twelve feet wide the quake

voraginem civibus castellorum saxorumque ruinas vel adhuc hostium incursiones fugientibus busta[4] paravit. uno in castello regionis Gavisae, quod Sarnonto dicitur, ruptis tunc terra venis et ad instar torridae fornacis exaestuans diutinum altrinsecus ferventemque imbrem evomuit.

Anastasius imperator subita morte praeventus maior octogenario periit: regnavit annos viginti septem menses duos dies viginti novem.

[*Daras civitate huiuscemodi condita in Mesopotamia. Daras quaedam possessio LX ab Amida civitate miliario ad austrum sita et quindecim milibus a Nisibino oppido ad occasum distans Amidensi ecclesiae reditum pensavit. huius ergo humilis villae casas Anastasius imperator ob condendam ibi civitatem dato pretio emit, missisque continuo praecipuis fabris*[5] *construi praecepit: Calliopium deinde Antiochenae urbis patricium huic operi praefecit. nempe hic collem in planitiem desinentem mira sagacitate ob fundamenta locanda sulcum sarculo designavit, murisque firmissimis fascia tenus consummatis undique texit. rivum quoque, qui ex praedii nomine, iuxta quod nascitur, Cordissus nominatur serpensque murmurat, quintoque miliario eundem collem novamque dividit civitatem, concesso utrique ostio prolabentem inclusit. publicis praeterea moenibus decoratae civitati pristinum nomen villae reliquit. ingens huius frontispicium civitatis in editiori loco constructa murisque continuata turris Herculea sic nomine dicta suspicitur Nisibin quidem ad orientem, Amidam huius ad aquilonem respiciens.*[6]]

[4]Mommsen prints 'iussa' (the reading of T and S) but suggests 'busta' as possible; Petschenig (1889, 154) proposed 'scissa'. The context points to 'busta' as the most likely.

[5]Mommsen printed the otherwise unattested 'praefabris'; however, his suggestion in the apparatus of 'praecipuis fabris' makes better sense of the circumstances of Anastasius' rapid building program at Dara.

[6]This account of Dara (preserved only in S) does not form part of the original chronicle, although it was printed in Mommsen's edition. Instead, it comes originally from Marcellinus' lost work on the locations of places (Croke, 1984, passim).

provided graves for a considerable number of the citizens fleeing from the ruins of the forts and rocky places and still fleeing the raids of enemies. In one fort of the region of Gavisa, which is called Sarnontum, the earth's channels were dislocated and after boiling up like a burning furnace disgorged a fiery shower which had built up for a long time on the inside.

2. The emperor Anastasius died suddenly, aged more than eighty. He reigned for twenty-seven years, two months and twenty-nine days.

[*Dara, a city of this kind, was founded in Mesopotamia. Dara, a certain estate located 60 miles south from Amida and fifteen miles west from the town of Nisibis, paid its dues to the church of Amida. So the emperor Anastasius bought the houses of this modest town at a fixed price for the purpose of founding a city there, and he immediately despatched outstanding workmen and ordered building to begin. He put Calliopius, who was later a patrician of Antioch, in charge of this work. Indeed, with wonderful perception, he marked out with a hoe a furrow for locating the foundations on a hill ending up on level ground; and he surrounded it on all sides to the edge of its boundaries with the erection of very strong walls. So too he enclosed the stream called Cordissus, which takes its name from the estate near where it originates, and which winds its way as it roars along, and at the fifth milestone it divides the same hill and the new city, falling into a concealed entrance at each end. Henceforth he allowed the city which had been endowed with communal walls to retain the name of the village. The so-called Herculean tower, the city's huge lookout, was built on higher ground and connected to the walls. It looked up to Nisibis to the east and looked back to Amida to its north.*]

XII IVSTINI AVG. ET EVTHARICI

[T][7] Iustinus a senatu electus imperator continuo ordinatus est.

Amantius palatii praepositus, Andreas, Misahel et Ardabur cubicularii Manichaeorum fautores et Iustini Augusti deprehensi sunt proditores. quorum duo Amantius et Andreas ferro trucidati sunt, Misahel et Ardabur Serdicam in exilium missi. Theocritus Amantii satelles, quem idem Amantius praepositus ad regnandum clam praeparaverat, comprehensus et in carcere saxis contusus ingentibus periit salsoque in gurgite iacuit, sepultura quoque cum inperio, cui inhiarat, caruit.

Vitalianus Scytha Iustini principis pietate ad rem publicam revocatus Constantinopolim ingressus est septimoque receptionis suae die magister militum ordinatus.

XII VITALIANI ET RVSTICI

Vitalianus consul septimo mense consulatus sui sedecim vulneribus confossus, in palatio cum Celeriano et Paulo satellitibus suis interemptus est.

XIIII IVSTINIANI ET VALERII

Famosissimum hunc consulatum Iustinianus consul omnium Orientalium consulum profecto munificentior his liberalitatibus edidit. nam ducenta octoginta octo milia solidorum in populum inque spectacula sive in spectaculorum machinam distributa, viginti leones, triginta pardos exceptis aliis feris in amphitheatro simul exhibuit. numerosos praeterea faleratosque in circo caballos iam donatis quoque impertivit aurigis, una dumtaxat ultimaque mappa insanienti populo denegata.

[7]At this point, affected by the inclusion of the previous entry on Dara, S preserves the entries found in T in abbreviated form, though with some additions (see Croke, 1984):

[S] *Iustinus imperator creatus.*

Amantii palatii praepositus et Andreas cubicularius uterque regni eius inimicus in insula decapitatus est.

Vitalianus Scytha urbem data acceptaque fide accitus ingreditur statimque magister militum ordinatus.

1 Sept. 518– 12th indiction, Justin Augustus and Eutharic
31 Aug. 519 *519*

1. Justin was elected emperor by the senate and immediately invested.
2. Amantius, a praepositus of the palace, Andreas, Misahel and Ardabur, the bedchamberlains, being adherents of Manichaeism, were seized upon as traitors to Justin Augustus. Two of them, Amantius and Andreas, were slain by the sword. Misahel and Ardabur were exiled to Serdica. Theocritus, an attendant of Amantius, whom the praepositus had been secretly grooming to rule, was seized and was crushed in prison by huge rocks, perished and was laid in the salty sea. He forfeited a burial as well as the empire to which he aspired.
3. Vitalian the Scythian, recalled to Constantinople by the emperor Justin's dutifulness to the empire, returned and was invested as Master of the Soldiery seven days after his return.

1 Sept. 519– 13th indiction, consulship of Vitalian and Rusticius
31 Aug. 520 *520*

In the seventh month of his consulship, the consul Vitalian died in the palace, along with his attendants Celerianus and Paul, after being stabbed sixteen times.

1 Sept. 520– 4th indiction, consulship of Justinian and Valerius
31 Aug. 521 *521*

The consul Justinian made this consulship the most famous of all eastern ones by being considerably more generous in his largesses. For two hundred and eighty-eight thousand solidi were distributed to the people or spent on spectacles or on their properties. He exhibited simultaneously in the amphitheatre twenty lions and thirty panthers, not counting other wild beasts. Above all, after already donating the chariots, he provided caparisoned horses in the hippodrome, one final race being the only thing denied the clamouring populace.

XV SYMMACHI ET BOETHII

I MAXIMI SOLIVS

Plerique lapidatorum, percussorum urbisque depopulatorum sua ob scelera deprehensi ferro, igni suspendioque expensi sunt, gratum bonis civibus spectaculum exhibentes.

II IVSTINI AVGVSTI II ET OPILIONIS

His cons. inopia olei magnam penuriam in populum inportavit.

III FILOXENI ET PROBI

Iohannes Romanae ecclesiae papa LI anno Petri apostolorum pontificumque praesulis quadringentensimo octogensimo quinto sessionis eius, Theodorico rege sese . . . . pro Arrianis suae caerimoniae reparandis, solus dumtaxat Romanorum sibimet decessorum urbe digressus Constantinopolim venit. miro honore susceptus est: dexter dextrum ecclesiae insedit solium diemque domini nostri resurrectionis plena voce Romanis precibus celebravit.

IIII OLYBRII SOLIVS

Totam quidem Antiochiam Syriae civitatem repens inter prandendum terrae motus invasit: alioquin occiduam urbis magnamque eius partem sinistris mox ventis undique flantibus flammasque coquinarum pro tempore aestuantes ruentia in aedificia miscentibus duplex torridumque exitium inportavit. Eufrasium quoque totius urbis episcopum adempto eius capite combusto simul obruit sepulchro: obelisco circi inverso et humi defosso.

1 Sept. 521– 15th indiction, consulship of Symmachus and Boethius
31 Aug. 522 *522*

1 Sept. 522– 1st indiction, consulship of Maximus alone
31 Aug. 523 *523*

Most of the stone-throwers, bandits and ravagers of the city, when they were caught, were put to the sword, burnt and hung because of their crimes, thereby providing a grateful sight for the good citizens.

1 Sept. 523– 2nd indiction, consulship of Justin Augustus (2nd) and Opilio
31 Aug. 524 *524*

In this consulship an oil shortage brought severe hardship upon the populace.

1 Sept. 524– 3rd indiction, consulship of Philoxenus and Probus
31 Aug. 525 *525*

Alone among all his Roman predecessors, John, the fifty-first pope of the Roman church, in the four hundred and eighty-fifth year of the see of Peter, foremost of the apostles and priests, left the city at the request of king Theodoric and came to Constantinople to bring back the Arians to his fold. He was greeted with magnificent honour. As the right-hand man he took his place on the right-hand throne of the church and he celebrated in full voice the day of the Lord's resurrection in the Roman ritual.

1 Sept. 525– 4th indiction, consulship of Olybrius alone
31 Aug. 526 *526*

A sudden earthquake struck the entire city of Antioch in Syria during meal-time. Moreover, it brought doubly fierce destruction to the great western part of the city from the easterly winds, which were soon blowing in on all sides and fanning the fires of the kitchens which were blazing at the time in the collapsing buildings. It also killed Euphrasius the bishop of the whole city when his head was crushed in a fiery grave, for an obelisk in the hippodrome was upturned and driven into the ground.

V MAVORTII SOLIVS

Anno regiae urbis conditae centesimo nonagensimo septimo Iustinus imperator Iustinianum ex sorore sua nepotem iamdudum a se Nobilissimum designatum participem quoque regni sui successoremque creavit kalendas Apriles: ipse vero quarto ab hoc mense vita decessit, anno imperii nono mense secundo.

VI IVSTINIANI AVGVSTI SOLIVS

Anno regiae urbis conditae centesimo nonagensimo octavo regium vestibulum priscumque in eo solium ob aspicienda probandaque in circo certamina structum victor Iustinianus princeps eminentiorem clarioremque quam fuerat et utramque senatorum ex more spectantium porticum solita magnanimitate redintegravit, bonis quidem agitatoribus praemium, ignavis autem in nobis severitatem innuens.

VII DECII SOLIVS

Parthis bella moventibus arma Romanus paravit exercitus finesque suos rebellans tutatus est. haec expeditio nostrorum paene per quinquennium tenuit, digressaque Oriente Africam petiit, contra Vandalos feliciter dimicatura.

VIII LAMPADII ET ORESTIS

Mundo Illyricianae utriusque militiae ductor dudum Getis Illyricum discursantibus primus omnium Romanorum ducum incubuit eosque haut paucis eorum interemptis fugavit. his autem deinde consulibus idem dux audaciae suae secundus in Thraciam quoque advolans praedantes eam Bulgares felicior pugnans cecidit, quingentis eorum in proelio trucidatis.

1 Sept. 526– 5th indiction, consulship of Mavortius alone
31 Aug. 527 *527*

In the one hundred and ninety-seventh year from the foundation of the royal city, on the first of April, the emperor Justin made Justinian a partner in the empire and his successor. The latter was his nephew, by his sister, and had for a considerable time been designated 'Most Noble' by Justin, who himself died four months later in the ninth year and second month of his reign.

1 Sept. 527– 6th indiction, consulship of Justinian Augustus alone
31 Aug. 528 *528*

In the one hundred and ninety-eighth year from the foundation of the royal city the emperor Justinian the Victor rebuilt the imperial box and its ancient throne designed for viewing and applauding the contests in the hippodrome, making it more elevated and brighter than it had been. With customary generosity he also reconstructed each portico where the Senators sat as spectators. There he distributed both rewards to good charioteers and also discipline to the idle amongst us.

1 Sept. 528– 7th indiction, consulship of Decius alone
31 Aug. 529 *529*

Since the Parthians were making war the Roman army made ready its arms and, renewing the fight, it safeguarded its territories. This expedition of ours lasted almost five years and, when diverted from the East, made for Africa to fight successfully against the Vandals.

1 Sept. 529– 8th indiction, consulship of Lampadius and Orestes
31 Aug. 530 *530*

Mundo, the Master of the Illyrian soldiery, was the first Roman general to set upon the Goths who had previously been traversing Illyricum and put them to flight, after quite a few of them had been killed. However, later in this consulship, this same leader, fortunate in his boldness, hastened into Thrace and also killed, by fighting bravely, the Bulgars who were plundering it; five hundred of them were slain in the battle.

IX POST CONSULATUM LAMPADII ET ORESTIS

His consulibus codex Iustinianus promulgatus est.

X ITEM POST CONSVLATVM LAMPADII ET ORESTIS

Hypatius, Pompeius et Probus genere consobrini divique Anastasii nepotes imperium, quod sibi singuli indigna ambitione exoptabant, idibus Ianuariis iam plerisque nobilium coniuratis omnique seditiosorum turba armis donisque ministratis inlecta dolis invadere temptaverunt atque per quinque continuos dies urbem regiam rapinis, ferro igneque per sceleratos cives sine certo interrege discursantes hostili impietate, ipsi se fideles rei publicae in palatio dissimulantes, depopulati sunt. quinta vero huius nefandi facinoris die, dum de foro Hypatius sceleratorum comitum manibus torque redimitus aureo et Pompeius comes eius sua sub veste loricatus ad invadendum conscendunt palatium, uterque eorum ante fores palatii captus est statimque piissimi principis nostri nutu catenatus trucidatusque poenas luit et ante imperium perdidit quam haberet, innumeris passim in circo populis trucidatis et tyrannorum sociis continuo proscriptis. ecclesia tunc incensa mox coepit ab eodem Augusto renovari.

XI IVSTINIANI AVGVSTI III

Post diuturnum immanemque laborem contra Medos Romanis gestum sudoribus tandem per Rufinum patricium perque Hermogenem magistrum officiorum, utrumque legatum a principe nostro missum, pax cum Parthis depecta est sponsione percussi foederis ab utroque imperatore invicem sibi muneraque deinde concordiae missa.

XII IVSTINIANI AVGVSTI IIII ET PAVLINI

Provincia Africa, quae in divisione orbis terrarum a plerisque in

1 Sept. 530– 9th indiction, after the consulship of Lampadius and Orestes
31 Aug. 531 *531*

In this consulship the Code of Justinian was published.

1 Sept. 531– 10th indiction, after the consulship of Lampadius and Orestes
31 Aug. 532 again *532*

Hypatius, Pompeius and Probus, the nephews through his sister of the divine Anastasius, because they were each fired with unworthy ambition, tried to usurp the throne on 13 January after many of the nobility had already sworn allegiance and a whole crowd of troublemakers had been enticed by arms, gifts and the guile of their accomplices. They pillaged the royal city for five successive days through looting, fire and sword by means of criminal citizens running about with warlike disloyalty and without any definite substitute emperor, while they themselves were pretending loyalty to the empire in the palace. Indeed, on the fifth day of this unspeakably abominable riot Hypatius, bedecked with a gold torque at the hands of his criminal companions, and his companion Pompeius with a breastplate concealed under his clothes, went up to invade the palace. They were both seized in front of the entrance to the palace, immediately put in chains and executed at the command of our most holy emperor. They paid the penalty and lost the empire before they could obtain it. Countless people were killed throughout the hippodrome and the allies of the usurpers were proscribed immediately. The church which was burnt at that time soon began to be rebuilt by the same Augustus.

1 Sept. 532– 11th indiction, consulship of Justinian Augustus (3rd)
31 Aug. 533 *533*

After the fierce, drawn-out struggle conducted against the Persians with Roman toil, peace was finally reached with the Persians through Rufinus the Patrician and Hermogenes the Master of the Offices, both ambassadors being sent by our emperor. By a term of this agreed treaty pledges of good faith were sent afterwards by each emperor to the other.

1 Sept. 533– 12th indiction, consulship of Justinian Augustus (4th) and
31 Aug. 534 Paulinus *534*

The province of Africa, which is placed by most people in the

parte tertia posita est, volente deo vindicata est. Carthago quoque civitas eius anno excidionis suae nonagensimo sexto pulsis devictisque Vandalis et Gelimer rege eorum capto et Constantinopolim misso, quarto Iustiniani principis consulatu, ipsius moderatione recepta est, sua cum patria firmius, quam dudum fuerat, redintegrata.

Quo tempore Theodahadus rex Gothorum Amalasuentham reginam creatricem suam de regno pulsam in insula laci Vulsinensis occidit. cuius mortem imperator Iustinianus ut doluit, sic est et ultus.

XIII BELISARII SOLIVS

Postquam Carthago Libyaque suo cum rege Gelimero per Belisarium est subiugata, de Roma Italiaque deliberat imperator: iterumque expeditio iterumque classis parata idemque ductor qui consul eligitur, rectoque navigio Siciliam properat, Catinam Syracusam sine mora, immo omnem pervadit Trinacriam. ibique comperiens quod in Africa civile bellum exoritur et miles in proprio duce insurgit, cum paucis ad Africam tendit, Solomoni qui praeerat subvenit: exercitum vero partim blandiendo, partim ulciscendo, inimicum tyrannum effugando, rei publicae consulit utilitati remensoque navigio Trinacriam redit.

Agapitus quinquagesimus Romanae urbis episcopus a Theodato rege Gothorum in legatione directus Constantinopolim venit.

Tzitta patricius in Mysia cum hoste Bulgarum congrediens ad Iatrum superior invenitur.

Epifanius episcopus regiae urbis ante adventum Romani praesulis moritur: cuius episcopatum contra canones Anthimus Trapezuntena ecclesia relicta invadit.

third part of the world's division, was liberated by God's will. The city of Carthage as well, in the ninety-sixth year since its destruction, was restored after the Vandals had been driven out and subjugated, and their king Gelimer captured and sent to Constantinople in the fourth consulship of the emperor Justinian, who received him in moderation since his country was stronger than it had been for some time.

ANONYMOUS ADDITION

At that time Theodahad expelled queen Amalasuintha, who had made him king of the Goths, from her kingdom to an island on Lake Bolsena and killed her. The emperor Justinian, being rightly aggrieved, avenged her death.

1 Sept. 534–31 Aug. 535 13th indiction, consulship of Belisarius alone *535*

1. After Carthage and Libya together with their king Gelimer had been subjugated by Belisarius, the emperor turned his attention to Rome and Italy. Another expedition and another fleet were prepared and the same general, who had been elected consul, set a course direct for Sicily and without delay invaded Catina, Syracuse and indeed the whole of Trinacria. When he found out there that civil war had flared up in Africa, and that the army was rebelling against its own leader, he took a few of his men and set out for Africa, and provided assistance for Solomon, who was in charge. Partly through encouraging his army and partly through punishing it he took measures for the good of the empire by putting the terrible tyrant to flight and, resetting his course, he returned to Trinacria.

2. Agapitus, the fiftieth bishop of the city of Rome, was sent on an embassy by Theodahad, king of the Goths, and came to Constantinople.

3. The patrician Tzitta was found engaging with the Bulgar enemy at Iatrus in Moesia and was victorious.

4. Epiphanius, bishop of the royal city, died before the arrival of the Roman pontiff. Anthimus left the church of Trebizond and, against ecclesiastical regulations, usurped Epiphanius' see.

XIIII POST CONSVLATVM BELISARII

Ebremud Theodati gener relicto exercitu regio in Britios ad Belisarium in Siciliam convolavit.
In Africa vero Solomone itidem cum exercitu dissidente Germanus succedit, Solomonem remittens ad principem.

Belisarius Campaniam transiens Neapolim vastat.
Gothorum exercitus Theodahadum regem habens suspectum Vitigis in regno asciscit: qui mox in campos Barbaricos regnum pervasit.
Expeditione soluta Romam ingreditur, ubi iam Agapito Constantinopoli defuncto Theodahadus rex Silverium episcopatui subrogarat: ibique residens dirigit Ravennam.

Theodatum occidit in loco qui dicitur Quintus iuxta fluvium Santernum et ipse subsequitur per Tusciam omnes opes Theodati diripiens, quas in Insula vel in Urbevetus congregaverat.
Ravennamque ingressus Matesuentham nepotem Theodorici sibi sociam in regno plus vi copulat quam amore.

Belisarius favente domino Romam ingreditur.
Germanus in Africa feliciter administrat.
Agapitus Constantinopolim, ut diximus, episcopus a Roma adveniens, Anthimum pellit, dicens eum iuxta ecclesiasticam regulam adulterum, qui sua dimissa ambierat alienam: in cuius loco Mennam presbyterum episcopum ordinavit et ipse extremum diem obiit: in nullo tamen, sicut ei a principe imminebatur, sentiens contra fidem.

Ipso namque anno ob nimiam siccitatem pastura in Persida denegata circiter quindecim milia Saracenorum ab Alamundaro cum Chabo et Hezido fylarchis limitem Eufratesiae ingressa, ubi Batzas dux eos partim blanditiis, partim districtione pacifica fovit et inhiantes bellare repressit.

1 Sept. 535– 14th indiction after the consulship of Belisarius
31 Aug. 536 *536*

1. Evremud, son-in-law of Theodahad, deserted the royal army in Bruttium and fled to Belisarius in Sicily.
2. In Africa, however, Germanus succeeded Solomon, who had likewise fallen out with his army, and sent him back to the emperor.
3. Belisarius crossed Campania and laid waste Naples.
4. Being distrustful of Theodahad, the Gothic army admitted Vitigis into the kingship and he immediately usurped the kingdom in the Barbarican plains.
5. With his campaign completed, king Vitigis arrived in Rome where, since Agapitus had already died in Constantinople, Theodahad had called Silverius to the episcopate. While living there he controlled Ravenna.
6. He killed Theodahad in a place called Quintus beside the river Santernus and advanced through Tuscany himself, plundering all the wealth which Theodahad had gathered in Insula and Urbs Vetus.
7. After entering Ravenna, he joined to himself as a partner in the kingdom Matasuentha, the niece of Theodoric, through duress rather than affection.
8. With the Lord's blessing, Belisarius advanced to Rome.
9. Germanus administered Africa successfully.
10. Bishop Agapitus, coming to Constantinople from Rome, as we said above, banished Anthimus, calling him an adulterer in ecclesiastical terms because he left one see and solicited another. In his place Agapitus ordained the priest Mennas as bishop and he himself reached his life's end. He contemplated nothing contrary to the faith just as he was adjoined by the emperor.
11. Indeed in that very year, on account of the excessive drought the pasture land of Persia was destroyed and about fifteen thousand Saracens with the phylarchs Chabus and Hezidus were driven across the border of Euphratesia by Alamundarus. There the general Batzas encouraged them partly by flattery and partly by peaceful restraint and repressed their desire for war.

XV ITERVM POST CONSVLATUM BELISARII

Vitigis tyrannus exercitu aggregato Romam obsidet: cui tunc faventem papam Silverium Belisarius ab episcopatu summovit et loco eius Vigilium diaconum ordinavit.

Temporeque longo Romam obsidente Vitigis Belisarius intus inedia vigiliisque laborans auxilium ab imperatore deposcit. cui directi sunt Martinus et Valerianus uterque magister militiae: nec sic tamen Vitigis obsidionem relinquit.

In Africa Germanus rebelliones milites cum Stotza tyranno inter Maurorum deserta bellando effugat.

In Oriente quoque Iohannes Cottistis arripiens tyrannidem, antequam adversi aliquid temptaret, Daras extinctus est.

Ecclesia maior Constantinopoli ab imperatore Iustiniano singulariter in mundo constructa dedicatur die VI kalendas Ianuarias.

INDICTIONE PRIMA IOHANNIS SOLIVS

Adhuc Vitigis in obsidione Romae morante Iohannes magister militum cum Batza, Conone, Paulo Remaque inlustribus magnoque exercitu apparato ad Italiam properant castraque ad Portum Romanum conlocant, laboranti Romae subveniunt. quorum adventum Vitigis cernens trium mensium temporis cum Belisario pacta confirmat suosque legatos ad imperatorem transmittit.
In qua pace Belisarius Campaniam redit, annonae copiam Romae inlaturus: reversusque Campania contrarium sibi de medio aufert Constantinum patricium.

Iohannes vero in portu quae posuerat castra deserens Samnitum regionem ingressus est Aternoque oppido expugnato Tremonem Gothorum ducem cum suis prosternit, Ortonam quoque similiter invadit. Picenum depraedans Ariminum occupat.

Quo audito Vitigis ab obsidione urbis, in qua adhuc post turbatam pacem consistebat, relicta Roma per Clodiae aggerem et

1 Sept. 536– 15th indiction, again after the consulship of Belisarius
31 Aug. 537 *537*

1. The usurper Vitigis gathered his army together and laid siege to Rome. Belisarius removed from his see Pope Silverius who was at that time favourable to Vitigis, and ordained the deacon Vigilius in his place.
2. After Vitigis had been besieging Rome for a long time Belisarius was hard-pressed within by hunger and patrols and asked the emperor for reinforcements. Martin and Valerian, both Masters of the Soldiery, were sent to him. However, Vitigis did not slacken off the siege.
3. In Africa, Germanus put the rebellious soldiers, together with the usurper Stotzas, to flight into the desert country of the Moors, through a clash of arms.
4. In the East too, John Cottistis was killed at Dara while usurping power before he could undertake any hostile action against the emperor.
5. The great church in Constantinople, built by the emperor Justinian in a manner unique in this world, was dedicated on 27 December.

1 Sept. 537– In the 1st indiction, John alone
31 Aug. 538 *538*

1. Vitigis was still lingering in the siege of Rome when the Master of the Soldiery John, together with the illustrious Batzas, Conon, Paul and Rema and a large well-equipped army, neared Italy and pitched camp at Portus Romanus, and then came to the assistance of hard-pressed Rome. On perceiving their approach Vitigis confirmed a three-month truce with Belisarius and sent his ambassadors to the emperor.
2. During this peace Belisarius went back to Campania to secure a supply of corn for Rome. When he returned from Campania he did away with the patrician Constantine, an opponent of his.
3. But John, leaving the camp which he had set up in the harbour, advanced into the Samnite region and, after attacking the town of Aternum, he stood with his men before Tremo, the Gothic general, and at the same time also invaded Ortona and, after pillaging Picenum, occupied Ariminum.
4. When he had heard this Vitigis left the siege of the city in which he had been still stationed after the peace was broken

annonariam Tusciam transit Appenninum et in Rubiconis fluminis ripa castra metatus Ariminum obsidet.

Unde proturbatus a Narsete de Constantinopoli et a Belisario de Roma venientibus fugit Ravennam.

Cuius nepos Oraio Mediolanum longa inedia deterit, Mundilam Paulumque duces ibi positos cum suos milites obsidens.

Narsete vero Arimino residente Belisarius accedens Romae ad exhiemandum in deditione suscipit Urbinum et Urbemvetus et insulam laci Vulsinensis.

II APPIONIS SOLIVS

Narsis revertitur Constantinopolim.
Belisarius obsidens Auximum septimo mense ingreditur, similiterque et Faesulam.
Gothi Mediolanum ingressi muros diruunt praedamque potiti omnes Romanos interficiunt, Mundilam Paulumque duces abducunt Ravennam.
Theudibertus Francorum rex cum magno exercitu adveniens Liguriam totamque depraedat Aemiliam. Genuam oppidum in litus Tyrrheni maris situm evertit ac praedat. exercitu dehinc suo morbo laboranti ut subveniat, paciscens cum Belisario ad Gallias revertitur.

Germanus de Africa Constantinopolim evocatur. Solomon ibi rursus dirigitur.
Calluc magister militum cum Gepidas primum feliciter dimicans secundo infeliciter ruit.

III IVSTINI IVN. SOLIVS

Parthi in Syriam ingressi multas urbes subvertunt: contra quos Germanus arma arripiens Iustinum filium eundemque consulem in ipsis fascibus secum ducit.
Antiochia magna depraedata demolitur a Persis.

Belisarius Ravennam ingreditur, regem Vitigis et reginam

and, leaving Rome, he crossed the Appenines over the rampart of Clodia and Tuscia Annonaria and, pitching his camp on the bank of the Rubicon river, he besieged Ariminum.

5. Being driven out of there by Narses coming from Constantinople, and by Belisarius coming from Rome, he fled to Ravenna.

6. His nephew Oraio weakened Milan through a lengthy starvation, besieging Mundilas and Paul, the generals stationed there together with their soldiers.

7. While Narses was encamped at Ariminum, Belisarius took Urbinum in surrender, as well as Urbs Vetus and the island of Lake Bolsena, on his way to Rome to spend the winter.

1 Sept. 538– 2nd indiction, consulship of Apion alone
31 Aug. 539 *539*

1. Narses returned to Constantinople.

2. After a seven month siege Belisarius entered Auximum and at the same time Faesulae as well.

3. The Goths entered Milan and tore down its walls, took booty and killed all the Romans. They led the generals Mundilas and Paul off to Ravenna.

4. Theudebert, king of the Franks, advanced with an enormous army and devastated the whole of Liguria and Aemilia. He subjugated and looted the town of Genoa located on the shore by the Tyrrhenian sea. Afterwards, in order to assist his disease-stricken army, he made an agreement with Belisarius and returned to Gaul.

5. Germanus was summoned to Constantinople from Africa. Solomon again took charge there.

6. Calluc, the Master of the Soldiery, fought against the Gepids at first successfully, and later unsuccessfully, and was killed.

1 Sept. 539– 3rd indiction, consulship of Justin the Younger alone
31 Aug. 540 *540*

1. The Parthians invaded Syria and overthrew many cities. Germanus took up arms and marched against them with his son Justin the consul, while he was actually in office.

2. Antioch the Great was ravaged and demolished by the Persians.

3. Belisarius entered Ravenna and, on the summons of count

cunctasque opes Gothosque nobiliores tollens secum ad imperatorem revertitur evocante se Marcello comite.

Solomon in Africa feliciter dimicans rebelliones proturbat.

Gothi trans Padum residentes Oraio Vitigis nepote et Heldebado ductantibus Vitigis regem cum regina opibusque palatii nec non et Gothos audientes sedibus propriis pulsos Orientemque per Belisarium abductos rebellare disponunt, regem sibi statuentes Heldebadum.

Contra quem debellaturus Bessa patricius Placentiam a Ravenna conscendit, Constantino Ravennam de Dalmatiis, ut praeesset exercitui, ab imperatore directo.

IIII BASILI SOLIVS ANNO PRIMO

Parthis persistentibus inimicis Belisarius Orientis suscipit expeditum Germano regresso ad urbem regiam.

Gothi Heldibado occiso Erarium sibi ordinant regem.

Solomon in Africa interficitur, Sergius loco eius dux successit belli moderatorque provinciae.

V POST CONSVLATVM BASILII ANNO SECVNDO

Milites clam Veronam ingressi dum avaritia inhiante de praeda concertant, a Gothis egredientibus de latebris cum suo dedecore civitate pelluntur.

Gothi Erario rege occiso Totilam in regnum manciparunt. qui malo Italiae mox Padum transit et ad Faventiam Aemiliae civitatem Romanum exercitum superat, duces effugat, Caesenam et Urbinum, Montem feretris et Petrapertusa occupat, huc illucque discurrens devastat Italiam.

Rursus in annonaria Tuscia ad Mucellos per Ruderit et Viliarid Bledamque duces suos Romanum exercitum superat. quo proelio Bessa patricius vulneratus evadit: ceteri vero fugientes per quaqua

Marcellus, returned to the emperor accompanied by king Vitigis and his queen and all their wealth, as well as the most noble of the Goths.

4. Solomon fought successfully and put down rebellions in Africa.

5. The Goths living across the Po, with their generals Oraio, the nephew of Vitigis, and Ildibadus, were ready to revolt on hearing that king Vitigis and his queen, with the wealth of the palace and the Goths, had been driven from their thrones and taken to the East by Belisarius. They elected Ildibadus as their king.

6. The patrician Bessas came up to Placentia from Ravenna to fight Ildibadus, after Constantine had been sent by the emperor to Rome from Dalmatia to take command of the army.

1 Sept. 540–31 Aug. 541 4th indiction, consulship of the first year of Basil alone *541*

1. Since the Persians continued to be hostile, Belisarius undertook the Eastern expedition after Germanus had returned to the royal city.

2. After Ildibadus had been killed the Goths elected Erarichus as their king.

3. Solomon was killed in Africa. Sergius succeeded him as general in the war and governor of the province.

1 Sept. 541–31 Aug. 542 5th indiction, 2nd year after the consulship of Basil *542*

1. While the soldiers who had secretly entered Verona were fighting over the booty in their covetous avarice, they were shamefully banished from the city by the Goths emerging from their hideouts.

2. When king Erarichus had been killed the Goths put Totila on the throne. To Italy's detriment, he soon crossed the Po and overwhelmed the Roman army in the city of Faventia in Aemilia, put the generals to flight, occupied Caesena and Urbinum, Mons Feretris and Petra Pertusa, and devastated Italy as he rushed from place to place.

3. Again in Tuscia Annonaria he overcame the Roman army near Mugellum, through his generals Ruderit, Viliarid and Bleda. In that battle the patrician Bessas was wounded and

salvati sunt.

VI POST CONSVLATVM BASILII ANNO III

Totila devastat Campaniam urbesque muratas evertens per suos Tiburem obsidet.
Mortalitas magna Italiae solum devastat, Orientem iam et Illyricum peraeque attritos.

In Oriente Persis adhuc tenentibus conflictum cum nostris Sergius in Africa inquietatur a rebellionibus cum Stotza et Mauris.

VII POST CONSVLATVM BASILII ANNO IIII

Totila obsidet Firmum et Asculum invasamque Neapolim desolat et Tibur.
Roma vero obsidetur a longe, in qua praeerat Iohannes magister militum.
In Oriente Belisario constituto exulatur Iohannes ex consule ordinario patricius atque praefectus praetorio et domus eius datur Belisario.

VIII POST CONSVLATVM BASILI ANNO QUINTO

Totila Firmum et Asculum sub iuramento ingressus est: milite Romano cum rebus suis dimisso crudelitatem suam in Romanos exercuit eosque omnes nudat et necat.

In Africa Iohannes inruens super tyrannum Stotiam interimit eum et ipse ab eius occiditur armigero. in qua tyrannide Iohannes quidam electus Stotias iunior vocitatur.

Belisarius de Oriente evocatus in offensam periculumque incurrens grave et invidiae subiacens rursus remittitur ad Italiam. qui veniens Romae dirigit Bessam. Iohannem mittit ad imperatorem.
Totilas vastato Piceno pugnansque ad Auximum vincit. indeque discurrens per Tusciam Spoletium destruit et Asisium Clusiumque

escaped while the others, who fled in all directions, were unharmed.

1 Sept. 542– 6th indiction, 3rd year after the consulship of Basil
31 Aug. 543 *543*

1. Totila devastated Campania and, destroying walled cities, he laid siege to Tibur with his own men.
2. A great pestilence ravaged the land of Italy, and also the Orient and Illyricum which had been already similarly affected.
3. In the East while the conflict between the Persians and our army continued, Sergius was being subdued in Africa by the rebellions of Stotzas and the Moors.

1 Sept. 543– 7th indiction, 4th year after the consulship of Basil
31 Aug. 544 *544*

1. Totila besieged Firmum and Asculum, invaded Naples and plundered it, as well as Tibur.
2. Rome, however, was under siege for a long time when the Master of the Soldiery John was in command there.
3. While Belisarius was stationed in the East, John the patrician and Praetorian Prefect, formerly consul, was exiled and his house given to Belisarius.

1 Sept. 544– 8th indiction, 5th year after the consulship of Basil
31 Aug. 545 *545*

1. Totila entered Firmum and Asculum under pledge. When the Roman soldiery had been sent away together with their equipment he exercised his cruelty towards the Romans by stripping and killing them all.
2. In Africa, John, making an attack on the usurper Stotzas, killed him and was himself killed by his armour-bearer. In that usurpation a certain John was elected and called Stotzas the Younger.
3. Belisarius was summoned from the East and, although running into enmity and serious danger and being exposed to envy, he was again sent back to Italy. On his arrival at Rome he put Bessas in charge and sent John to the emperor.
4. After Picenum had been devastated Totila was victorious in a battle near Auximum. Rushing from there through Tuscany he destroyed Spoletium, took the towns of Assisi and

oppida tenuit et obsidet Perusiam.

VIIII POST CONSVLATVM BASILI ANNO SEXTO

Vigilius papa LVIIII ab apostolo Petro evocatus ab imperatore Roma egreditur et Siciliam venit.
Totila occupata Lucania et Brittios Neapolim subvertit, Romam obsidet.
De Africa Sergius evocatur et Ariovinda neptem imperatoris acceptam ibi iudex dirigitur.

In Oriente cum Parthis foedus initur per Constantianum magistrum militiae et exercitus revertitur Constantinopolim.

X POST CONSVLATVM BASILI ANNO VII

Gothi legationem mittunt ad imperatorem per episcopum civitatis Asisinatium nomine Aventium.
Iohannes magister militum ad Italiam properat.
Bilisarius a Ravenna egressus venit Dyrracio indeque directo Iohanne Calabriam ipse per Siciliam Romae perrexit.

Papa Vigilius ingressus est Constantinopolim VIII kalendas Februarias.
Totila dolo Isaurorum ingreditur Roma die XVI kal. Ianuarias, muros evertit, domos aliquantas igni comburens ac omnium Romanorum res in praedam accepit: hos ipsos Romanos in Campaniam captivos abduxit. post- quam devastationem quadraginta aut amplius dies Roma ita fuit desolata, ut nemo ibi hominum nisi bestiae morarentur. sic veniens Belisarius murorum partem restaurat venienteque Totila ad pugnam resistit.

Eodem quoque anno de Africa neptis revertitur imp. vidua occiso viro eius Areovinda a Gunthario tyranno, qui cum Stotzia iuniore tractans eum occiderat. sed Artabanes utrosque comprehensos Guntharium occidit, Iohannem id est Stotiam iuniorem vinctum transmittit ad principem. post aliquantos dies mittitur Africam Iohannes et Artabanis evocatus praesentale accipit magisterium.

Clusium and besieged Perusia.

1 Sept. 545– 31 Aug. 546

9th indiction, 6th year after the consulship of Basil *546*

1. Vigilius, the fifty-ninth pope from the apostle Peter, was summoned by the emperor, left Rome and came to Sicily.
2. Totila occupied Lucania and Bruttium and overran Naples, and besieged Rome.
3. Sergius was summoned from Africa and Ariobindus, having married the emperor's niece, was put in charge as governor there.
4. In the East a treaty was sealed with the Parthians through Constantianus, the Master of the Soldiery, and the army returned to Constantinople.

1 Sept. 546– 31 Aug. 547

10th indiction, 7th year after the consulship of Basil *547*

1. The Goths sent an embassy to the emperor through the bishop of the town of Asinatum, Aventius by name.
2. John, the Master of the Soldiery, hastened to Italy.
3. Belisarius left Ravenna and came to Dyrrachium, from where John was directed to Calabria and he himself reached Rome by way of Sicily.
4. Pope Vigilius entered Constantinople on 24 January.
5. Through the treachery of Isaurians, Totila entered Rome on 17 December, knocked down the walls, put several homes to the torch and received the possessions of all the Romans as booty. He led these very Romans off as prisoners into Campania. After this destruction Rome was so desolated that for forty days or more neither man nor beast stayed there. So, when Belisarius came he rebuilt part of the walls and on Totila's approach opposed him in battle.
6. Also in that year, the emperor's niece returned from Africa. She was widowed after her husband, Ariobindus, had been killed by the usurper Guntharic, while he was negotiating with the younger Stotzas. But Artabanes, having seized both, killed Guntharic and had John, that is Stotzas the Younger, bound and sent to the emperor. After several days John [Troglita] was sent to Africa and Artabanes was summoned to receive the office of Master of the Soldiery in the imperial presence.

XI POST CONSVLATVM BASILII ANNO VIII

Iohannes magister militum in Campania praedans Gothos nonnullas liberat senatrices. qui postea patitur nocturnum Totilae superventum Bulgarum suorum proditione.

Verus quoque magister militum et ipse in parte alia Calabriae infestum sustinuit Totilan et Valerianus ab imperatore in eorum solacia . . .

1 Sept. 547– 11th indiction, 8th year after the consulship of Basil
31 Aug. 548 *548*

1. John, the Master of the Soldiery, set free some senators' wives while he was plundering the Goths in Campania. Afterwards, through the treachery of his Bulgars, he was attacked at night by Totila.

2. Verus, also a Master of the Soldiery but in another part of Calabria, made the dangerous Totila stand his ground and Valerian was sent by the emperor to their relief ...

At this point the manuscript (T) breaks off.

COMMENTARY

PREFACE

Eusebius of Caesarea The chronicle of Eusebius of Caesarea marked a major achievement in the development of Christian historiography. It was a complex work which set out in a tabular format the whole of human history from the time of Abraham until the late third century AD, when it was first written, before being updated subsequently in the reign of Constantine (in fact to 326). Although not extant in its original format and language, it is clear that the chronicle was organised by a sequence of kingdoms through the correlation of successive kings of (originally) the Hebrews, Athenians, Egyptians, Sicyonians and Argives. Later were added the kingdoms of the Macedonians, Lacedemonians and Romans. Eventually these kingdoms disappeared from the chronicle as they were, for the most part, absorbed into the Roman realm so that from the time of Julius Caesar to the end of the chronicle Eusebius recorded each regnal year of each Roman emperor. The chronological framework of the chronicle was the 'year of Abraham' (i.e. from the birth of Abraham), with each year from Abraham recorded and each tenth year underlined. From the first Olympiad (776 BC) Eusebius noted each Olympiad in a separate heading inserted between years of Abraham. Eusebius did not believe that one could be certain about the chronology of the period between Adam and Abraham so he began with Abraham (details in Barnes, 1981, 111–20; Mosshammer, 1979; Adler, 1989; Croke, 1982a and 1983c).

beginnings of ... regions The content of Eusebius' chronicle was varied. M.'s description of it might be interpreted as indicating that it divided human history into epochs (e.g. from Moses to Solomon, Solomon to the rebuilding of the temple in Jerusalem, from Darius to Christ in the 15th year of Tiberius [Eus., *praef.*; Helm, 16–17]), that it provided a date for every event recorded and a framework into which other events could be inserted at any time, and that it covered all the ancient kingdoms in full. The historical entries included in Eusebius' chronicle concentrated on the key-dates for important writers and thinkers (especially Christian writers), natural disasters and other portents, the construction of famous and important buildings, wars and invasions, imperial births, deaths and marriages; and for the Roman period it ranged across all the provinces East and West.

Jerome The fourth-century ascetic and Christian scholar Jerome was one of the first Western scholars to appreciate the significance of Eusebius' chronicle and included it in c. 381 as part of his extensive program of translating Eusebius' works for a Latin audience (Kelly, 1975, 72–4). In translating Eusebius' elaborate format Jerome took the opportunity to simplify it and at the same time to add a few relevant Roman entries into appropriate points of the chronicle. Then he continued the chronicle from 327 in the reign of the first Christian emperor, Constantine (305–37), to the death of the emperor Valens in 378 using the same chronology as Eusebius, i.e. years of Abraham, Olympiads and imperial regnal years. In addition, Jerome followed Eusebius in determining the sort of entries suitable for inclusion in the chronicle. Jerome's continuation therefore comprises a record of relic translations, battles and sieges, eclipses, famines and earthquakes and other prodigies, famous scholars and writers, imperial deaths and accessions and specifically ecclesiastical events such as the exile and return of bishops, the dedication of churches and the development of heresies; as well as usurpations and invasions of Roman territory. M. clearly felt a close identification with the outlook and culture of Jerome ('our Jerome', cf. **380** and **392.2**). In terms of content, his chronicle followed the pattern of Eusebius and Jerome.

five thousand five hundred and seventy-nine years 5579 was the total number of years recorded by Jerome at the very end of his chronicle for the period from Creation to AD 378 and was calculated backwards as follows — from Abraham to AD 378 there were 2395 years; from the Flood to Abraham 942 years; from Adam to the Flood 2242 years (Helm, 250.1–26). M. evidently accepted Jerome's calculation although the exact chronology of history had long been a controversial question and remained so in the time of M. The paramount concern of Christian chronographers had been to establish the date of Creation and express it in terms of the year of Christ's Incarnation. Hence, a whole range of different dates based on different methods had been developed, the most popular of which was that of Julius Africanus which placed the Incarnation in the middle of the sixth millennium (5500 from Creation); but the commonly accepted era at CP when M. was writing was that of 5508, that is, the world was created 5508 years before the Incarnation (the different eras are set out in Grumel, 1958, 219–24). The era used by Eusebius in his *Chronicle* was an unconventional one of 5200 which was never subsequently taken up by Byzantine scholars and it is not clear how Eusebius arrived at that date in the first place, although it was probably based on a lunar cycle of 8 years (Grumel, 1958, 24–5). Nonetheless, the Eusebian era became standard in the West by virtue of being that used in the chronicle of Jerome, the fountainhead of the Western chronographical tradition. When M. speaks of 'both chroniclers' he means the combined work of Eusebius and Jerome.

Marcellinus The author's honorific titles were probably not included in the original edition of the chronicle in 519 but were only added to the up-dated edition in 534, having been acquired as a result of his service at the imperial court in the time of the emperor Justin (early 520s) when he acted as *cancellarius* to the patrician Justinian (Cass., *Inst.* 1.17). The title *comes* (count) indicates that he was enrolled in one of the three orders of counts, while *vir clarissimus* (most distinguished man) indicates that he was a man of senatorial status at CP although not necessarily entitled to a seat in the Constantinopolitan senate. By the sixth century both these titles belonged to *cancellarii* (Seeck, 1889, 1459).

indictions and consuls In specifying that he is concentrating only on the eastern provinces of the Roman empire M. means to distinguish his chronicle from that of Eusebius/Jerome which covered the whole classical world ('almost all regions'); by specifying 'indictions' and 'consuls' he is indicating another departure from his model, which was structured in terms of Years of Abraham, Olympiads and imperial years. Rather than follow Jerome's complex layout of listing individual years in a single column and then linking events to them, M. preferred a simpler structure (as had been utilised by previous continuators of Jerome, such as Prosper of Aquitaine) by inserting the events directly under each successive year, with each year marked firstly by its indiction and then by its consuls. This simplification is presumably what he intended by his claim of 'simple straightforward calculation'. The *indiction* was a period of tax assessment (in the modern sense of the financial year) beginning on 1 September in one calendar year and ending on 30 August of the following calendar year. The year began with a liturgy for the indiction (*SEC*, 1.4–2.5 with Janin, 1966, 73). Originating in Egypt in the early fourth century, its use spread until it became the official form of reckoning in the Byzantine realm by the sixth century. Indictions formed a cycle of fifteen years although successive cycles do not seem to have been numbered as (say) Olympiads were. *Consuls*, on the other hand, had for over a millennium been the two leading Roman magistrates who gave their name to the year from 1 January to 31 December. Originally the most powerful and influential office in the state, in the early sixth century the consulship was still highly prized in the Roman world and was frequently the prerogative of the emperor himself (Bagnall et al., 1987, 1–12). In M.'s day imperial statute ensured the official use of consuls and indictions in the dating of documents (cf. *Nov. Just.*, 47 [31 August 537]). By using two overlapping dating systems (January to December and September to August) M. made it more difficult for his readers to be certain about exactly when an event occurred when no month is given, especially since one usually assumes that the consulship is the correct date. Yet the evidence of the chronicle suggests that M. frequently dates events primarily by the correct indiction but not necessarily the correct consulship (see e.g. **429.2, 430.3, 454.1, 465.1, 469**).

one hundred and forty years M. is continuing the chronicle of Jerome beginning in 379 (coss. Ausonius and Olybrius) and finishing in 518 (cos. Magnus), which is 140 years counting inclusively.

sixteen years The updated edition of the chronicle began in 519 (coss. Justin and Eutharic) and ended in 534 (coss. Justinian and Paulinus), which is 16 years counting inclusively. This paragraph was obviously added when the updated edition was produced in 534 but it is not necessary to suppose that any other part of the preface was added or modified at this time, except M.'s honorific titles (*comes* and *vir clarissimus*).

379.1 The emperor Valens (*PLRE* 1: 930–31) had perished at the battle of Adrianople (9 August 378), after which Theodosius (*PLRE* 1: 904–5) was summoned from his estates in Spain to Sirmium (Sremska-Mitrovica) where he was proclaimed emperor by Gratian on 19 January 379 (Cons. Const., s.a. 379.1 [IX 243]; F. Vind. Pr., 497 [IX 297]; Soc., 5.2; Phil., 9.17; Chron. Pasch., 561.1–4; Pac., 9–11; Them., *Or.* 14; *Epit.*, 47.3; Theod., 5.5.1–6.3; Barb. Scal. 316 [IX 297]). Theodosius' domain of the Eastern empire included the dioceses of Asiana, Pontica and Oriens, to which were now added Dacia and Macedonia. The comparison between Theodosius and Trajan was originally propagated in the East by the orator Themistius in 383 (*Or.* 16. 204d–205a [294]) and was subsequently picked up by Pacatus (*Pan.* 4.5) and the anonymous *Epitome de Caesaribus*. For the context: Syme, 1971, 101–3. It was also reflected in Theodosius' construction at CP of a forum and a column modelled on those of Trajan at Rome (Müller-Wiener, 1977, 258). Theodosius did not in fact come from Italica but from Cauca (Coca) in Gallaecia (Hyd., 1 [XI 14]). It would appear that M. (followed by Jord., *Rom.* 315) has inferred 'Italica' from the fact that it was the hometown of Trajan, and Theodosius was taken to be part of Trajan's family. Alternatively, such an interpretation may have been inherited by M. from his source. M. provides a generalised tribute to Theodosius' piety which reflects that emperor's Byzantine reputation (cf. Jo. Mal., 13.37 [344.13–14]; Chron. ad 724 [106.5–12]; Theoph., AM 5871 [66.16–20]). Marcian is third emperor by counting only Eastern emperors (Arcadius, Theodosius II, Marcian). In reckoning Theodosius as the 39th Roman emperor M. was evidently following a standard Eastern list which omitted simultaneous emperors (cf. Chron. Pasch., 560.19–20; Hyd., 1 [XI 14], rather than Orosius 7.35.1, who had Theodosius as 41st emperor).

379.2 Once emperor, Theodosius set out from his base in Thessalonike to engage the tribes invading the Balkans (Wolfram, 1988, 131; Heather, 1991, 149–50). He defeated the Goths and took hostages (Soz., 7.4), erected trophies and returned towards CP, only to fall ill at Thessalonike and be detained there for nearly a year (Soc., 5.6). M. is here copying from Oros., 7.34.5 although he may possibly have relied on his Constantinopolitan source for the precise year. This entry probably refers to the victory announcement in CP, on 17 November 379 (Cons. Const., s.a. 379.3 [IX 243]; cf. Phil., 9.19). The victory was also announced in Rome (Symm., *Ep.* 1.95). For details: McCormick, 1986, 41–2.

380 In speaking of 'our church', 'our Jerome' (cf. Praef. and 392.2), 'us' and 'us Catholics' M. is identifying himself closely with the traditional Catholic position. Gregory of Nazianzus in Cappadocia was a key figure in the development of Eastern theology. In 379 he arrived in CP as bishop of the orthodox community which had been out of favour in the imperial capital for just on 40 years since the accession of Eusebius of Nicomedia as bishop in 339. The Catholic centre of worship during this period was the house known as *Anastasia* (Resurrection) and it was there that Gregory preached regularly (Theoph., AM 5871 [67.12–15]), including the 'Five Theological Sermons' which became so influential in Orthodox theology and which M. himself had possibly read. It was during this period that Jerome spent some time at CP on his way back to Italy from Palestine and was captivated by Gregory's teaching (Kelly, 1975, 84 ff). The Anastasian church was later enlarged by Marcian and became one of the more important CP churches.

After engaging the Tervingi of Fritigern, with the help of reinforcements from the West, a victory was announced (Cons. Const., s.a. 380.1 [IX 243]). Theodosius returned to CP in triumph on 24 November 380 (Soc., 5.6; Cons. Const., s.a. 380.2 [IX 243] with McCormick, 1986, 42 and Heather, 1991, 152–3). On the following day he asked the Arian bishop of CP, Demophilus, to declare his acceptance of the Council of Nicaea (325). The bishop refused and left the city on 26 November (Soc., 5.7; Phil., 9.19 with Holum, 1982, 17), whereupon the churches of Hagia Sophia and the Holy Apostles were restored to the Orthodox (Theoph., AM 5874 [68.7–13]), presumably in December as M. states. An imperial law restoring churches everywhere followed shortly after on 10 January 381 (*CTh.* 16.5.6).

381.1 The 'Second Ecumenical Council', as it came to be known much later, was held in CP from May to July 381. It was summoned by Theodosius to deal with a range of heresies and to bring all the Eastern bishops into doctrinal unity. M. singles out for mention only the heresy of Macedonius, bishop of CP, who insisted that the Holy Spirit was of a substance separate from the Father and the Son (cf. Jo. Mal., 13.40 [346.4–5]: 'the Holy Spirit' synod; Chron. Pasch., 562.9–16). It is interesting too that M. indicates Damasus as the contemporary pope because he was not present, the council being only for Eastern bishops, and Damasus never in fact recognised the council. The council, and the creed which became associated with it, developed into an important part of Eastern tradition (Kelly, 1972, 296 ff). Only much later were its canons accepted by the West.

During the course of the council Gregory of Nazianzus, who recently had been elected bishop of CP, resigned his position rather than have factions in the synod continue to challenge the canonical propriety of his election (Soz., 7.7 with Liebeschuetz, 1990, 160–3). Like Ambrose at Milan in 374, Nectarius (*PLRE* 1: 621) was not even a baptized Christian when nominated as bishop so he had to be immediately baptized and ordained (Theod., 5.8; Soc., 5.8; Soz., 7.7–9; cf. Theoph., AM 5876 [68.21–69.30]). M. does not mention the famous third canon of the synod establishing CP as the see second to Rome and its bishop as patriarch.

381.2 Theodosius' former enemy Athanaric (*PLRE* 1: 120–1) was expelled by his own people, the Tervingi, and arrived in CP on 11 January 381 (Cons. Const., s.a. 381 [IX 243]), died on 26 January and was given an elaborate state funeral by Theodosius (Cons. Const., s.a. 381.2 [IX 243]; Them., *Or.* 15.190; Oros., 7.34.6–7; Prosp., 1177 [IX 461]; Zos., 4.34.4–5; Jord., *Get.* 142–5; Soc., 5.10; Ammianus, 27.5.10; Jord., *Get.* 144 with Wolfram, 1988, 72–4 and Heather, 1991, 154).

382.1 The emperor Valentinian I (*PLRE* 1: 933–4) had died on 17 November 375 while campaigning against the Quadi near Brigetio on the Danube (Amm., 30.6.1 ff) and his body was received in CP on 28 December 376 (Cons. Const., s.a. 376 [IX 243]). In 382 his sarcophagus was transferred, with proper imperial solemnity, on 21 February (Cons. Const., s.a. 382.1 [IX 243]) to the church of the Holy Apostles (Johnson, 1991, 501–2; Grierson, 1962, 42), which had become the resting place for emperors.

382.2 Through his general Saturninus (*PLRE* 1: 807–8) Theodosius negotiated an important treaty with the Goths whereby they settled as *foederati* in Roman territory on certain conditions (Wolfram, 1988, 133–4; Heather, 1991, 157 ff. and Blockley, 1992, 40–1). M. is here copying Oros., 7.34.7 except for the date, 3 October 382 (Cons. Const., s.a. 382 [IX 243]), which most likely refers to the day the agreement was ratified and publicly proclaimed in CP.

382.3 Pope Damasus, having occupied the see of Peter since October 366, died not in 382 but on 11 December 384, and it is because of this inaccuracy that M.'s dates for subsequent papal accessions are incorrect. Since Damasus died in the 18th year of his pontificate and since M. must have realised that his accession occurred in 366 because it is recorded in the *Chronicle* of Jerome (Helm, 244e) under that year, then one can only conclude that M. made a mistake in copying or locating the date in Jerome. M.'s list of popes apparently included only names and reign lengths in years, not exact years of accession. So it is likely that his list had only '16 years' for Pope Damasus (i.e. 366–382). Following Jerome (Helm, 244e) M. reckons Damasus as 35th pope, but to do this he must delete (at least) Liberius and Felix as he claims (cf. Mommsen, 1896/7, 168). Liberius and Felix had disputed the see of Peter in the time of Constantius II although Jerome had recorded Liberius (Helm, 237b).

383.1 Siricius (December 384–26 November 399) was an active and forceful pope, the first in fact to issue decretals on matters of liturgy and church discipline. He also established the so-called 'vicariate of Thessalonike' by assigning the bishop of that city responsibility for the Balkan bishoprics (Kelly, 1986, 33–4). M. records the length of Siricius' papacy (14 years 3 months) in terms of full years, but by following his erroneous date for Damasus (382.3) he places Siricius' accession a year too early.

383.2 Arcadius (*PLRE* 1: 99) was born to Theodosius and his first wife Flaccilla in c. 377. The boy's coronation, an important dynastic event (see Holum, 1982, 28–9), took place at the 'seventh milestone', the Hebdomon, a suburb of CP outside the walls of the city. The Hebdomon had an imperial palace, several churches and its original field (*campus tribunalis*) for the assembly and exercise of imperial troops (Janin, 1964, 446–9). It was here that Valens had been crowned in 364 and several emperors afterwards, including Honorius in 393 and Theodosius II in 402. Arcadius' coronation day was 16 January 383 (Cons. Const., s.a. 383.1 [IX 244]; cf. Chron. Pasch., 562.19–563.2; Soc., 5.10; Prosp., 1179 [IX 461]); Oros., 7.34.9) not 19 January (Seeck, 1919, 26).

383.3 The emperor Gratian (*PLRE* 1: 401) had marched from Italy into Gaul to counter the revolt of the British general Maximus (*PLRE* 1: 588) but was forced to retreat and was captured in flight and killed in Lyons, on 25 August 383 (F. Vind. Pr., 503 [IX 297]; Barb. Scal. 321 [IX 297]; Chron. Gall. 452, 9 [IX 646] with Paschoud, 1979, 413–5 [n.172]). M. could easily have acquired this information from an Eastern source (cf. Soc., 5.11.9; Soz., 7.13; Zos., 4.35.3–6) rather than from an Italian one as proposed by Mommsen (1894, *margin*).

384.1 The long reign of the bellicose Persian king Sapor II (*PLRE* 1: 803) had ended in 379 and he had been succeeded (379–83) by his aged brother Artaxerxes II (*PLRE* 1: 111) and then his son Sapor III (*PLRE* 1: 803), both of whom sought to make peace with the Romans. In recording this Persian embassy to announce the accession of Sapor III, M. uses the language of Oros., 7.34.8 but the Persian embassy is well known from Eastern sources (Them., *Or*. 19.227c; Soc., 5.12; Cons. Const., s.a. 384.1 [IX 244]; Chron. Pasch., 563.9). It will have been a grand ceremonial occasion, as indicated by the description of the reception of Persian envoys at CP in the Byzantine *Book of Ceremonies* (Const. Porph., *de caer*. 1.89–90). On this occasion the Persian ambassadors brought precious stones, silk and 'triumphal animals for your chariot' (Pac., 22.5). The Persians must have been in CP around mid-late August since it was at the same time (September) according to M. (cf. Soc., 5.12) that Theodosius' son Honorius was born and since by 31 August Theodosius was on an expedition through the Balkans (Matthews, 1975, 178).

384.2 Honorius (*PLRE* 1: 442), the second son of Theodosius and Flaccilla, was born at CP on 9 September 384 (Cons. Const., s.a. 384.2[IX 244]; F. Vind. Pr., 503 [IX 297]; Barb. Scal., 322 [IX 297]; Soc., 5.12.3; Chron. Pasch., 563.9–11) while Theodosius was preparing a campaign (Soz., 7.14).

385 Following the invasion of Cappadocia, Cilicia and Syria by the Tzanni (Jo. Mal., 13.41 [347.8–10]), Theodosius sent envoys to the East to resolve the vexed question of the sovereignty of Armenia and a Persian embassy once more came to CP. The various negotiations resulted in the partition of Armenia between Romans and Persians (Blockley, 1987, 222 ff. and 1992, 42–5). It was perhaps as a result of these negotiations that Theodosius received pledges of loyalty from 'kings whose domains encircle the Eastern frontier' (Pac., 32.2 with Nixon, 1987, n. 108 [p.92]).

386.1 On behalf of Theodosius, Fl. Promotus (*PLRE* 1: 750–1) defeated the Goths in battle and took many prisoners (Zos., 4.35.1, 38; Cons. Const., s.a. 386.1 [IX 244] with Wolfram, 1988, 134–5). They were transported to Phrygia and were probably the very Goths who mutinied in 398 (Liebeschuetz, 1990, 30). The emperor and his young son, Arcadius, entered CP in a triumphal parade on 12 October 386 (Cons. Const., s.a. 386.2 [IX 244] with McCormick, 1986, 43 and Lippold, 1966, 122–3). The victory was saluted by Claudian (*IV Cons. Hon*., 623 ff., 634 ff.) and commemorated at CP by the erection of a triumphal column in the Forum of Theodosius (Theoph., AM 5878 [70.20–1] with Janin, 1964, 81–2). M.'s information is derived from Oros., 7.34.9 and his annalistic Constantinopolitan source.

386.2 There is something amiss with this report. Theodosius did not marry Galla, the daughter of Valentinian I and Justina, until after the death of his first wife

Flaccilla in 386 (Zos., 4.44.2–4; Soc., 4.31.17–18 with Bury, 1923, 198, n. 1; Oost, 1968, 44 ff. and Holum, 1982, 44–7). For the date: Seeck, 1920, 52, n. 34. Galla fled to Thessalonike, together with her mother (Justina) and brother (Valentinian II) and from there went to CP, where she married Theodosius in 387. So, as normally supposed, M. and Chron.Pasch. have the date wrong (probably reflecting an original error of their common source). On the other hand, there may be some event (perhaps an imperial *adventus*) associating Galla with CP in 386 which is concealed in the tradition lying behind the statement of M. and the confused account of Jo. Mal., 13.37 [16–19] and the Chron. Pasch., 563.13–18 (with Mommsen, 1894, 62, n. 1), in which the order of Theodosius' marriages is reversed. M. would appear to be referring only to Galla's arrival in CP.

387.1 With all due pageantry the young Arcadius celebrated the commencement of the 5th year of his reign in 387, which included the special games and displays on the exact anniversary of his *dies imperii*, 16 January (Cons. Const., s.a. 387.1 [IX 244]). Commemorative coins were minted in honour of the occasion (Burgess, 1988, 85).

387.2 M. expresses in the words of Oros., 7.35.2 the fact that Theodosius decided to put down the rule of the usurper Maximus (*PLRE* 1: 588) and arrived in Italy in 387. For details: Matthews, 1975, 223–7.

388.1 Valentinian II (*PLRE* 1: 934–5) did not accompany Theodosius to the West but went separately by sea (Zos., 4.45.4). Maximus was certainly killed at Aquileia on 28 August (Oros., 7.35.3; Zos., 4.46.3; cf. Soc., 5.14; Cons. Const., s.a. 388.1 [IX 245]; Prosp., 1191 [IX 462]; Theoph., AM 5880 [70.27–9]) but not his son Victor, as M. perhaps implies. Victor was hunted down in Gaul by the Frankish general Arbogast (*PLRE* 1: 95–7) and killed there (Zos., 4.47.1; Cons. Const., s.a. 388.2 [IX 245]). The victory over Maximus was subsequently celebrated at Rome and CP (McCormick, 1986, 44–5) and continued to be so commemorated until M.'s time (cf. Proc., *Wars* 3.4.16).

388.2 Maximus' general Andragathius (*PLRE* 1: 62–3) was sent by Maximus to intercept the imperial ships but on discovering Maximus' defeat threw himself overboard (Zos., 4.47.1; Soc., 5.14; Soz., 7.14). The exact location of the ships is not known. Here M. virtually copies the account of Oros., 7.35.5.

389.1 Theodosius summoned his five-year old son Honorius from CP immediately after the defeat of Maximus (Soc., 5.14; Soz., 7.14) and together they entered Rome in a ceremonial triumph on 13 June (Cons. Const., s.a. 389.1 [IX 245]; F. Vind. Pr., 512 [IX 298]; Chron. Pasch., 564.8–10; Theoph., AM 5881 [70.31–3]).

389.2 There does not appear to be any corroborative evidence for this ferocious hailstorm nor any indication of where it struck, although it was presumably at CP. Perhaps it is included in the general catalogue of prodigies recorded by Phil., 10.11.

Similar occurrences of freak weather are recorded at other times, such as the immense hail at CP on 30 September 404 (Soc., 6.19; Chron. Pasch., 569.1–3) and the storms in April 407 (Chron. Pasch., 570.3–8) and July 408 (Chron. Pasch., 570.15–17), and were worth recording in chronicles because they gave rise to a substantial ritual of supplication led by the emperor (Croke, 1981b and 1990). Jerome had recorded a similar hailstorm at CP in 367 (Helm, 245c).

389.3 M. appears to be recording here the appearance of the same comet described in detail by Phil., 10.9. It may also be the same one noted in F. Vind. Pr., 514 (IX 298); cf. Newton, 1972, 682.

389.4 The temple of Serapis was destroyed (in 391 not 389) thanks to the organization of bishop Theophilus of Alexandria (Soc., 5.16–17; Soz., 7.15; Chron. Gall. 452, 28 [IX 650]; Theoph., AM 5882 [71.7–20]). The impetus for its destruction came from the resolutely anti-pagan edict of Theodosius (*CTh.* 16.10.10) which was published in Egypt on 16 June 391 (*ibid.*, 16.10.11).

390.1 This cigar-shaped, or 'hanging-column' object in the heavens which shone for thirty days was obviously a startling phenomenon. It is reported in similar terms in Western chronicles (F. Vind. Pr., 514 [IX 298]; Chron. Gall. 452, 26 [IX 648]; Chron. Gall. 511, [IX 649]).

390.2 This information is unique and it is not clear whether Galla (*PLRE* 1: 382) was expelled by her teenage stepson from the city or just the palace, but in any event the expulsion is likely to have been the result of some personnel changes at court arising from her marriage to Theodosius (cf. Oost, 1968, 50) or perhaps from the emerging independence of Arcadius. The expulsion must have occurred while Theodosius was still in Italy. M.'s information on Galla (cf. **386**) is probably reliable and based ultimately on local sources.

390.3 The obelisk, originally honouring the Pharaoh Thutmose III, still survives in the hippodrome (Janin, 1964, 189–91). Both the emperors Constantius II (337–61) and Julian (361–3) had tried to bring it to CP but Theodosius finally succeeded. It was erected in 30 days under the supervision of Proculus (references in *PLRE* 1: 746–7 with Rebenich, 1991, 447–76). As for the column and silver statue of Theodosius, it stood in the Augusteon until the time of M. In fact it was still standing after the Nika riots in January 532. Later, however, Justinian replaced the statue of Theodosius with one of himself as Achilles. This celebrated statue was perhaps the original silver statue of Theodosius recast to portray Justinian (Janin, 1964, 74–5). Since the statue of Justinian is said to have been 'bronze' then he may simply have 'bronze-plated' Theodosius' statue; alternatively he may have re-used another statue of Theodosius from the Forum Tauri (Mango, 1959, 351–6; 1993, 1–8).

391.1 Returning from Italy Theodosius entered the imperial capital on 10 November 391 (Soc., 5.18; Zos., 4.50.1). The ceremonial *adventus* would have been similar to Theodosius' later entry into Rome (MacCormack, 1981, 50–2). When an emperor arrived at CP the imperial entourage processed through the Golden Gate.

391.2 M. is here mainly relying on Oros., 7.35.10 to which he adds the date, incorrectly recorded (or perhaps a copyist's error) as 15 March rather than 15 May. In addition this entry is mistakenly inserted under 391 rather than 392, but we cannot be certain that the mistake is not that of an early copyist since it is also the date given in several manuscripts of Prosper and in F. Vind. Pr., 516 [IX 298], cf. Theoph., AM 5882 (71.1–7). For the circumstances of Valentinian's death: Croke, 1976, 235–44 and Paschoud, 1979, 455–8.

391.3 Arbogast held the initiative in the West after Valentinian's death and proclaimed as emperor on 22 August 392 a Roman professor of rhetoric, Eugenius (F. Vind. Pr., 517 [IX 298]; Zos., 4.54.4; Phil., 11.1–2; cf. *PLRE* 1: 293). 391, rather than 392, for Eugenius' proclamation is also the date in Chron. Alex., s.a. 391. That M. ascribes the initiative to Eugenius suggests his dependence on a later Eastern source (cf. Soc., 5.25) rather than Orosius.

392.1 M. is again relying on the account of Oros., 7.34.11–12, except that he calls Eugenius Caesar rather than Augustus. The lesser title seems to be M.'s way of indicating his view that that there could be only one Augustus at a time (cf. **402.2**). Arbogast (*PLRE* 1: 95–7) campaigned in Gaul against the Franks in particular (Paul., *v. Amb.* 30; Greg. Tur., *HF* 2.9).

392.2 This is one of the longest entries in the chronicle, which is merely an indication of M.'s special affinity for 'our Jerome' (cf. **Praef** and **380**), by which he means Catholic, orthodox or perhaps even Illyrian. The proposition of Vaccari, 1958, 32–34 that the shortened version of this entry in the St Omer manuscript (S) of M. represents the original edition of the chronicle to 518 cannot be sustained (Croke, 1984). M.'s entry is virtually a thumbnail sketch of Jerome and his writings, but it makes no mention of any of the polemical battles of Jerome, particularly that with Rufinus. Most of M.'s information comes from the entry written by Jerome himself for his *de viris illustribus* 135, a work composed in 392 (hence M.'s date).

393 Honorius was proclaimed Augustus not Caesar on 23 January (F. Vind. Pr., 521 [IX 298]; Soz., 7.24.1; cf. Soc., 5.25.8 [10 January]), at the Hebdomon outside CP, just as Arcadius had been in 383. M. implies that the eclipse followed soon after but it was not until 20 November and it was at Ravenna that the eclipse was total (Newton, 1972, 452). It is also reported in F. Vind. Pr., 520 [IX 298] — incorrectly dated to 27 October — and Claud., *Stil.* 170 ff.

394.1 Theodosius collected together a large army and set out on the expedition against Eugenius with a promise of victory (Soz., 7.22; Eun., fr. 60.1 [88–91]; Zos., 4.57.1–3; Soc., 5.25). Honorius did not accompany Theodosius, as M. insinuates, but remained behind at CP (Soc., 5.25).

394.2 Eugenius and Arbogast had blocked the main Alpine routes into Italy and met the forces of Theodosius by the Frigidus river in one of the more sensational encounters of late Roman history. In the ensuing battles on 5 and 6 September the forces of the Eastern emperor proved victorious. Eugenius was captured on 6 September and decapitated, while on 8 September Arbogast took his own life (F. Vind. Pr., 522 [IX 298]; Zos., 4.58.1–6; Soc., 5.25.16; Soz., 7.24; Theoph., AM 5885 [73.25–7]). M. follows the wording of Orosius here.

394.3 There appears to be no other record of this earthquake, which must be dated to September–November 394. It was perhaps on this occasion that the tetrarchic palace at Thessalonike was destroyed (Vickers, 1973, 120, n. 80).

394.4 The Arcadian Baths, named after the young emperor, were opened in this year. They were located on the eastern slope of the first hill of the city and were a prominent landmark for those approaching the city by sea. See Janin, 1964, 311–2 for the topography and subsequent history of the site.

395.1 From this year until 469 Mommsen printed the Greek text of the Chronicon Paschale alongside the Latin text of M. in order to show their close similarities in describing events, which is to be explained by their ultimate dependence on the same local Constantinopolitan chronicle.

Having summoned Honorius from CP after the defeat of Eugenius, Theodosius died at Milan on 17 January 395 (Cons. Const., s.a. 395.1 [IX 246]; F. Vind. Pr., 525 [IX 298]; Soc., 5.26.4; Soz., 7.29.4; Theod., 5.25; Phil., 11.2; Chron. Pasch., 565.11–13; Theoph., AM 5886 [74.9–19]) — of dropsy (Hyd., 25 [XI 16]).

395.2 The body of Theodosius was carried from Milan and was honourably received into CP by Arcadius on 8 November (*Epit.* 48.20; Amb., *de ob. Theod.*, 35; Zos., 4.59.4; Chron. Pasch., 566.1–2; Soc., 6.1.4; Chron. Edess., 39 [6]). It was laid to rest the following day in a porphyry sarcophagus in the church of the Holy Apostles (Müller-Wiener, 1977, 405), not the church of St Laurence (Hyd., 25a [XI 16]). This day became the annual Byzantine commemoration of Theodosius (*SEC*, 205.24–5).

395.3 Following the death of Theodosius, Honorius ruled in the West and Arcadius in the East. It was alleged that Theodosius had entrusted Honorius to the protection of his Vandal general Stilicho, and Arcadius to the Praetorian Prefect Rufinus but this is probably propaganda (Cameron, 1970, 38–40). M. is copying here from Oros., 7.36.1 (not noted by Mommsen, *ad loc.*)

395.4 M. repeats the accusation levelled against Rufinus at the time, namely that he bribed Alaric and his Goths (some sources say Huns) to invade Greece (Eun., fr. 64.1 [192–3]; Soc., 6.1.3; Soz., 8.1; Phil., 11.3; Zos., 5.5.4–7; Claudian, *In Ruf.* with Cameron, 1970, 71–4).

395.5 On 27 November Arcadius and his courtiers, including Rufinus, greeted the army returning from the West at the Hebdomon, the imperial parade-ground seven miles from the centre of CP, as was customary (Soc., 6.1.3; Soz., 8.1; Chron Pasch., 566.4–5). It had been arranged by Honorius or Eutropius (Cameron, 1970, 90–2), however, that the military count Gaïnas should lead a contingent of soldiers in assassinating Rufinus on their arrival outside CP (Eun., fr. 64.1 [94–5]; Zos., 5.7.3–6 cf. Chron. Gall. 452, 34 [IX 650]). It had become usual in the case of rebels and usurpers to have their heads and limbs paraded around the capital as part of the ceremonial of victory. Rufinus' hands were displayed to the crowds, who were asked mockingly to give to the insatiable one (Phil., 11.3; Zos., 5.7.6).

396.1 Following Rufinus' execution, his wife and daughter were allowed to retire to Jerusalem (Zos., 5.8.2–3). For the context see Hunt, 1982, 159–60, 190.

396.2 To posterity the eunuch Eutropius (*PLRE* 2: 440–4) became a paragon of capricious avarice. In putting this entry in 396 M. is presumably borrowing from an account which linked Eutropius to his conniving treatment of Abundantius (*PLRE* 1: 4–5) and Timasius (*PLRE* 1: 914–15) in precisely that year (Bury, 1923, 118, n. 1).

396.3 This was obviously a terrifying quake to judge from the contemporary account of it recorded by Oros., 3.3.2. M., however, does not rely on Orosius on this occasion but rather his local CP source (cf. Glycas, 478.20–1) which will have provided the date lacking in Orosius. There are no localised reports of damage and the quake was probably connected to a massive volcanic eruption elsewhere (Cameron, 1987, 352–4).

397 Flaccilla (*PLRE* 2: 472), the first child of Arcadius and Eudoxia (married 27 April 395) was born on 17 June (Chron. Pasch., 567.1–2) and is never heard of again. She was certainly dead before 408.

398.1 Anastasius (27 November 399–19 December 401) occupied the see of Rome for only a short period and his pontificate was dominated by the conflict between Jerome and Rufinus over Origenism. He strongly supported the bishop of Thessalonike against the encroaching influence of CP (Kelly, 1986, 36–7). M. has placed his accession a year too early because he was forced by his papal list to count in whole years, that is 13 years from the accession of Siricius (cf. **383.1**), his predecessor.

398.2 M. makes no mention of Ambrose, bishop of Milan, in the course of the 380s and early 390s when he was deeply involved in developments at court in Milan and had delivered funeral orations for both Valentinian II and Theodosius. Instead M.

records his death only and a year too late at that. Ambrose died in 397 (Paul., *v. Amb.* 48). Among Western ecclesiastics, Ambrose occupied an important place in the Eastern tradition. There was a Greek version of Paulinus' life and there were several Greek hymns composed for his feast-day. His celebrated encounter with the emperor Theodosius at Thessalonike was commemorated at the Byzantine court (Const. Porph., *de caer.* 2.26). M.'s dating error is perhaps explained by confusing Ambrose's feast day (7 December) with his death (4 April); that is, if M. was under the impression that Ambrose died on 7 December in this indiction then he would have to put his entry under the following consulship (398).

398.3 M. here introduces one of his heroes, John Chrysostom, by summarising his career to this point when he was consecrated bishop of CP on 26 February 398 to succeed Nectarius (Soc., 6.2; Soz., 7.2–3). John was born in Syrian Antioch c. 347 of a noble family, studied under Libanius, turned from law and was ordained reader by bishop Meletius in 370 and deacon in 381. During his diaconate he published famous treatises on Virginity, S. Babylas and the Priesthood. In 386 he was ordained to the priesthood. By the time of his elevation to CP he had established a reputation as a powerful speaker and strict moralist who lived an austere life himself. Subsequently, M. mentions his exile from CP and death (**403.3**), followed by the introduction of his annual memorial (**428**) and the transfer of his body back to CP (**438**).

398.4 Gildo, *magister militum per Africam* (*PLRE* 1: 395–6), had responded to the overtures of Eutropius in switching his allegiance from the Western to the Eastern court, thus threatening Rome's African corn supplies. His brother Mascezel fled to Milan in fear of Gildo but left behind his two sons, whom Gildo had killed. When Gildo prevented cornships from sailing in summer 397 the senate declared him a public enemy, and the following spring an expeditionary force was assembled under the command of Mascezel to return to Africa to challenge Gildo, who was quickly defeated and put to death (F. Vind. Pr., 528 [IX 298]). M.'s account is simply a condensed version of that in Oros., 7.36.2–11. For further details: Cameron, 1970, 92–123; Bury, 1923, 121–4; Paschoud, 1979, 118–19.

399.1 Eutropius' successful campaign in 398 against the Huns in the Caucasus won him the consulship for 399. In noting the notorious consulship of the eunuch Eutropius, M. quotes Claudian, *In Eutr.* 1.8. There is no reason to insist that M. did not know Claudian's work since his poems were read in CP in the sixth century, as we know from Priscian and John the Lydian, *de mag.* 1.47. The 'portents' refer to a range of horrendous happenings in the late 390s (Cameron, 1987, 352–4). Eutropius' consulship was publicly revoked (Soc., 6.5; Soz., 8.7). Because it is out of sequence (i.e. after, not before, the consulship of Theodorus) Eutropius' consulship must have been added by M. to his list (Bagnall et al., 1987, 399).

399.2 Pulcheria (*PLRE* 2: 929–30), the second child of Arcadius and Eudoxia, was born on 19 January 399 (Chron. Pasch., 567.5–6).

399.3 In this year the general Gaïnas (*PLRE* 1: 379–80 with Paschoud, 1979, 122–3) was implicated in the revolt of his Gothic relative Tribigild (*PLRE* 2: 1125–6) in Phrygia and sent his incompetent subordinate Leo (*PLRE* 2: 661–2) to quell the revolt. Leo was killed and Gaïnas openly sided with Tribigild, who crossed into Thrace and died shortly afterwards. Meanwhile, Gaïnas had arranged that on a pre-determined signal his Gothic supporters in CP should rise up and slay all the imperial soldiers in the capital (Zos., 5.18.1–10; Soc., 6.6; Soz., 8.4; Theod., 5.32; Phil., 11.8). As M. reports, Gaïnas feigned an illness so that he could leave the city (Zos., 5.19.1) but confusion ensued and the Goths left in the capital were either killed or sought asylum in a nearby orthodox church (cf. Cameron/Long, 1993, 385, n. 254), whereupon the roof-tiles were removed and they were showered with lethal missiles and firebrands (Zos., 5.19.4–5). These latter events took place in mid-400 and are brought into M.'s compressed account because he dated the revolt to the year of its original outbreak in Phrygia (Liebeschuetz, 1990, 111–25).

400 M. here continues the narrative of Gaïnas' revolt. Once the planned uprising had failed Gaïnas fled initially to Thrace, then came down into the Chersonese with a view to crossing over to Asia. He was opposed by the imperial forces now under the control of another Gothic general Fravitta (*PLRE* 1: 372–3). In the attempt to cross the Hellespont many of the Goths were cut down or drowned, while Gaïnas himself fled back through Thrace where he was blocked and killed by the Hunnic king Uldin (Soc., 6.6; Soz., 8.4 with *PLRE* 2: 1180). M.'s use of the Greek form 'Cherronesum' suggests a Greek source for this information, which is paralleled by the Chron. Pasch., 576.15. Gaïnas was defeated and killed in late December (Cameron/Long, 1993, 331). M.'s 'February' is therefore an error. It cannot be construed as February 401 (so Liebeschuetz, 1990, 119).

401.1 Uldin sent Gaïnas' head to CP and, as had become usual in the case of rebels, it was ceremoniously paraded around the imperial capital in triumph on 3 January (Chron. Pasch., 567.18–19, cf. Zos., 5.22.3; Phil., 11.8; Soc., 6.6; Soz., 8.4 with McCormick, 1986, 51).

401.2 The astonishing sight of massive icebergs floating down the Propontis after breaking off from the frozen Euxine sea was doubtless recorded as some sort of portent (cf. Phil., 11.7). The sea was frozen for twenty days (Chron. Pasch., 568.1–2) or thirty days according to M.

401.3 Theodosius II, son of Arcadius and Eudoxia, was born on 10 April (F. Vind. Pr., 531 [IX 299]; Soc., 6.6.40; Soz., 8.4; Chron. Pasch., 567.20–1; Jo. Ant., fr. 190 [*FHG* 4, 612]; Theoph., AM 5893 [76.6–7]).

402.1 Innocent (21 December 401–12 March 417) was extremely active in expanding the authority and influence of the papacy, especially its teaching authority. He supported John Chrysostom in exile and formalised the papal vicariate of Thessalonike, which assured the allegiance of the Balkan bishops to Rome rather than CP. Innocent was absent when Alaric and his Goths sacked Rome. M.'s date is a year too early because of his papal list, which included only whole numbers for papal reigns, that is Innocent's predecessor Anastasius ruled for four years, on M.'s reckoning (cf. **382.3**).

402.2 On January 10 the nine-month old Theodosius was made Augustus (not Caesar, as M. says) at the Hebdomon (F. Vind. Pr., 535 [IX 299]; Chron. Pasch., 568.5–8), like his father Arcadius in 383 and his uncle Honorius in 393. He had been baptised four days earlier.

402.3 M. may be mistaken in recording an earthquake at CP in 402 since there is no other evidence for it; most likely he is confusing it with the quake which occurred in 403 (Theod., 5.34, cf. Cameron/Long, 1993, 102) or else that in 400 (cf. Cameron, 1987, 354–5; Cameron/Long, 1993, 93–102).

403.1 Marina (*PLRE* 2: 723), the third daughter of Arcadius and Eudoxia, was born on 11 February (cf. Chron. Pasch., 568.10–11 dating her birth, perhaps incorrectly, to 10 February). M. also records her death in **449**. Nothing more is known of her.

403.2 By the time M. was writing his chronicle this porphyry column and the silver statue of the empress Eudoxia on top of it had been standing for about 120 years (details in Janin, 1964, 76–7 and Müller-Wiener, 1977, 52). Its original ceremonial dedication had incurred the wrath of John Chrysostom, the bishop of CP, and led to his banishment (Soc., 6.18.1; Soz., 8.20.1; Pall., *Dial.* 9–12; Theoph., AM 5898 [79.4–12], with Bury, 1923, 155). The column was located in the Pittakia district north-east of the Augusteon, that is near Hagia Sophia (cf. M.'s 'near the church'). In that region in 1847 the statue's pedestal was unearthed and it is now in the garden of the Hagia Sophia museum. On it was found a bilingual inscription (*CIL* III.736 = *CIG* 8614), in which the monument was dedicated by the City Prefect Simplicius (*PLRE* 2: 1014).

403.3 M. offers a very compressed version of the complicated series of events leading to the final exile of John Chrysostom in 404 (Holum, 1982, 69–77). He chooses to ignore proceedings leading to the 'Synod of the Oak' in 403 in which John's opponents, led by Theophilus the bishop of Alexandria, had him deposed and sent into exile (Soc., 6.15–16; Soz., 8.13–18). On the intervention of the empress Eudoxia he was recalled to CP, but before long his enemies were prosecuting him once more with the support of the empress, who was indignant at John's outrage over the games for the dedication of her silver statue (Soc., 6.18 with Bury, 1923, 138–60). He was originally exiled to Cuccusus in Armenia where he kept in good contact with both Antioch and CP. Eventually this spot was not considered isolated enough and he was then transferred to Pityus on the Black Sea, but he failed to reach his destination and died at Comana. It was reported that on the night before his death there appeared to him a former bishop of the town, the martyr Basiliscus, who advised John of his impending death (Soz., 8.28). All this information M. acquired from the *Dialogus* of Palladius.

404.1 In the angry aftermath of John's exile the church of Hagia Sophia caught alight on 20 June and was virtually burnt to the ground in a vast conflagration which engulfed much of the surrounding area, including the senate house (Soc., 6.18; Soz., 8.22; Zos., 5.24.3–6 cf. Jo. Mal.,13.47 [Tusculan Fragments]; Chron. Pasch., 568.14–9; Theoph., AM 5898 [79.15–16]). Whether or not the fire was deliberately lit by John's supporters remains an open question, although at the time they were made the scapegoats (Bury, 1923, 156–7). Again M. is here drawing on Palladius' *Dialogus* (61–3).

404.2 Eudoxia died on 6 October (Soc., 6.19.4–6; Soz., 8.27.1–2; Chron. Pasch., 569.3–6; Theoph., AM 5898 [79.29]) probably from a miscarriage (Holum, 1982, 77–8) and was buried on 12 October in the Church of the Holy Apostles. An immense hail-storm on 30 September was taken by some to foreshadow the death of the empress (Soc., 6.19; Soz., 8.27; Chron. Pasch., 569.1–3).

405 In 404 the Isaurian tribesmen launched an invasion into neighbouring Pamphylia and into Syria (Jo. Mal., 14.21 [363.15–19]). A force under the general Arbazaicus (*PLRE* 2: 127–8) drove back the raiders and destroyed their homes (Zos., 5.25.1–4; Soz., 8.24; Phil., 11.8; Jord., *Rom.* 321) in 405 or late 404, which would mean that M. has placed this in the correct indiction but the wrong consulship. It was probably as a result of his victory that Arbazaicus acquired the epithet 'Isaurian' (Blockley, 1983, 148, n. 168), having led his troops by special appointment as 'legatus' as M. notes (cf. *PLRE* 2: 128).

406.1 The five-year old Theodosius celebrated the commencement of the fifth year of his reign (*quinquennalia*) on 11 January 406 (Chron. Pasch., 569.21–570.2 with Burgess, 1988, 86).

406.2 Radagaisus (*PLRE* 2: 934), who was probably a Gothic king, assembled a force of 200,000 to cross the Danube under pressure from the Huns and advanced to Italy in 405 (Zos., 5.26.3–4; Oros., 7.37.4 ff.; Add. Prosp. Haun., 405 [IX 299] with Heather, 1991, 227–9). As a pagan he sacrificed regularly (Aug., *civ. Dei*, 5.23). M., following his usual procedure, copied Orosius and placed this entry under 406 because that is when the episode concluded with the defeat of Radagaisus (cf. Bury, 1923, 67, n. 3).

406.3 The forces of Radagaisus were overwhelmed near Fiesole by the combined contingent of the Hunnic king Uldin (*PLRE* 2: 1180), who had defeated Gaïnas in 401, and the Gothic king Sarus (*PLRE* 2: 978–9), both of whom were fighting on behalf of the Roman general Stilicho (Prosp., 1228 [IX 465]). Although it was Stilicho who celebrated the victory in grand style (Bury, 1923, 168), M. does not mention him, which suggests that here he is following the tradition hostile to Honorius and Stilicho. Radagaisus was decapitated on 23 August (Chron. Gall. 452, 52 [IX 652]; Chron. Gall. 511, 546 [IX 653) while there is no other evidence for M.'s claim that the prisoners were sold (cf. Oros., 7.37.12).

407 M. is the only evidence for the construction of this cistern (Janin, 1964, 210), located under the city's main artery, the Mese (='platea/plateia'), which ran through the Forum of Constantine. The porphyry column of Constantine (details in Janin, 1964, 77–80) was the most magnificent monument in the forum and some idea of its grandeur is still evident in its preserved state as the 'burnt column'.

408.1 Although Stilicho (*PLRE* I: 853–8) had been *magister militum* for twenty-three years this is the first time he is mentioned by M., who provides his usual summary entry based on Oros., 7.38.1–6, followed by Jord., *Rom.* 322 and *Get.* 154. M. is the only source to draw attention to the fact that neither marriage with Stilicho's daughters was consummated, which may be ascribed to impotence on the part of Honorius or possibly self-abnegation (Oost, 1968, 66 and Holum, 1982, 49 but see Cameron, 1970, 153, n. 1). That Stilicho stirred up barbarian groups against the Romans and that he planned to put on the throne his son Eucherius (*PLRE* 2: 404–5) were part of a wider imperial propaganda campaign to justify his execution (cf. O'Flynn, 1983, 58–9).

408.2 The tremors reported in CP from Rome (cf. Theoph., AM 5900 [80.5]) were later seen to portend the city's capture by the Goths in 410 (Add. Prosp. Haun., 408 [IX 299], cf. Exc. Sangall., 537 [IX 299]).

408.3 Arcadius died on 1 May (Chron. Pasch., 570.13–7; Soc., 6.23; Soz., 9.1; Phil., 12.7; Zos., 5.31.1; Prosp., 408 [IX 465]; Theoph., AM 5900 [80.7]). M. counts the thirteen years of Arcadius' sole rule in the East (395–408).

409 This is the same fracas as that described in Chron. Pasch., 571.5–11 but mistakenly dated to 412 instead of 409. During the riot the populace set fire to the *praetorium* of the City Prefect, Fl. Monaxius (*PLRE* 2: 764–5), and dragged his official carriage through the city. Details in Seeck, 1920, 598, n. 24 and Whitby/Whitby, 1989, 62, n. 210.

410 M. draws essentially on Oros., 7.39.1–15, 40.2 in his compact account of the sack of Rome by Alaric followed by Placidia's abduction and later marriage to Athaulf (cf. Olymp., fr. 6 [156–9]). The Goths entered Rome on 24 August and plundered the city for three days. Many buildings, including the Basilicas of SS Peter and Paul, were spared (details in Seeck, 1920, 414–15 and Bury, 1923, 183–4); other parts of the city were burned, including the palace of the Valerii on the Caelian hill (*v. Mel. Iun.*, 14). The sack of Rome had a profound and lasting effect not only on the Western part of the Roman empire but also in CP and the East (details in Kaegi, 1968).

411.1 The tenth anniversary of Theodosius began on 10 January 411 but the twentieth of Honorius did not begin until 10 January 412 and was therefore anticipated. Burgess, 1988, 85 suggests a contemporary error on the part of the Eastern court. This anniversary was an early instance of Theodosius' direct involvement in public ceremonial (Holum, 1982, 92).

411.2 Fl. Claudius Constantinus (*PLRE* 2: 316–17) was proclaimed emperor by the army in Britain in 407 and then proceeded to seize Spain and Gaul where he made his headquarters at Arles. In 408 he made Caesar his son Constans (*PLRE* 2: 310) a former monk (Zos., 6.4.1; Olymp., frs. 13 [170–3],16 [176–9]; Soz., 9.11, Greg. Tur., HF 2.9). M. copies all the details from Oros., 7.40.4,7.

411.3 Constantine was besieged at Arles, captured and led off to Rome but he was killed on the way (Oros., 7.42.2; Soz., 9.15.1; Prosp., 411 [IX 466]; Add. Prosp. Haun., 411 [IX 300]; Chron. Gall. 452, 66 [IX]; Hyd., 50 [XI 18]; Greg. Tur., HF 2.9; Proc., *Wars* 1.2.37; Theoph., AM 5903 [81.21–2). His head was stuck on a pole and ceremoniously paraded into the imperial capital Ravenna on 18 September (Cons. Const., s.a. 411 [IX 246]). Constans was killed in Vienne (Olymp., fr. 17.1 [176–9]; Oros., 7.42.4; Soz., 9.13; Prosp., 1243 [IX 466]).

412.1 Jovinus (*PLRE* 2: 621–2) was proclaimed emperor in 411 with extensive barbarian support and in the following year elevated his brother Sebastianus (*PLRE* 2: 983) as co-emperor. In 413 they were besieged and captured by Athaulf and put to death at Narbonne (Oros., 7.42.6; Olymp., frs. 18 [182–3], 20.1 [182–5]; Hyd., 51, 54 [XI 18]; Add. Prosp. Haun., 413 [IX 300]; Prosp., 1251 [IX 467]; Theoph., AM 5904 [81.25–7]). It is curious that M. dates the deaths of these usurpers to 412 rather than 413, his usual pattern being to record under the first or last year episodes drawn out over more than one year (McCormick, 1986, 56). Oddly enough the Ann. Rav., 127 also dates the demise of the usurpers to 412 and records the ceremonial arrival of their heads in Ravenna on 30 August.

412.2 Priscus Attalus (*PLRE* 2: 180–1) was originally proclaimed emperor at Rome in 409 relying on the support of Alaric and his Goths, only to be deposed the following year by Alaric. In 414, however, he was proclaimed emperor again with Gothic support. The following year he was captured, had his hand cut off and was sent into exile (Oros., 7.42.9; Prosp., 1256 [IX 467]; Phil., 12.4–5; Soz., 9.9; Chron. Pasch., 572.8–12 with Bury, 1923, 194–8; McCormick, 1986, 56–8). This victory was also celebrated at Rome (Prosp., 1263 [IX 468]) and at CP, by the City Prefect Ursus on 28 June 416, with theatrical and other spectacles (Chron. Pasch., 573.15–17). Perhaps it was the defeat of Attalus, rather than John (425) or Maximus (388) which was celebrated on the Golden Gate at CP (Janin, 1964, 269–70; Müller-Wiener, 1977, 297). M.'s date is completely wrong, perhaps because the events occurred so close together in Oros., 7.42.

413 In 413 Heraclian (*PLRE* 2: 539–40) was *comes Africae*, a post he had held since 408 when he was responsible for the murder of Stilicho. Possibly fearful of being killed by Constantius in revenge for Stilicho (O'Flynn, 1983, 70), he revolted. His attempt to make himself emperor in 413 involved cutting off trade between Africa and Italy then sailing to Italy with a fleet of 3,700 ships (Oros., 7.42.12–13; Soz., 9.8). Near Otricoli Heraclian was defeated by another military count Marinus (*PLRE* 2: 724) and returned to Carthage where he was put to death (Oros., 7.42.14; Olymp., fr. 23 [186–7]; Hyd., 56 [XI 18]; Cons. Const., s.a. 413 [IX 246]; Prosp., 1249 [IX 467]; Chron. Gall. 452, 75 [IX 654]; Phil., 11.6; Jord., *Rom.* 325; Theoph., AM 5904 [81.27] with Bury, 1923, 195–6). The date of his death was probably 7 March (Ann. Rav., 127). M.'s account is a compressed but verbatim extract from Orosius.

414.1 Pulcheria was crowned Augusta on 4 July (Chron. Pasch., 571.14–16 cf. Phil., 12.7; Soz., 9.1). For the detailed context: Holum, 1982, 97–9 and Cameron/Long, 1993, 399–403.

414.2 Vallia (*PLRE* 2: 1147–8) made peace with the Romans in 416, after an abortive attempt to move the entire Gothic force to Africa. Then, in exchange for hostages, he handed over Placidia to the court of her brother in Ravenna (Prosp., 1259 [IX 463]). Again M.'s wording takes full account of Orosius 7.43.12. It is not apparent why M. should record the event under the incorrect year.

415.1 The 'Great Church', Hagia Sophia, was rededicated in this year, having being rebuilt after the fire following the exile of John Chrysostom in 404. The *encaenia* or dedication ceremony took place on 10 October with the bishop of CP, Atticus, presiding. The new church was a five-sided basilica with a columned entrance (Müller-Wiener, 1977, 84–5) and it stood until it was destroyed during the Nika riots in 532. The new church may have seen the deposition of the newly-discovered relics of Joseph the son of Jacob and Zachariah the father of John the Baptist (Chron. Pasch., 572.13–573.2 with Whitby/Whitby, 1989, 64, n. 218 and Schneider, 1936, 77–85). The procession bringing the relics was accompanied by the City Prefect Ursus (*PLRE* 2: 1192).

415.2 M. copies from Genn., 46 but is able to locate the discovery of Stephen's relics from the original account of Lucianus, which dated the events precisely. As with the account of the discovery of the head of John the Baptist (s.a. 453), M. is probably showing his familiarity with the original account of the discovery of Stephen's relics written by Lucianus but translated into Latin by a Spanish priest Avitus (*PL* 41, 805–16, cf. Hyd., 58 [XI 120]; Cons. Const., s.a. 415 [IX 246]). Yet, even if he was unfamiliar with Lucianus' account, he would obviously have found the date and other details in his local chronicle source (Cons. Const., s.a. 415 [IX 246]). The relics had been found at Jemmala, north-west of Jerusalem, near Diospolis where a synod was then in session, and had been introduced by bishop John of Jerusalem to the church of Sion (Hunt, 1982, 212–20). The discovery of the relics was commemorated annually at CP on 16 September (*SEC*, 52.4–6).

416.1 In taking leave of Orosius, on whose history he had relied for Western events to this point, M. again turns to Genn., 39, which singles out for mention the arrival of Orosius back in Africa from Jerusalem bearing some of the Stephen relics discovered the previous year (Lacroix, 1965, 33, 37; Hunt, 1982, 213–14). Gennadius' longer account of Orosius' history is briefly summarised by M. (cf. Pintus, 1984, 804).

416.2 Again M. merely copies a Gennadian entry (*de vir. ill.*, 52) in full and verbatim (cf. Pintus, 1984, 804–5). The treatise of Atticus, bishop of CP 406–25, was directed to Pulcheria, Marina and Arcadia. It does not survive but it doubtless contained a discussion of Mary as the ideal model of faith and virginity and probably justified the term 'theotokos', which was soon to lead Nestorius into perceived heresy (Holum, 1982, 138–40).

417.1 There seems to be no other evidence for this eclipse.

417.2 There is recorded elsewhere (Chron. Pasch., 574.7 ff.) a severe earthquake which struck on Good Friday 20 April. It was probably the same quake which destroyed Cibyra (Whitby/Whitby, 1989, 65, n. 223)

417.3 Zosimus (18 March 417–26 December 418) enjoyed only a short pontificate but his divisive and strong-headed style created a series of difficult situations, especially over his establishment of the vicariate of Arles (Kelly, 1986, 38–9). He was pope for less than two years, not the 'three years' recorded by M. Although M. records Zosimus' accession in the correct year this is more by accident than design. His list of popes recorded their papal tenure in whole years (cf. 382.3) so M. counted fifteen years for Zosimus' predecessor, Innocent, reckoning (incorrectly) from 402 (s.v.).

418.1 This is a puzzling entry which may well involve an insoluble textual problem. Perhaps the name of the rebel has been omitted or is somehow concealed in 'idemque'. Nonetheless, as military count Plinta (*PLRE* 2: 892–3; Ensslin, 1951, 457–8) put down an evidently large revolt, although M. is our only witness to these events. It was presumably on the strength of this accomplishment that Plinta acquired the consulship for the following year and a promotion to the position of *mag. mil. praes.*, a position he held until 438. A Goth himself he was related to the Alan family of Ardaburius and was one of the most powerful of courtiers (Soz., 7.17.14).

418.2 An eclipse of the sun occurred on July 19 and is recorded in sources both Eastern (Phil.,12.8; Chron. Pasch., 574.13–15) and Western (Hyd., 64 [XI 19]; Exc. Sang., 543 [IX 300]; Chron. Gall. 452, [IX 656]). The eclipse was total at Rome but only partial at CP. M.'s information is not from an Italian source (cf. Newton, 1972, 452–3 contra Mommsen).

418.3 This appearance of a comet followed closely upon the eclipse (Exc. Sang., 543 [IX 300 with n. 3] with Newton, 1972, 453). M.'s 'seven months' should be 'seventh month' (cf. Newton, 1972, 539).

419.1 Valentinian III (*PLRE* 2: 1138–9), son of Constantius (*PLRE* 2: 321–5) and Galla Placidia, was born on 3 July according to M., although the correct date may be 2 July (Phil., 12.12; Theoph., AM 5911 [83.23–4] with Oost, 1968, 162 with n. 75).

419.2 In this year there was a devastating earthquake in Palestine (Phil., 12.8) which was reported in a letter circulated from Jerusalem and written by the city's bishop Praylius (Hyd., 66 [XI 19], cf. Cons. Const., s.a. 419 [IX 246] with the name of the bishop incorrect).

419.3 There is no other evidence for this appearance of Christ on the Mount of Olives and it is not easy to see why M. has included it, unless it was one of those religious events commemorated annually at CP. It may therefore be somehow connected with the similar appearance in 351 which was celebrated annually on 7 May (*SEC*, 661.28–662.27 with Hunt, 1982, 155–6).

420.1 Boniface (28 December 418–4 September 422) spent the first few months of his pontificate securing imperial approval for his election against the claims of Eulalius who was elected at the same time. Although old and feeble he strongly advocated Roman primacy and authority. In particular he set about withdrawing the vicariate of Arles but at the same time he reasserted the vicariate of Thessalonike against the attempt of Theodosius II to transfer episcopal authority from Rome to CP (*CTh.* 16.2.45). M. places his accession under 420 because that was (incorrectly) three years from the accession of his predecessor (**417**, cf. **382.3**).

420.2 M. is the only source to report the murder of Maximinus (*PLRE* 2: 741) who was probably *magister militum per Orientem*. Nothing more is known of Maximinus or his death.

420.3 For some time the Christian communities within the Persian empire had been hindered, which resulted in deputations to the Persian court seeking tolerance. Following closely upon the accession to the Persian throne in 420 of Vararanes V (*PLRE* 2: 1150) a general persecution of Christians was set in motion by the Persian court and with the encouragement of the intolerant Persian nobility (Blockley, 1992, 56–7). The Christians were being perceived as a threat because of the number of conversions among high Persian officials (Theod., 5.39.6; Soc., 7.18).

421.1 The marriage of Theodosius II to the Athenian philosopher's daughter Eudocia took place on 7 June (Chron. Pasch., 578.13–7) and became subsequently the centre of a legendary Byzantine tradition (cf. Jo. Mal., 14.3–5 [352.8–356.5]). For details: Holum, 1982, 112–21.

421.2 The spiral column of Arcadius was erected in his forum in 402/3, to commemorate the victory over Gaïnas, but now Theodosius II was adding a statue of Arcadius on top of the column (Janin, 1964, 71–2 and Müller-Wiener, 1977, 250–3). The official dedication of the new monument took place on 10 July (Chron. Pasch., 579.15–18). The seventeenth-century drawings of the spiral sculptures are discussed in Liebeschuetz, 1990, 273–8 [with plates] and McCormick, 1986, 117.

421.3 The cistern referred to here was constructed by the City Prefect Aetius (*PLRE* 2: 19–20), although in *Patria* (Preger, 1901, 72–3) he is confused with the more famous Western general Aetius (*PLRE* 2: 21–2) who was consul in 432, 437 and 447. For details see Janin, 1964, 203–4 and Cameron/Herrin, 1984, 276. It was possibly the cistern dedicated to Pulcheria on 12 February 421 (Chron. Pasch., 578.10–12).

421.4 Around 420 Roman suppression of Persian fire cults on Roman territory resulted in Persian persecution of Christians on their territory and support by the Saracen phylarch Aspebetus (*PLRE* 2: 169–70) for those Christians fleeing the persecution. In this atmosphere the emperor Theodosius repudiated the current treaty with the Persians and mobilized the army: the praesental army under Ardaburius (*PLRE* 2: 137–8) was sent to support the troops of the *magister militum per Orientem* Anatolius (*PLRE* 2: 84–6). Ardaburius' troops advanced from Amida (Diyarbekir) into Persian Arzanene then back into Mesopotamia, laying siege to Nisibis, while the troops of Anatolius marched north and besieged Theodosiopolis (Erzerum). Later the Persian king repelled Ardaburius' men from Nisibis and the army of Ardaburius soon defeated some Persians, for which a victory was 'announced' at CP on 6 September (details: Chron. Pasch., 579.19–20; Soc., 7.18 with Holum, 1977, 167–71 and Croke, 1984a, 68–70). This may be the occasion which gave rise to the *ludi* subsequently celebrated each 3 September, that is, the date of the original victory not its announcement on 6 September (McCormick, 1986, 58, n. 79).

422.1 Licinia Eudoxia (*PLRE* 2: 410), daughter of the emperor Theodosius and his new bride Eudocia, was born sometime in this year, although the exact date is not known.

422.2 Maximus (*PLRE* 2: 745) had usurped power in Spain in c. 420 and was now finally captured, along with his ally Jovinus (*PLRE* 2: 622). They were brought to Ravenna and figured in the ceremonial for Honorius' tricennalia (Chron. Gall. 452, 89 [IX 656]; Ann. Rav., 127 with McCormick, 1986, 59). Honorius' consulship in this year was designed to coincide with his tricennalia, for which there are extant solidi (Burgess, 1988, 85).

422.3 As a consequence of moving troops from Thrace to the Eastern frontier to counteract an incursion of the Persians in 421, the emperor Theodosius II settled some Goths from Dacia in Thrace. Subsequently, in 422, the Huns and Sarmatians under King

Rua in Pannonia invaded Illyricum and advanced through the Succi pass as far as CP (Olymp., fr. 27 [190–3]; Theod., 5.37), whereupon a peace was concluded and troops were transferred back from the East (*CTh.* 7.8.13). The Huns agreed to keep the peace for a tribute of 350 pounds of gold annually (details in Croke, 1977, 347–67 and Blockley, 1992, 59–60).

422.4 On 6 September 421 a victory over the Persians was announced in CP (s.a. **421.4**), although this was the result only of an interim military success. Before long both sides called a halt to hostilities (Holum, 1977, 169). The terms of the settlement were that each side agreed not to receive federate Saracens of the other and not to construct new fortifications near the frontier; the Romans also agreed to resume payments to the Persians for guarding the passes through the Caucasus, while the Persians agreed to cease persecuting Christians in their territory (details in Soc., 7.20–1 with Holum, 1977, 170–1 and Blockley, 1992, 57–9). The peace was finalised by the Roman general Procopius (Croke, 1984a, 70–2). It is possible that Theodosius II founded special games to commemorate the victory, which continued to be celebrated in the West (McCormick, 1986, 58 and 119).

423.1 Pope Celestine (10 September 422–27 July 432) moved on the policy lines of his predecesor Boniface. He outlawed Novatians in Rome and combated Pelagians everywhere. Celestine was effective in re-asserting papal control over the vicariate of Thessalonike, and was invited to adjudicate on the conflict between Cyril of Alexandria and Nestorius which resulted in anathemas for Nestorius. Although his delegates arrived late for the Council of Ephesus, he did endorse and support the decisions of the council (Kelly, 1986, 42). His accession is placed in 423 because M. was counting three years from the accession of his predecessor Boniface (**420**, cf. **382.3**).

423.2 It is not apparent why under this particular year M. should include a notice of Evagrius' work which he has copied verbatim and in full from Genn., 51 (cf. Pintus, 1984, 805). Perhaps he had himself read Evagrius' treatise.

423.3 The earthquakes referred to here occurred on 7 April (cf. Chron. Pasch., 580.6–8). There is no indication of precise location but the very failure of the Chron. Pasch. to be specific suggests that CP was among the places affected by the quake (cf. Downey, 1955, 597). It may have been the same quake which caused devastation in Crete (Jo. Mal., 14.12 [359.18–360.6]). There is no other evidence for the subsequent famine. The quake may be the reason that financial appropriations were made from the revenues of shops in the portico of Zeuxippos for rebuilding the city early the following year (*CTh.* 15.1.52 [9 January 424]).

423.4 Since nothing is known about the philosophers Philippus (*PLRE* 2: 875) and Sallust (*PLRE* 2: 971) it is hard to explain their inclusion in the chronicle. The only other testimony to their existence occurs in Ann. Rav. 127–8 which ascribes their deaths not to disease but to murder 'between Claternae and Bologna'.

423.5 Honorius died of dropsy at Ravenna, not Rome (Oost, 1968, 178, n. 29), on 15 August (Soc., 7.22.20; Olymp., fr. 39 [202–3]; Phil.,12.13; Chron. Gall. 452, 91 [IX 658]; Theoph. AM 5915 [84.14–16], although Theodosius delayed the announcement of his death at CP (Soc., 7.23). The comet is presumably that of 13 February.

424.1 In 421 the Western emperors Honorius and Constantius III, husband of Galla Placidia, had elevated Galla to the rank of Augusta, a title which Theodosius was not prepared to recognize in the East. Before the death of Honorius on 15 August 423 Galla, together with her son Valentinian and daughter Honoria, was sent into exile and sought refuge at the court of Theodosius (Olymp., fr. 38 [200–3]; Prosp., 1280 [IX 470]; Chron. Gall., 452, 95 [IX 658]. Following the usurpation of John formal recognition was given by Theodosius to Galla's title of Augusta as a prelude to restoring the Western throne to her family (details in Oost, 1968, 176–183; Holum, 1982, 128–9). M. is evidently recording here what was probably an official announcement at CP of the recognition of Galla's title.

424.2 The five-year old Valentinian was proclaimed Caesar or junior emperor at Thessalonike on 23 October (Olymp., fr.43 [206–7]; Soc., 7.24; Phil., 12.13) by the *magister officiorum* Helion (*PLRE* 2: 533), and at the same time it was arranged that on reaching marriagable age Valentinian would marry Eudoxia (*PLRE* 2: 410–2), the three-year old daughter of Theodosius and Eudocia (Oost, 1968, 183–5). Theodosius had originally set out for Italy but fell ill at Thessalonike and later returned to CP (Soc., 7.24, 25).

424.3 The chief secretary of the Western court John (*PLRE* 2: 594–5) was proclaimed emperor at Rome on 23 November 423 (Ann. Rav., 128) but was never recognised in the East, hence M.'s 'usurped'. The reason M. includes this notice under 424 may simply be that it occurred in that part of the indiction which fell in the previous year (September–December 423); alternatively, it may be that the usurpation of John was not announced in CP until 424. Theodosius had previously kept secret from the public for some time the news of Honorius' death (Soc., 7.23) and may well have sought to do the same in the case of John's claim to the throne. Certainly the ambassadors sent by John to secure Theodosius' recognition were treated with contempt (Soc., *ibid.*).

425.1 In order to put an end to the regime of John, an Eastern army under the generals Ardaburius (*PLRE* 2: 137–8) and his son Aspar (*PLRE* 2: 164–9) was despatched to Italy and landed at Salona on the Dalmatian coast. From there Aspar's forces proceeded overland, while those of Ardaburius crossed over by sea but went astray in unfavourable winds and were captured by the forces of John (Phil., 12.13). Ardaburius himself was imprisoned in Aquileia which was eventually put under siege by Aspar. Thanks to Ardaburius's success in encouraging defectors among John's contingent in the city, Aspar was able to capture Aquileia. John was taken prisoner and subsequently mutilated and killed. M.'s comment that John was defeated by the 'treachery rather than manliness' of Ardaburius and Aspar may betray the trace of a hostile source. The news of John's defeat reached CP while Theodosius was presiding at games in the hippodrome, whereupon the games were disbanded and the spectators removed to the church singing hymns of praise (Soc., 7.23).

425.2 Valentinian was proclaimed Augustus on 23 October at Ravenna (Hyd., 85 [XI 21]; Soc., 7.25; Phil., 12.13; Chron. Pasch., 580.13–15; Theoph. AM 5916 [85.8–9]).

426 Sisinnius was consecrated patriarch of CP on 28 February (Soc., 7.26; Theoph. AM 5921 [87.6]; Zon., 13.22). He was famous for his piety and his care for the poor.

427.1 This is one of the more enigmatic passages in the chronicle, especially since it is the only testimony (followed by Jord., *Get.* 166) for the Huns' occupation of the Pannonian provinces after 377 (Stein, 1959, 473–4). Its historicity has been denied by some but is generally accepted as reflecting a situation that arose in the wake of the movement of the Goths into the Balkans in 376 in flight from the Huns (Thompson, 1948, 26; Maenchen-Helfen, 1973, 78–81). M. dates the occupation from the time when the peoples of Alatheus (*PLRE* 1: 32) and Saphrax (*PLRE* 1: 802) attacked Pannonia and settled there. Some of these were Huns. Their forced removal in 427 may be explained by their recent support for the usurpation of John; so too, their removal may have been negotiated as a pre-condition for the transfer of western Illyricum to the Eastern court (cf. Bury, 1923, 272). It was probably the *magister militum* Felix (*PLRE* 2: 461) who was responsible for the expulsion of the Huns at this time (O'Flynn, 1983, 175, n. 21). By 427, however, these Huns formed the nucleus of their emerging power-base and the reinstatement of Roman dominion in Pannonia was short-lived. M.'s information (and that of Jordanes) on this episode probably derives from their common Byzantine source rather than a Western document (as argued by Nagy, 1967, 159–86).

427.2 The Baths named after the reigning emperor Theodosius were originally built, it seems, by Constantius II and named after him (Janin, 1964, 219–20). This rebuilding, or final stage of completion, was sponsored by the City Prefect Hierius (*PLRE* 2: 557) and the dedication ceremonial took place on 3 October (Chron. Pasch., 580.19–581.3).

428.1 After the death of Sisinnius on 24 December 427 (Soc., 7.28) the priest Nestorius was summoned from Antioch and consecrated bishop of CP on 10 April 428 (Soc., 7.29). He had studied under Theodore of Mopsuestia. A monk imbued with the Antiochene approach to theology (that is, stressing a literal/historical rather than allegorical, interpretation), Nestorius had previously been a famous preacher at Antioch. M.'s judgment on Nestorius stresses that for all his eloquence he was not a sound theologian.

428.2 Having recorded the exile of John Chrysostom under 403 M. now notes the original public commemoration of his *memoria/mneme* in 428. The feast may have originated at Antioch and was instituted at CP when Nestorius became patriarch. There is, however, a problem with the date 26 September. In the tenth century this feast of Chrysostom was held each year on 13 November (*Typ.* I, 98.2–106.2; 217.37–220.4; *SEC*, 46.8–16) but it was not always so. Originally it was held on 14 September, the date of Chrysostom's death and the traditional date of the finding of the Holy Cross by the empress Helena, but when the feast of the Exaltation of the Holy Cross became more prominent (presumably in the time of Heraclius) the feast of Chrysostom was switched to 13 November, the day the news of his death had reached CP in 407 (cf. van Ommeslaeghe, 1978, 338). If M. is referring to the feast which was still held on 14 September in his day then there may be an error in transmission: that is, XIV may have been corrupted into XXVI.

429.1 M. reports the death of Antonius, bishop of Germae on the Hellespont, murdered by the heretical Macedonians whom he was persecuting. The Macedonians or *Pneumatomachoi* as they were more commonly called, had been outlawed by the Council of CP in 381 for their insistence that the Holy Spirit was not God but a creation of God. Obviously they were still active in 428 and able to provoke opposition, although they were soon finally eliminated by Nestorius, who confiscated their churches in CP and elsewhere. Soc., 7.31 reports these events in much the same way as M., who was probably following his local Byzantine source.

429.2 Augustine, bishop of Hippo in Africa, died on 28 August 430 aged 76 years (Poss., *v. Aug.* 31). M. incorrectly reports his death a year too early, yet another indication of the inadequacy of his sources for events in the West. Evidently, all he had to go on was the indiction so he places Augustine's death in the correct indiction but wrong consulship.

430.1 Theodosius celebrated his thirtieth anniversary by anticipation since it fell officially only on 10 January 431.

430.2 Fl. Constantius Felix (*PLRE* 2: 461) was *magister militum* and *patricius* from 425 (cf. O'Flynn, 1983, 77–8) and a favourite of Placidia. With his wife Padusia and a certain deacon named Grunitus he was struck down on the steps of the Basilica Ursiana at Ravenna for allegedly plotting against the general Aetius (Prosp., 1303 [IX 473]; Hyd., 94 [XI 22]; Jo. Ant., fr. 201.3 [*FHG* 4, 615]). Aetius had probably engineered the whole episode (Bury, 1923, 243; Oost, 1968, 229–30).

430.3 M.'s account concerns not so much the council of Ephesus itself; rather it is about the background to it, especially the letter of Pope Celestine of August 430, in which he offered Nestorius ten days from the receipt of the letter to recant his views on the 'Mother of God'. The letter was also sent to Cyril of Alexandria with a copy to the other Eastern patriarchs (text [ed. E. Schwarz] in *ACO* i.2 [1925], 7-12; partial translation in Stevenson, 1966, 279–80). The council of 150 bishops (not 200, although that is also the figure in Chron. Pasch., 581.13) summoned to Ephesus the following year proceeded controversially to condemn Nestorius before the Antiochene or Roman representatives had arrived (Soc., 7.34). Nestorius was replaced by Maximian as bishop of CP in August 431. M. may have been familiar with this letter at first hand since he relies on the same document for his notice of Sisinnius in 426 (Holder-Egger, 1877, 94).

431.1 Flaccilla (*PLRE* 2: 473), the daughter of Theodosius II, was still only a child when she died (Cameron, 1982, 262). The exact year of her birth is not known, although it will have been after 422 when her elder sister Eudoxia (*PLRE* 2: 410–12) was born, but perhaps before the birth of her brother (or half-brother) Arcadius (*PLRE* 2: 130). M.'s failure to mention Arcadius may stem from the fact that his parentage was doubtful and therefore that his birth had been expunged from the records (Cameron, 1982, 267). It is possible, however, that Arcadius never actually existed and that the sources have therefore been misinterpreted (cf. Holum, 1982, 178, n. 14 who denies his existence altogether).

431.2 The context of this fracas is most unclear but presumably the mention of 'our church' is meant to refer to Hagia Sophia in which case it is probably to be connected with the account of Soc., 7.33. The barbarian domestics of some local magnate sought refuge from ill-treatment in the church, drew their swords and could not be persuaded to leave. After some days there they killed one of the clerics and then slew themselves, or perhaps incinerated themselves, if that is what M. intended by his description. This account is likely to have been borrowed by both M. and Socrates from a local CP source (cf. Holder-Egger, 1877, 105). It was surely this incident which led to a law issued on 23 March 431, iterating the sanctity of a church as a place of refuge and forbidding any armed person from entering therein (*CTh*. 9.45.4).

431.3 The imperial procession to the public granaries was an important ceremonial occasion as described in the *Book of Ceremonies* (*de caer*., 2.51). The emperor and Praetorian Prefect travelled by chariot in formal procession and checked the measurements of grain available in the granaries. The date of this procession is not known but it was perhaps in the summer before the harvest. The granaries were located in the Strategion (Guilland, 1969, 1.168–9). It was an obvious occasion for the populace of the city to vent their anger at a time when food supplies were low.

432.1 Pope Sixtus III (31 July 432–19 August 440) invested much time in attempting to reconcile the breach between East and West opened up after the Council of Ephesus, which resulted in the reconciliation of Cyril and John of Antioch in 433, and then into asserting papal authority over Illyricum. When Proclus became patriarch of CP in 434 he began to lure the Illyrian bishops into his orbit so that Sixtus had to remind them of their obligation to bishop Anastasius of Thessalonike. In rebuilding Rome after the sack in 410, he is probably best known for the basilica of S. Maria Maggiore and the Lateran baptistery (Kelly, 1986, 42–3).

432.2 Aetius (*PLRE* 2: 21–9) and Boniface (*PLRE* 2: 237–40) were both established and powerful generals at the Western court but they had developed a deep-seated rivalry. Boniface had been in charge of affairs in Africa until a series of setbacks against the Vandals, whereupon he was made *magister militum* before returning to Italy. There, soon after, he was confronted in battle five miles from Rimini by Aetius. Placidia's role in instigating this conflict as a means of containing the influence of Aetius is noted by M. (cf. Hyd., 99 [XI 22] with Oost, 1968, 230–33 and O'Flynn, 1983, 78–81). While Boniface may have been a *patricius* in 432 (cf. O'Flynn, 1983, 80 with 176, n. 26 and 177, n. 44), Aetius did not acquire that honour before 435 (*PLRE* 2: 24). M. is therefore anticipating.

432.3 Despite actually defeating Aetius, Boniface received a fatal wound in the encounter (Prosp., 1310 [IX 473–4]; Hyd., 99 [XI 22]; Chron. Gall. 452, 111 [IX 458]; Add. Prosp. Haun. 432, [IX 301]; Jo. Ant., fr. 201.3 [*FHG* 4, 615]). The authenticity of M.'s information about the specially-made long sword used by Aetius to wound Boniface has been doubted (Oost, 1968, 233, n. 87; cf. O'Flynn, 1983, 176, n. 28) but there is no reason to reject it. Pelagia (*PLRE* 2: 856–7), of Arian Gothic background, had been the second wife of Boniface. Her subsequent marriage to Aetius produced a son, Gaudentius (*PLRE* 2: 494 with Clover, 1970, 30 ff.). The source of Pelagia's wealth is unknown.

433 This was a truly savage fire to burn over a three-day period (Soc., 7.39 says two days and two nights). It spread from the Neorion harbour (or gate?) on the Golden Horn to engulf the largest public granaries and the Achillean baths (Soc., 7.39 and Chron. Pasch., 582.4–6 with Janin, 1964, 235–6; Müller-Wiener, 1977, 58 and Mango, 1985, 18, n. 30, 40). A church of the Novatians managed to escape the blaze and this deliverance was celebrated annually on 17 August (Soc., 7.39). The dates for the fire given by Soc. (17 August) and the Chron. Pasch. (21 August) are inconsistent. Perhaps the fire raged on August 17, 18 and 19; or else August 19, 20, 21. All three accounts probably depend ultimately here on a local CP source.

434 This is one of the most controversial entries in the chronicle. Justa Grata Honoria (*PLRE* 2: 568–9), the daughter of Galla Placidia and Constantius and therefore sister of Valentinian III, was born in 418 so was of marriageable age by 434; as Augusta since the age of six (424) she had her own separate household. The events described by M. (her affair with Eugenius, her expulsion from the palace and her offer to the Hun king Attila) were considered by Bury, 1919 (cf. 1923, 289) to be misdated. According to Bury, the events described are correctly dated to the second indiction but they belong to the 2nd indiction of the next indiction cycle, that is fifteen years later (1 September 449–31 August 450). This means that the source used by M. for this entry must have contained an indictional date only, and that there was no other chronological indication which would enable him to date it to the correct consulship; that is, it was not an annalistic chronicle with the event inserted under the correct year, either by indictions or consuls, but some other less exact source, perhaps like that of Malalas who so frequently dates events merely by indictions (Jeffreys, 1990, 149–51). M.'s date was followed by Jord., *Rom.* 329 and *Get.* 223–4. Bury's argument has usually been accepted, while at the same time M.'s statement on Honoria's pregnancy and her expulsion to CP has been rejected (e.g. *PLRE* 2: 416, 568–9; Oost, 1968, 283–5), as having 'all the earmarks of Byzantine court gossip' (Maenchen-Helfen, 1973, 130).

The matter is, however, not so simple. In the first place M. is not recording Honoria's marriage to Herculanus (*PLRE* 2: 544–5), which the other sources (Priscus, John of Antioch) date firmly to 449. Instead, he is describing a separate incident — her pregnancy by Eugenius (*PLRE* 2: 416) and exile to CP. Bury's explanation for the 434 date, as he himself conceded, means that the reported exile in CP of Honoria must be rejected as fictitious. Such a conclusion is questionable (cf. Oost, 1968, 283, n. 115). Moreover, the inclusion of this entry in the chronicle is best explained by the very act of Honoria's presence in CP at some stage. M. was probably depending here on a local CP source (Holder-Egger, 1877, 105). It seems unlikely that M. and Jordanes should invent this episode, since it hardly served their purpose to do so. Furthermore, the chronological problem lies rather with John of Antioch than M.; that is to say, by compressing and abbreviating the account of Priscus, John gives the mistaken impression that Honoria's affair with Eugenius was followed closely by her betrothal to Herculanus (Priscus, fr. 15; Jo. Ant., fr. 199.2 [*FHG* 4, 613]; cf. Holum, 1982, 1–2). When this is realised it means that the Eugenius scandal and a subsequent period of exile in CP can be assigned to 434, as Gibbon (1896, 456–7) supposed. This then explains the date of M., who under 434 simply compounds events stretching out over a number of years. Such a method of composition is common in the chronicle (cf. **435.2**). Thus, the fact of Honoria's exile to CP in 434 can be reinstated. The only anticipated part of the account is Honoria's approach to Attila, which belongs in the period 449/50 (Priscus, frs.17 [300–3]; 20.1 [304–7]; 20.3 [306–9]).

435.1 There is some uncertainty about the construction of this forum. Since the region of the Helenianae can be located fairly precisely (Tiftixoglu, 1973, 49f.), this can only mean that the Forum of Arcadius no longer existed. So in 435 Theodosius II must have extended the Forum, surrounding it with arcades and porticoes and decorating it with numerous statues. Yet 'aedificatum' seems to imply more than simply 'renovation' or extension (cf. **447.1** where 'reaedificatio' means 'extension'). Perhaps a complete reconstruction was undertaken and it was re-dedicated as the 'Forum of Theodosius'. Like the fora of Constantine and Theodosius (Forum Tauri), the central monument of this forum was a column at the base of which stood statues of the emperors Theodosius II, Valentinian I and, later, Marcian (Janin, 1964, 71). The column of Arcadius is described as resembling that of Theodosius and was covered with bas-reliefs, drawings of which survive (Liebeschuetz, 1990 — with plates). Although the column has disappeared, its base survives, built into a wall.

435.2 Sebastian (*PLRE* 2: 983–4) was the son-in-law of the *magister militum* Boniface (*PLRE* 2: 237–40), who succeeded to Boniface's post in 432 only to forfeit it the following year on the re-emergence of Boniface's rival Aetius (*PLRE* 2: 21–9). He then fled to the Eastern court at CP (Hyd., 104 [XI 22]). Precisely when he left CP to return to the West is a matter of controversy. It used to be thought (e.g. *PLRE* 2: 984) that M. has placed Sebastian's departure from CP in the correct indiction but in the wrong cycle by linking it with his death in 450 (cf. a similar instance in **434**). Clover (1979, 65–76) has shown, however, that M.'s date must be correct and that it makes sense of other developments in the Mediterranean at that time. Upon leaving CP in 435 Sebastian and his men conducted a campaign of piracy in the Hellespont before being attracted to Toulouse in 438/9 and subsequently (445) into Vandal Africa (Hyd., 129, 132 [XI 24]). There Sebastian was killed in 450 (Hyd., 144 [XI 25]). His death is anticipated by M. under 435.

436 M. is the sole source of information for the imperial expedition to Cyzicus. Presumably it occurred in the best sailing period up to June (Seeck, 1919, 365). M.'s comment about Theodosius' 'generosity' suggests a disaster of some kind, probably an earthquake like that which occurred there in 460 (cf. **443.2**). For the sedentary Theodosius such a trip was indeed rare and probably recorded in the local chronicle source (Holder-Egger, 1877, 105).

437 Valentinian and Eudoxia had originally been betrothed in 424 as part of the settlement process involved in restoring Valentinian to the Western throne (Oost, 1968, 242–5). The formal process for the marriage was set in train in 436 by the Roman aristocrat Volusianus (*PLRE* 2: 1184–5). It was originally arranged that the wedding be in Thessalonike but subsequently Valentinian agreed to come to CP. In late summer 437 the emperor and his entourage left Ravenna for the East, perhaps travelling via Rome, if that explains M.'s mention of Rome; otherwise it is simply a mistake for Ravenna. Their formal *adventus* or arrival into CP occurred on 21 October (Soc., 7.44.3; Chron. Pasch., 582.14–15) and the marriage itself on 29 October with all the pomp and ceremony normally surrounding such an occasion (Prosp., 1328 [IX 475]; Chron. Pasch., 582.13–18). The newly-wed imperial couple arrived in Thessalonike in November and stayed until the following spring, presumably in the imperial palace (cf. Croke, 1981a, 480–3).

438.1 M. is the only source of information for this Contradis (not in *PLRE*). In 437 and 438, as we learn from Prosp., 1330, 1332 (IX 476), there was an outbreak of piratical activity in the Mediterranean and this is probably to be linked to similar unrest in the Hellespont at this time (cf. Clover, 1979, 71–2). This is evidently the background to Contradis' activity. M.'s notice presumably derives from a local CP source reporting the announcement and celebration of Contradis' defeat and death (cf. Holder-Egger, 1877, 105).

438.2 Here, as elsewhere in the chronicle, M. is noting the original occurrence of an event still commemorated annually in his own time. Since 428 the memory of John

Chrysostom had been celebrated at CP (cf. **428**). In 437 bishop Proclus of CP had persuaded the emperor Theodosius to have John's remains transferred to the capital. They arrived and were formally received by the emperor and his sister Pulcheria in the established *adventus* ceremonial on 28 January 438 (Soc., 7.45: 27 January; Theod., 5.36 with Holum, 1982, 184–5). His bones were then deposited in the church of the Holy Apostles (Theoph., AM 5930 [93.4]). Thereafter on the same day each year the arrival of Chrysostom's remains in the capital on 28 January was celebrated with a liturgical procession through the city (*SEC*, 425.23–30; *Typ*., I 212–4 with Janin, 1966, 77) and celebrated likewise throughout the East (e.g. *PO* 10.118).

438.3 This notice records the elaborate ceremonial welcome for Valentinian and Eudoxia when they arrived in Ravenna after spending the winter months since their wedding in Thessalonike (see **437**). They will have entered Ravenna most probably in March/April (cf. Chron. Gall. 511, 595 [IX 661]), although the exact date is not recorded. M. probably took his information from a CP source recording the announcement in CP of the arrival of the imperial couple in Ravenna.

439.1 Since the fortieth anniversary of Theodosius' reign (= fifth quinquennial celebrations) was not due to commence until 10 January 440, it have must have been celebrated by anticipation (as sometimes happened) a year earlier in 439.

439.2 The empress Eudocia had set out on her pilgrimage to the Holy Land after the wedding of her daughter Eudoxia in early Spring 438 and had included a successful stop-over in Antioch on the way (Soc., 7.4.7 with Holum, 1982, 185–7). Early the following year, as recorded here by M., she returned to the capital with some relics of St Stephen in a formal *adventus* (Hunt, 1982, 229–33; Holum, 1982, 189), just as in 421 other relics of Stephen had been ceremonially received into the city (Holum, 1982, 103–9). The relics were apparently deposited at the commencement of construction of the church of St Laurence (Holum, 1982, 137; Cameron, 1982, 278) — or else they were deposited in the martyrium of Stephen in the imperial palace (cf. Hunt, 1982, 233, n. 73). M.'s 'are venerated' indicates his familiarity in his own day with the annual liturgical commemoration celebrated on 2 August (Janin, 1966, 83) at CP (*SEC*, 349–350) and elsewhere (*PO* 10.83).

439.3 This is the first mention of the Vandals in the chronicle. There is no indication that they were previously in Spain and had arrived in Africa years before. While other sources confirm the capture of Carthage in this year (Chron. Pasch., 583.5–7), M. alone adds that Geiseric achieved this with the help of his allies. The Vandals entered the city on 19 October. M.'s '23 October' may just be a scribal error, that is X for XIV (cf. Courtois, 1955, 171, n. 4).

440.1 Paulinus (*PLRE* 2: 846–7) had been *magister officiorum* in 430 and probably again in 440 (Cameron, 1982, 267, n. 162), having long been a companion of the emperor Theodosius. Indeed he it was who introduced Theodosius to his wife Eudocia two decades previously. According to Malalas, in one of his most celebrated passages, Paulinus was exiled by the emperor and put to death on suspicion of adultery with the empress (Jo. Mal., 14.6,8 [356.17–358.4]). As noted by *PLRE* 2: 847 'the chronology is very uncertain and the story of the adultery may be no more than a contemporary rumour'. There is no reason, however, to doubt M.'s statement that Paulinus was executed in Caesarea and on the emperor's orders, which is corroborated by Theophanes and Nestorius. Relying on his local CP source (cf. Holder-Egger, 1877, 105), M. is here merely reporting the serious fact of a high imperial official executed on imperial command. He suggests no reason and it is possible that none was suggested in his source, which must have listed the event under the year 440. No reason is given for Paul being at Caesarea, but as *magister officiorum* he could have been en route to the Eastern frontier to engage in treaty negotiations (following the outbreak of the Persian war?) or some other official business. Although it has been argued that M.'s date must be wrong (e.g. Bury, 1923, 230; Holum, 1982, 194, n. 83), because Paulinus cannot have been killed while Eudocia and the Praetorian Prefect Cyrus were still at court (i.e. before 441), there is strong reason for upholding it (Seeck, 1921, 246, 449–50 and especially Cameron, 1982, 258–63). It is not necessary to suppose that Eudocia and Cyrus were originally implicated in the circumstances leading to Paulinus' exile, despite the embroidered accounts of later chroniclers. If there is any chronological reliability in the story of Malalas then it was some incident which took place on the feast of the Epiphany (6 January) 440 which inculpated Paulinus. Perhaps it had something to do with the fact that on this day *magistri* were traditionally appointed, so perhaps it was the very installation of Paulinus as *magister officiorum*. It was evidently during the elaborate ceremonial procession to Hagia Sophia on that occasion (*de Caer*., 1.3.26), from which Paulinus was excused, that there occurred some incident between him and Eudocia which proved their undoing. Eudocia remained in the capital and returned to Jerusalem later in the year or early the following year, while her favourite Cyrus remained and became consul in 441, although he too was expelled in the course of his consulship (Cameron, 1982, 257–58 whose reconstruction is to be preferred to that of Holum, 1982, 190–93, which places too much reliance on the evidence of Malalas and the Chronicon Paschale for the prefectures of Cyrus).

440.2 Pope Leo the Great (August/September 440–10 November 461) was one of the most influential and celebrated popes, who worked to enhance the papacy by acting decisively against Manichaeans and other heretics and by asserting the primacy of Rome over the Eastern patriarchates and the Balkans, as well as in Africa, Spain and Gaul. He met both the Hun king Attila (452) and the Vandal king Geiseric (455), which resulted in the former turning away from Rome and in the latter desisting from sacking the city. Leo's *Tome* (449) was a crucial document in attempts to establish the orthodox position on the nature of Christ at the Council of Chalcedon. His support for the position of the Eastern court remained loyal, despite Canon 28 which gave Rome and CP ecclesial parity (details in Kelly, 1986, 43–5; cf. Friend, 1972, 100–2, 145–7).

441.1 M. groups together in a single entry a number of different invasions of imperial territory which occurred in rapid succession. The Persians had encroached on Roman ground early in 440 and peace had been agreed on by the middle of 441 (Croke, 1984a, 65); the Huns subsequently launched their attacks into Illyricum. The Huns must have invaded in spring/early summer 441, because after a one-year truce there was another invasion in 442 (s.v.), which was itself over by the end of summer 442. One assumes the raids of the Tzanni, Saracens, and Isaurians occurred in 441 but they may have originated in 440. None of these nations posed a major military threat to the Romans at this time but they continued to harass them for a number of years (Croke, 1983, 304–7). Although these invasions have been placed even *before* the invasion of the Persians (Lee, 1987, 188–9), it is more likely that M.'s compressed entry is designed to imply that the Tzanni, Saracens and Isaurians invaded in concert with the Persians, or took advantage of the Persian conflict to invade of their own volition. Unrest among the Saracens led to their subsidies being reassured (Blockley, 1992, 63). M. continues with a note on the treaties concluded by Anatolius and Aspar. It is now clear that Aspar (*PLRE* 2: 164–9) must have made a one-year peace (as M. notes) with the Huns in the Balkans (Maenchen-Helfen, 1973, 110), while Anatolius (*PLRE* 2: 84–6) made a settlement, possibly for one year also, with the Persians (Blockley, 1992, 61–2). The view that Anatolius' treaty was with the Huns (rather than the Persians) in 441 is based on a mistaken understanding of M.'s statement (cf. Croke, 1981, 160–64).

441.2 The circumstances behind the death of the *magister militum* John (*PLRE* 2: 597) are not clear. It is not necessary to suppose, as does *PLRE* 2: 597, that John was killed purely because he was a Vandal at a time when a Roman force was being assembled to do battle with the Vandals who were posing a threat to the empire; nor to suppose that it could be connected with 'preparations for a naval expedition to oust the Vandal Geiseric from Carthage' (Whitby/Whitby, 1989, 73, n. 245). Rather, it seems (*pace* Seeck, 1919, 291–2) that Arnigisclus was a refugee subject of the Huns who had been selected by John to be handed over to the Huns in order to secure the peace of 441. The death of John was therefore the desperate vengeance of Arnigisclus. If that is so, and it is quite likely in view of Attila's constant demand that refugees from the Hun confederation be returned, then it seems that Arnigisclus had the sympathy of the Eastern court for his treachery went unpunished. Certain sources (Theoph., AM 5943 [103.31]), despite some confusion, would appear to implicate the eunuch Chrysaphius (*PLRE* 2: 295–7), the emerging influence at the imperial court. In other words he may have encouraged Arnigisclus (*PLRE* 2: 151) to do away with John. Arnigisclus, probably a Goth, was perhaps *comes rei militaris* and took John's place as *magister militum per Thracias* based at Marcianople (Croke, 1983, 302, n. 30), as Chrysaphius had perhaps promised. M. indicates that some treachery was involved in the murder of John, and the fact that Zach. Rhet., 2.5 attributes his death to the 'servants of Ariobindus (*leg.* Arnigisclus)' may suggest that John was lured into a trap.

441.3 Upon advancing across the Danube, probably at Margum, the Huns under their kings Bleda and Attila moved into Sirmium and Singidunum on the one hand

and then up the Margus valley as far as Naissus on the other (Priscus, frs. 5–6 [228–233]). They apparently captured and looted many other towns along the way (Thompson, 1948, 20 ff. and Maenchen-Helfen, 1973, 109–10). The invasion was halted with the one-year peace negotiated by Aspar (see **441.1** above). Soon after, the capital of the Praetorian Prefecture was transferred from Sirmium to Thessalonike (Croke, 1978, 255–6) and a new palace was built there for the prefect (Croke, 1981a, 480–3).

442.1 This may be the same comet recorded by Hyd., 126 (XI 24), although Grumel, 1958, 470 separates them.

442.2 In 441 the Huns had only ravaged Illyricum. When the one-year peace had expired (spring/summer 442), or was about to expire, Attila again threatened to invade if Hunnish deserters and tribute were not produced. Theodosius refused and Attila immediately crossed the Danube at Drobeta, which was sacked. The Huns then attacked Ratiaria (noted by Priscus) and moved along the Danube road into northern Thrace, taking the towns in their way — the legionary base of Oescus, Novae, Sucidava, Nicopolis ad Istrum (Croke, 1981, 160 with nn. 8 and 9). In response the contingent assembled under Areobindus and Ansila to engage the Vandals in Africa sailed back from Sicily in order to provide reinforcements (Prosp., 1346 [IX 479]), and it subsequently halted the Huns' advance. Hostilities had ceased by August 442 and a peace with the Huns was then worked out by the *magister officiorum* Nomus (Croke, 1981, 168–70).

443.1 There is no other evidence for this extremely cold and lengthy weather. M. is likely to have found the information in a local chronicle, and its significance probably stemmed from the supplication liturgies which will have been held to seek relief from the harsh consequences of the weather (cf. **389.2**).

443.2 The emperor, on one of his rare journeys outside the capital, travelled to the diocese of Asiana, through Heraclea Salbake (*Nov. Theod.*, 23.5.21) and Aphrodisias (Roueché, 1986, 130–2; cf. Whitby/Whitby, 1989, 73, n. 249 on possible motives for the journey). M. records his ceremonial *adventus* on returning to CP on 27 August and will have found this in his local chronicle (cf. Chron. Pasch., 583.18–584.2).

443.3 The Baths of Achilles were the oldest in CP and were located near the Strategion (details in Janin, 1964, 216). They had been burnt out in the fire on 21 August 433 (s.v.) and were apparently rebuilt; hence their opening here described by M. Their inauguration took place on 11 January 443 (Chron. Pasch. 583.17). There are no extant remains of the baths.

444.1 Theodosius' ninth quinqennium (45 years) actually began on 10 January 445. So it was obviously anticipated in this year.

444.2 The emperor's sister Arcadia (*PLRE* 2: 129) had been born on 3 April 400 and had lived the life of a pious recluse until her death in 444 (cf. Jo. Nik., 87.25).

444.3 There is no other evidence for the heavy rains and flood in Bithynia. M.'s local CP chronicle source will have noted the official report of the situation in CP and the imperial munificence in response (cf. **389.2**).

444.4 The empress Eudocia had retired to Jerusalem in early 441 or so and had transported her entourage there (Cameron, 1982, 264), including the clerics Severus and John. The affluent 'count of the domestics' Saturninus (*PLRE* 2: 979–80) had been sent there by the emperor and executed Severus and John before falling victim to the empress' revenge (cf. Priscus, fr. 8 [93–4]; Theoph. AM 5942 [102.1–6]). It is not certain what gave rise to Saturninus' mission, although it was possibly connected with some discovery at CP in which Eudocia was implicated; or else to report back to the emperor on her burgeoning reputation (Bury, 1923, 231). As punishment for her execution of Saturninus the empress was deprived of her 'royal ministers', probably the *praepositus* and others (Holum, 1982, 194), but she retained her imperial title throughout the remainder of her life in Jerusalem (on which: Hunt, 1982, 237 ff.) until her death in 460. M. obviously found it incredible to think that an empress could have been so enraged as to murder Saturninus, if there is any force in his comment 'nescio quo excita dolore'.

445.1 There is some uncertainty about the year of Bleda's death (*PLRE* 2: 230). It is reported as 444 by Prosp., 1353 (IX 480) as 446, by Chron. Gall. 452, 131 (cf. Jord., *Get.* 181 and Theoph., AM 5942 [102.16]), but M.'s 445 date is evidently the correct one (Thompson, 1948, 88, n. 3; Maenchen-Helfen, 1973, 104–5). It is possible, however, given M.'s indictional dating system, that he means to place the Hun king's death in the period 1 September–31 December 444, which would accord with the date of Prosper. There is no confusion about Attila's responsibility.

445.2 M. is the only evidence for both the sedition at CP and the mortality among men and cattle. The linking together by M. of these events suggests that severe famine and pestilence may have been the original cause of both, exacerbated in all likelihood by Vandal raids. If so, then this oppressive condition continued to afflict CP until 447 (cf. **446.1** and **447.1** below). There is no need to assume that this event represents the first conflict of the circus factions at CP (as does Cameron, 1973, 233). Rather it was just another food riot (cf. **409, 431**).

446.1 M.'s consular date ('Valentinianus VII et Aetius III') is completely wrong. It should be 'Aetius III and Symmachus'. The error is to be explained (cf. Bagnall et al., 1987, 446) by the addition of the first name (Aetius) to the consul of the previous year (Valentinian).

This famine and plague may be the same as that mentioned in Hyd., 126 (XI 241). It may also have been prolonged by the earthquake early the following year (**447.1**).

446.2 Although there is no corroborative evidence for this fire, there is no need to doubt its occurrence. It is precisely the sort of information M. will have found in his local CP chronicle source. Schneider, 1941, 383, n. 2 was wrong to omit it from the catalogue of CP fires on the grounds that it is a duplication of the fire of 404. By 'templum' M. presumably means the church of Hagia Sophia.

447.1 This destructive earthquake hit CP and environs on Sunday 26 January in the early hours of the morning when the public places were empty, which explains why no-one was hurt there (details in Croke, 1981b, 132–40). The most severe damage occurred along the Mese from the Troad porticoes near the wall of Constantine to the bronze tetrapylon near the Forum of Theodosius. The city walls demolished on this occasion were those along the land wall of Theodosius, mainly constructed early in the century. In fact about half the wall (fifty-seven towers) was seriously damaged and required rebuilding (Janin, 1964, 265; Müller-Wiener, 1977, 287–8). The 'recently constructed walls' were the sea walls located between the land walls of Constantine and Theodosius (Müller-Wiener, 1977, 312). The column and statue of Theodosius in the forum of Thedodosius was not damaged, but the statues and huge stones which were toppled probably belonged to the basilica of Theodosius and/or his triumphal arch. There is no evidence of damage in other places besides CP, except that the Long Wall across the Chersonese was destroyed sufficiently to allow the Huns to breach it (Evag., 1.17). The subsequent plague and famine are referred to in the life of Anatolius, patriarch of CP at the time (*vita Anatolii* 17 [*AASS*: July, vol. 1, 583B]) and it may have been the impact of the disease on the Huns which caused their withdrawal from CP (references in Maenchen-Helfen, 1973, 122–3). This earthquake was subsequently commemorated each year at CP with a liturgical procession and it was during this very procession ten years later that the emperor Marcian took ill and died (Croke, 1978a, 5–9).

447.2 As M. indicates, the Hun invasion of 447 was more devastating and more extensive than those of 441 and 442 and he wrote about it 'with a vigour which he rarely displays elsewhere' (Thompson, 1948, 94). Having been settled in northern Thrace after 442, the Huns this time moved right through Thrace into the Chersonese, thereby threatening the very province (Europa) in which the imperial capital was located. More than 100 towns were captured (Call., *v. Hyp.*, 139.21 ff.) or at least 70 according to Chron. Gall. 452, 132 (IX 662).

447.3 In a much acclaimed feat (performed with the aid of personnel provided by the circus factions), the earthquake-damaged walls (s.a. **447.1**) were rebuilt by the Praetorian Prefect Constantine (*PLRE* 2: 317–18) within sixty days (i.e. by the end of March), as we know from several inscriptions placed on the restored gates of the wall (Croke, 1981b, 133–4). The urgency for the rebuilding was probably provided by the fact that the Huns were in the vicinity and were threatening CP; indeed the serious damage to CP's defences may have provided the impetus for their raid (*ibid.*, 138).

447.4 M. would appear here to be recording the furthermost point of the Huns' invasion. It has been suggested (by Blackman, 1968, 92, n. 120) that by Thermopylae M. was not indicating the famous pass but another place closer to the Danube. Given the route of the Huns' invasion in 447 (cf. **447.2**), it is clear that they would have reached Thermopylae in Thessaly, where they were probably halted by the well-guarded wall there (cf. Hohlfelder, 1977, 174, 177, n. 26).

447.5 In 441 Arnigisclus (*PLRE* 2: 151) had succeeded John as *magister militum per Thracias* with his headquarters at Marcianople. When Attila's Huns mobilised again in 447, Arnigisclus marched out of Marcianople and engaged with the Huns by the river Vit (Utum) in the province of Dacia Ripensis. Despite his brave showing the Roman general was killed (cf. Jord. *Rom.* 331, Chron. Pasch., 586.5). He was succeeded by Theodulus (*PLRE* 2: 1105–6 with Croke, 1981, 167 and 1983, 302, n. 30).

448.1 M. is the sole evidence for this donation from India.

448.2 There is no other evidence for this fire but it was clearly destructive. Antiochus (*PLRE* 2: 104) was Praetorian Prefect of the East but was out of office by November. The fire must have occurred early in the year if its damage was cleared and restored by Antiochus as Prefect. The Troadesian porticoes were famous marble porticoes stretching west from the Forum of Arcadius, and they formed an important part of ceremonial processions in and out of CP (Janin, 1966, 93). The 'gates' referred to are presumably the entrances to the portico at either end.

448.3 There is a problem with the punctuation here. This entry would appear to be connected temporally with the previous entry. In other words the Hunnish legates were in CP at the time Antiochus was refurbishing the incinerated part of the city (before November). After the 447 invasion a treaty was agreed on, under which the Romans supplied tribute to the Huns (Blockley, 1992, 63–6). The terms were negotiated in 448 by Edeco, on behalf of Attila (Priscus, fr. 11.1 [242–3]), so that by mid-late 448 they were still haggling with the emperor over the unpaid tribute (Croke, 1983, 307–8).

449.1 Marina (*PLRE* 2: 723) was one of the daughters of Arcadius and Eudoxia and therefore sister of the emperor Theodosius and Pulcheria. Born in 403, she devoted her life to spiritual matters, as part of the pious imperial household (cf. Arcadia in 444.2), and died on 3 August 449 (Chron. Pasch., 586.18–20; Theod. Anag., 353; Jo. Nik., 87.23).

449.2 What M. calls the 'Second council of Ephesus' was convoked by the emperor Theodosius II in order to address the charges against Eutyches, who had been condemned for his supposedly docetic/monophysite views by a council at CP the previous year (cf. Vict. Tonn., 448 [XI 184–5]; Prosp., 1358 [IX 480]; Theod. Anag., 347 [98.28–99.13]). Dioscorus, the bishop of Alexandria was the driving force behind the council and he ensured that Pope Leo's *Tome* was not read or discussed and that the previous ruling of the Patriarch of CP, Flavian, was overturned. He was, however, dependent on the influence of the *cubicularius* Saturninus (*PLRE* 2: 980), which presumably smoothed his reputation at court. The name given the council by Pope Leo — *latrocinium* or 'robber council' — has stuck.

449.3 Ariobindus (*PLRE* 2: 145–6) had been a distinguished general and patrician, and was consul in 434. He had led armies against the Persians, Vandals and Huns. Taurus (*PLRE* 2: 1056–7) had been a Praetorian Prefect and patrician, and was consul in 428. It is not clear why they should be so strongly linked in this case except to signify that both distinguished patricians died in the same year.

450.1 Theodosius died on 28 July of spinal injuries sustained from falling off his horse two days earlier while out riding by the river Lycus in CP (Theod. Anag., 353; Chron. Pasch., 589.17–590.5; Chron. Gall. 452, 135 [IX 662]; Theoph., AM 5942 [103.6–9]; Evag.,1.22; Jo. Mal., 14.27 [366.19–367.5]). M. counts only his period as sole Augustus, 408–450.

450.2 Marcian (*PLRE* 2: 714–15) was proclaimed emperor on 25 August, less than a month after the death of Theodosius, during which time the smooth succession was worked out by Pulcheria and her supporters. Since Marcian was one of the associates of the *magister militum* Aspar his cause was advanced with the support of the army, whereupon he was married to Pulcheria, who then elevated him to the throne at the Hebdomon outside CP (Chron. Pasch., 590.8–10.; Theod. Anag., 354 [100.11–13]; Proc., *Wars* 3.4.7; Evag., 1.22; Jo. Mal.,14.28 [367.6–11]; Theoph., AM 5943 [103.27–8]; Zon., 13.24.1–3). For details: Holum, 1982, 208–9. His reign became a 'golden age' in Byzantine tradition (e.g. Theoph., AM 5946 [108.12–15]).

450.3 The eunuch Chrysaphius (*PLRE* 2: 295–7) was one of the most powerful figures at CP in the 440s, although this is the only time he is mentioned by M. Pulcheria's resentment of Chrysaphius dated back to the time (c. 443) he had tried to have her become a deaconess but he had remained a favourite of the emperor Theodosius who resisted a request from Attila for him to be turned over to the Huns (Priscus, fr. 15.5 [300–1]). Only with the death of Theodosius was Pulcheria in a position to have him removed. As M. reports, it was at the behest of Pulcheria that Chrysaphius was struck down by Jordanes (*PLRE* 2: 620–1), son of the Vandal general John (*PLRE* 2: 597), whose murder had probably been inspired by Chrysaphius in 441 (s.v.). Chrysaphius' murder took place before the elevation of Marcian, presumably in early August, not long after the death of Theodosius (Prosp., 1361 [IX 481]; Coll. Avell., 99.11; Theod. Anag., 353 [100.8]; Jo. Mal., 14.32 [368.5–8]; Chron. Pasch., 590.6–7; Nic. Call., 14.49). Vict. Tonn., 450.2 (XI 185) suggests that Chrysaphius was murdered before Marcian's elevation.

451 This council was convoked and presided over by the emperor Marcian and his wife Pulcheria, with the aim of resolving the dispute over Eutyches' alleged claims that Christ's humanity was not consubstantial with that of mankind and that after the Incarnation he was of a single nature. It was held from late September at Chalcedon opposite CP in the basilica of St Euphemia, a fourth century church built outside the walls of the city around the shrine of the saint (Janin, 1953, 31–60; 1964, 493 ff.). Eutyches had acquired influence at court through his godson Chrysaphius and used that influence to promote the interests of the Alexandrian patriarch Dioscorus. He had in turn been supported by Dioscorus at the 'Robber Council' in 449, which had exonerated him on the charge of heresy. At Chalcedon Eutyches was condemned along with the 'Robber Council'. About 350 bishops attended, not 630, and the first formal meeting was held on 8 October. Pope Leo was not present but his legates Paschasinus and Boniface attended. Leo's *Tome* or letter to Flavian formed the basis for the Christological definition accepted at Chalcedon. Dioscorus was deposed, excommunicated and exiled to Gangra in Paphlagonia, whereupon his supporters fomented trouble in Alexandria (Evag., 2.5; Nic. Call., 15.8). Similar summary acounts of the council can be found in Vict. Tonn., 451 (XI 185); Prosp., 1369 (IX 482); Theod. Anag., 360 (101.18–28); Theoph., AM 5944 (105.21–106.14).

452.1 Marcian's law on the consulship is preserved in *CJ* 12.12.3 and is referred to in a novel of the emperor Justinian (*Nov. Just.*, 105 praef.). The consular games had become a very expensive burden by the fifth century and emperors were only too keen to encourage the channelling of such funds into necessary public works (Cameron, 1982, 126; Bagnall et al., 1987, 9). Marcian's law represents an important step in that process, which was to come to completion under Justinian. The aqueduct was presumably the aqueduct of Valens (Mango, 1985, 40–2), which had perhaps become derelict in part, or had not been properly repaired after the earthquake in 447.

452.2 The three large stones mentioned by M. may have been meteorites. Although they are not elsewhere recorded, there is other less precise evidence of unusual happenings in this year which may be a reference to the same phenomenon.

452.3 After the settlement with the Romans in 448/9 Attila and his Huns resolved to turn West, either spurred on or enticed by the alleged offer of Honoria (cf. 434). Although M. does not follow the movements of the Huns in the West, his Eastern source will have noted for him the capture of Aquileia after a siege (Jord., *Get.* 219–20; Prosp., 1365 [IX 482]; Proc., *Wars* 3.4.29–35; Agn. 42 [IX 302]; Add. Prosp. Haun., 452, [IX 302]; cf. Chron. Gall. 511, 617 [IX 663]; Chron. Gall. 452, 139, 141 [IX 662]; Theoph., AM 5945 [107.5]).

453.1 This entry on the discovery of the head of John the Baptist by monks from the Spelaion monastery in Emesa is one of the longest entries in the chronicle. Indeed its unusual length makes one suspicious about whether it did form part of the original chronicle or whether it was a later interpolation. Since, however, it is included in full in all the best manuscripts there are no real grounds for doubt. So its unusual length and detail may be taken to indicate an incident of special interest to M. There were many known relics of John the Baptist by the fifth century and more than one head! M.'s account describes the rediscovery of the head at Emesa in 453 (Ced., 562, cf. 574; Chron. Pasch., 591.7–12). As with his earlier report of Lucianus' account of the discovery of Stephen's relics (s.v. **415.2**), M. demonstrates here his access to a separate document describing the events in question. This document was a *relatio* which included Marcellus' own account of the discovery of the head (*PL* 67, 420C–430D). This was obviously a popular document and it was translated into Latin in M.'s day by Dionysius Exiguus (*ibid.*), although it is clear that M. will have based his account on the original Greek version (cf. Holder-Egger, 1877, 89–90). There is a clear link between the accounts of M. and the Chron. Pasch., who both date the recovery of John's head to the consulship of Vincomalus and Opilio (453). M.'s date has been impugned (by Ducange originally) on the grounds that, since 24 February 453 did not fall in the middle of Lent (as M. says), then it must have been the previous year, while the date of the Chron. Pasch. has been discarded as a doublet for the establishment of an earlier head of John at the Hebdomon in 391 (Whitby/Whitby, 1989, 82, n. 270). The testimony of Marcellus' *relatio*, however, shows that both dates are in fact correct. In the first place he tells of the original appearance of John at the monastery in Emesa on 18 February in the '763rd year' [Seleucid year: 1 October 452–30 September 453] and the 6th indiction [1 September 452–31 August 453]', with the head itself recovered to bishop Uranius of Emesa on 24 February (*PL* 67, 424). To the dating of Marcellus' *relatio* the Chron. Pasch. adds the '501st year of Antioch' [452–453]. The weight of the testimony is therefore in favour of February 453. Yet there is one discrepancy: the *relatio* (followed by M. and Chron. Pasch.) dates the event to the 'mid week of Lent', which cannot be true for 453 but would make sense for 452 (as noted by Whitby/Whitby, *loc.cit.*). One can only conclude that, either from ignorance or for effect, the author of the *relatio* was mistaken in this detail. Preference must be given to the document's other more exact dates. So, John first revealed himself at the monastery at Emesa on 18 February 453 (which means that the Chron. Pasch. doublet of 18 February in both 391 and 453 is reversed, i.e. 453 is correct but not 391) and his head was unearthed to the monks on 24 February 453. The immediacy of the events was reinforced by their annual commemoration on 24 February at CP (*SEC*, 524.8–10; cf. *Typ.*, I.244–6) and elsewhere in the East (*PO* 10.38 [Syriac Martyrology]). Following the discovery of the head and its installation at the cathedral, the city of Emesa became an independent metropolitan see under the patriarchate of Antioch.

453.2 Pulcheria died in July 453 (Chron. Pasch., 591.6; Hyd., 157 [XI 27]; Theoph., AM 5945 [106.25–9]; Jo. Mal., 14.34 [368.18–19] and Theod. Anag., 363 [102.21–4]) but the exact date is not known. The Basilica of St Laurence was located in the Pulcherianae (Janin, 1964, 137). It was begun earlier (s.v. 439) and only brought to completion shortly before the death of Pulcheria. Subsequently, the emperor Leo instituted a memorial to Pulcheria (*Paras.*, 45).

454.1 Attila (*PLRE* 2: 182–3) is remembered by M. not as the scourge of the empire or of the West but more narrowly as the scourge of the very province in which was located the imperial capital (Europa). This obviously reflects his local source. There was considerable uncertainty about the death of Attila. On the one hand it was reported that he died from some sort of haemorrhage (Jord., *Get.* 254–8; Jo. Mal., 14.10 [359.1–3]; Chron. Pasch., 588.1–4; Theoph., AM 5946 [108.5–10]) and on the other that he had been murdered by his new wife on their wedding night (Hyd., 154 [XI 27]). M. prefers the latter version, although he records both. Modern scholars disagree on the year of Attila's death, some (e.g. Maenchen-Helfen, 1973, 143), preferring 453 which is that of most sources (e.g. Vict. Tonn, 453.2 [XI 185]; Prosp., 1370 [IX 482–3]) and others (e.g. Thompson, 1948, 148) opting for M.'s 454. The confusion could well be solved by presuming that here, as elsewhere (e.g. **445** for Bleda, cf. **429.2**, **430.3**), M.'s source gave only an indictional date and so he has placed the event in the right indiction but in the wrong consulship. This would mean therefore that Attila's death is to be placed in the period September to December 453.

454.2 Aetius (*PLRE* 2: 21–9) here reappears in M. for the first time in twenty-two years and then only to record his death. The circumstances leading to the death of Aetius were treacherous (Oost, 1968, 301–3), with the emperor Valentinian and the patrician Maximus ultimately responsible, as M. notes both here and in the following entry (**455.1**). Aetius and his friend the Praetorian Prefect Boethius (*PLRE* 2: 231) were killed on 21 (or 22) September (Hyd., 162 [XI 27]; Vict. Tonn., 454 [XI 158]; Add. Prosp. Haun., 454 [IX 303]; Prosp., 1373 [IX 483]; Theoph., AM 5946 [108.3–5]). M.'s evaluation of Aetius as the 'main salvation of the Western world', whose death marked the end of the 'Western Kingdom' which 'has not yet been restored', is a striking one (cf. Jord., *Get.* 191) and has received a good deal of attention in recent years (e.g O'Flynn, 1983, 103; Clover, 1970, 38 ff.; cf. Bury, 1923, 300). Generally it has been taken to indicate the perspective of the senatorial aristocracy of Rome itself and their hankering after the return of a military strongman to restore the Western empire from a barbarian king to their own tutelage. This view, in so far as it is based exclusively or primarily on M., is misconceived. In the first place there is nothing remarkable in M.'s statement: Aetius was plainly the most powerful man in his day (e.g. Cass., *Variae* 1.4.11) and the security of the Western provinces, especially Italy, rested on his shoulders (cf. Bury, 1923, 251). Moreover, this fact was as evident in the East as in the West and other sources of Eastern provenance (e.g. Jo. Mal., 14.10 [358.14]; Jo. Ant., fr. 201.1 [*FHG* 4, 614]; Jord., *Get.* 191; Theoph., AM 5946 [108.3–5]) clearly articulate the same view as M. There is therefore no reason to doubt that here, as elsewhere, M. is reflecting the viewpoint of the Eastern empire and his own preference for strong military leaders.

455.1 The emperor Valentinian III was killed on 16 March 455 in the military parade ground at Rome, the Campus Martius, with the army looking on (Hyd., 162 [XI 27]; Jord., *Rom.* 334; Vict. Tonn., 455 [XI 186]; Prosp., 1375 [IX 483–4]). Optila (*PLRE* 2: 810) and Thraustila (*PLRE* 2: 1117–8) were probably imperial bodyguards (*protectores*) and had easy opportunity to strike down the emperor. They were Hunnish or Gothic in origin and had previously been outstanding soldiers under Aetius before being taken on by the emperor after the death of their master in the previous year. It was Optila who killed the emperor while Thraustila was responsible for the death of the chief of the imperial bedchamber, Heraclius (*PLRE* 2: 541), who had earlier induced Valentinian to murder Aetius (Prosp., 1373 [IX 483]; Jo. Ant., fr. 201.1 [*FHG* 4, 614]).

455.2 Petronius Maximus (*PLRE* 2: 749–51) was one of the most distinguished Roman aristocrats of his time, having twice been consul, Praetorian Prefect and Prefect of the City of Rome. Maximus assumed the throne on 17 March, the day after the murder of Valentinian, in which he was implicated (F. Vind. Pr., 573 [IX 303]; F. Vind. Post., 573 [IX 303], Add. Prosp. Haun., 573 [IX 303]; Hyd., 162 [XI 27]; Vict.Tonn., 455 [XI 186]; Jo. Mal., 14.26 [365.22–3]; Theoph., AM 5947 [108.22–30]; Evag., 2.7; Jord., *Get.* 235; *Rom.* 334, Jo. Ant., frs. 200–1 [*FHG* 4, 614], Proc., *Wars* 3.4.36; Nic. Call., 15.11). His brief reign was terminated on 31 May, when he was stoned and dismembered by the crowd while trying to flee from Rome on the arrival of the Vandals (Vict. Tonn., 455 [XI 186]).

455.3 Geiseric and his Vandals entered Rome in June (F. Vind. Pr., 574 [IX 304]; F. Vind. Post., 574 [IX 304]; Add. Prosp. Haun., 574 [IX 304]) and spent two weeks looting the city (Vict. Tonn., 455 [XI 186]; Prosp., 1375 [IX 484]). On their departure for Carthage they took with them Eudoxia, Valentinian's thirty-three-year old widow (briefly married to the sixty-year old Maximus), and her young daughters Placidia and Eudocia (Jo. Mal., 14.26 [366.5–10]; Hyd., 167 [XI 28]; Jord., *Rom.* 334). The claim that Eudoxia had actually invited the Vandals to take Rome as part of a campaign of vengeance for the death of her husband is unfounded (Oost, 1968, 305; but see Bury, 1923, 324, n. 2). It was a prevalent view in the East, where M. would have picked it up. Marcian sent a delegation to Carthage to secure their release (Priscus, fr.31 [332–5]) and later planned a military campaign against the Vandals, but died before it could be implemented (Theod. Anag., 367 [103.15–20])

456.1 There is no other evidence for this plague of locusts, although the destruction of the crops would have had devastating consequences.

456.2 Eucherius who was bishop of Lyons (from the mid-430s) joined the monastic community at Lérins and became a practised ascete. He wrote both ascetical and exegetical works. M.'s entry is taken from Genn., 63. It is not apparent why it should appear under 456, unless this was the year of his death (cf. Pintus, 1984, 810–12).

457.1 Marcian's reign receives no systematic coverage in the chronicle. He died on 27 January 457 (see Croke, 1978a, 5–9), but his reputation as one of the 'good emperors' lasted for far longer, as M. indicates (s.v. 379; see also Bury, 1923, 236). Leo (*PLRE* 2: 663–4) was commander of a military contingent stationed at Selymbria (Silivri) when elevated to the throne on 7 February 457 (Chron. Pasch., 592.17–19; Theoph., AM 5950 [110.19–21]; Jord., *Rom.* 335; Theod. Anag., 367 [103.16–20]; Cand., fr. 1 [*FHG* IV 135]; Jo. Mal., 14.35 [369.1–4]).

457.2 Majorian (*PLRE* 2: 702–3) had served under Aetius but had retired before the latter's death, whereupon he was summoned back by Valentinian and made *comes domesticorum*. Although favoured as a successor on Valentinian's death, he was unsuccessful. At the accession of Leo he was made *magister militum* and just a few weeks later on 1 April was elevated to the purple as Caesar, followed by his proclamation as Augustus on 28 December. Leo's involvement in Majorian's proclamation, specifically stated by M., is uncertain (O'Flynn, 1983, 107–11), but it is clear that he was not recognised as Augustus by the Eastern court. This explains the fact that he is described by M. as Caesar, followed by Jord., *Rom.* 335.

458 Having come to power, the emperor Leo was anxious to establish the mood of the bishops of the East with regard to the settlement of Chalcedon, especially since the death of Marcian had unleashed anti-Chaledonian forces at Alexandria, Antioch and Jerusalem which resulted in the replacement of Chalcedonian bishops and the death of the patriarch Proterius at Alexandria (Vict. Tonn., 457.3 [XI 186]; Theoph., AM 5950 [110.24–111.6]). Leo sent this letter around the bishops and was gratified to find that the majority agreed with the formula of Chalcedon (details in Allen, 1981, 108–111; Zach. Rhet., 4.5–6, cf. Vict. Tonn., 468 [XI 187–8]).

459 Isaac of Antioch was one of the most prolific Syrian literary figures in the fifth century. Born in Amida (Diyarbekir) and educated in Edessa (Urfa), Isaac was in Rome in the early fifth century and wrote a poem on the Saecular Games of 404. Later he did produce polemical verse against Nestorius and Eutyches (Baumstark, 1922, 63–6). Most of his extant works are poetic, including his lament on the destruction of Antioch in this earthquake, in imitation of that of Ephrem on Nicomedia (Baumstark, 1922, 43). This particularly severe quake resulted in the emperor's financial support for rebuilding (Jo. Mal., 14.36 [369.5–9]; Evag., 2.12). It was even serious enough to be noticed in Spain (Hyd., 215 [XI 32]). M.'s date for this earthquake has often been taken to be 459, which has caused confusion, whereas it should be dated to September 458, the date given by Theoph. (AM 5950 [110.22–3]; cf. Downey, 1961, 476–80, 597–604); that is, M.'s source probably only dated the event by indiction. Despite having access to other sources for this quake, he copied this entry from Genn., 66 almost verbatim (cf. Pintus, 1984, 806). This earthquake, like that at Antioch in 526, was reported publicly at CP, which explains its presence in M.'s chronicle.

460 Cyzicus, metropolis of the province of Hellespont and in close proximity to CP, probably was affected in the earthquake which, according to Evagrius 2.14 (based on Priscus), destroyed parts of Thrace, the Hellespont, Ionia and the Cyclades and was 'so severe as to cause the overthrow of Cnidus and Cos'. Immensely heavy rains at CP and in Bithynia accompanied the quake, and islands in the lake of Nicomedia were submerged. Evagrius dates these events to the time of the 'Scythian war', that is, conflict between the empire and the Ostrogoths in 459–60 (Stein, 1959, 356; Allen, 1981, 112). This quake will have been recorded because of the imperial munificence associated with its aftermath, which perhaps included an imperial visit as occurred in 436 (s.a.).

461.1 Pope Hilary (19 November 461–29 February 468) consolidated the authority of Leo, whom he had represented at the Second Council at Ephesus in 449, but was lucky to escape alive. His struggle against the champions of Arianism in Italy involved him in standing up to the emperor Anthemius. A document which reaffirmed the councils of Ephesus and Chalcedon and the Tome of Pope Leo was circulated among Eastern bishops by Hilary (Kelly, 1986, 45).

461.2 Majorian was returning to Italy from fighting the Alans in Gaul when he was deposed by his *magister militum* Ricimer (*PLRE* 2: 942–5) at Dertona by the river Hyra on 2 August (Chron. Gall. 511, 635 [IX 664]). Not long after, on 7 August, he was murdered by Ricimer who replaced him with Libius Severus (Vict. Tonn., 463.2 [XI 187]; F. Vind. Pr., 587–8 [IX 305]; Chron. Gall. 511, 636 [IX 664]; Theoph., AM 5955 [112.26–8]; *PLRE* 2: 1004–5) at Ravenna on 19 November 461 (O'Flynn, 1983, 111). Severus was not recognised by the Eastern emperor Leo and M. describes his accession as an usurpation (cf. Jord., *Rom.* 336). Similarly, M. refers to Majorian only as Caesar and never Augustus, which would appear to indicate Majorian's subordinate status in relation to the Eastern emperor, at least in M.'s view.

462 This Jacob (*PLRE* 2: 582–3) was apparently the most famous physician of his day. He was the pupil of his father Hesychius (*PLRE* 2: 554) and his skill in the theory and practice of medicine led to him being consulted by the emperor. Statues of him were erected at CP and Athens. M. presumably was familiar with those at the Baths of Zeuxippus at CP (Jo. Mal., 14.38 [370.15]). M. is the only source for the incident described here in which the emperor Leo was offended at Jacob's apparent lack of respect for the majesty of the emperor.

463 In M.'s consular list there is an error here which cannot be explained (cf. Bagnall et al., 1987, 56, 463). Instead of recording Vivianus as sole consul M. has added 'and Felix'. It may be an early scribal error or corruption since 'et Bibiani' occurs in some manuscripts (Mommsen, 1894, 88 app. crit.). Prosper Tiro was from Aquitaine and was perhaps a monk. His voluminous writings embrace epigrams, poems, theological treatises and a chronicle which M. does not mention, perhaps because he did not know of it (Schanz-Hosius, 1921, 492–501). M.'s entry is copied from Genn., 84. It is not apparent why he should place the entry in 463 (cf. Pintus, 1984, 807), unless he otherwise knew that was the year of Prosper's death.

464 Beorgor (*PLRE* 2: 224), king of the Alans in Gaul, was killed by the *magister militum* Ricimer on 6 February 464 at the foot of the mountain near Bergamum (Cass., 1278 [XI 158]; F. Vind. Pr., 593 [IX 305]). Seven years previously the emperor Majorian had recruited Alans from Gaul for his unsuccessful strike at the Vandals. The Alans, now under Beorgor, soon began threatening parts of Gaul and north Italy. After the death of Majorian en route from engaging them, the Alans invaded Italy in 464, where they were defeated by Ricimer and saw their king killed (Bachrach, 1973, 32–3). As noted by O'Flynn, 1983, 112, M. simply characterises Ricimer as a barbarian king,

465.1 This fire was one of the most devastating of all the disasters which CP experienced in its early centuries (*Vita Dan. Styl* 45; Theod. Anag., 394 [110.21–5]; Jo. Mal. 14.43 [372.11–6]; Evag., 2.13; Chron. Pasch., 595 and 598; Theoph., AM 5954 [112.19–24] with Schneider, 1941, 383–4). Evidently it began, like that in 431 (s.v.), in the docks of the Neorion harbour along the Golden Horn and swept right across the city to the harbour of Julian. It burnt an area which covered eight of the city's fourteen regions and caused the imperial court to flee temporarily across the Golden Horn to St Mamas, where a palace was constructed (Janin, 1964, 141, 473–4). The fire was commemorated annually with a liturgy on 1 September (*SEC*, 6.3–9). This conflagration is frequently dated to 465 (e.g. Bury, 1923, 321) but actually occurred in September 464, since the precise dates of the Chron. Pasch. put the fire on '2nd September, a Wednesday in indiction 3', which corresponds exactly to 2 September 464 (Whitby/Whitby, 1989, 87, n. 285). Here, as so often elsewhere, M. places the event in the correct indiction but wrong consulship. As with earthquakes (cf. **459, 460**), the rationale for the inclusion of such a disaster is the ceremonial response to it, especially the 'grieving' (described in *v. Marcell.* 31; *v. Dan. Styl.* 45–6; Theoph., AM 5954 [112.19–24]).

465.2 The emperor Libius Severus died at Rome on 14 November 465, never having been recognised by the emperor at CP. Whether he was murdered by Ricimer or died of natural causes remains an open question (O'Flynn, 1983, 112–15). M. reflects the Eastern imperial perspective in his characterisation of Severus' reign as an usurpation. M.'s notice of Severus' death may be added to the sources listed in *PLRE* 2: 1005.

466 Theodoret of Cyrrhus was a key figure in the theological debates of the fifth century, being exiled by Dioscorus of Alexandria at the 'Robber Council' of 449 at Ephesus and re-instated at the Council of Chalcedon. His main work directed against Eutyches and Dioscorus was the *Eranistes*. M.'s entry is copied from Genn., 88 but there is no clear reason why M. should want to date the entry in 466 since Gennadius' statement was no more precise than 'in the reign of Leo I'. Theodoret had died eight years before.

467.1 Anthemius (*PLRE* 2: 96–8) was designated as emperor in the West by Leo then sent with an army to Italy. He was proclaimed emperor three miles from Rome on 12 April 467 (Hyd., 235 [XI 34]; Cass., 1283 [XI 158]; F. Vind. Pr., 598 [IX 305]; Theoph., AM 5957 [114.21–4]). As he was the nominee of Leo, there was no confusion about Anthemius' recognition in the East. So M. calls him simply 'emperor'.

467.2 Pope Simplicius (3 March 468–10 March 483) occupied the see of Peter at a crucial time in relations between the papacy and the imperial court. In particular he challenged the attempts of Acacius, patriarch of CP, to claim parity with Rome. Simplicius was especially active in Italy and was one of the great papal builders (Kelly,

1986, 46). M.'s date for Simplicius' accession is incorrect because he begins from the last year of his predecessor, counting by whole years only (cf. 382.3).

467.3 There is no other evidence for this quake at Ravenna in 467, unless it is the same one recorded by Evag., 2.14 (probably taken from Priscus).

468 Marcellinus (*PLRE* 2: 708–10) was a powerful general based in Dalmatia, probably as *magister militum*, in the mid-450s and maintained his authority there until this year (468). Although originally independent, Marcellinus later supported the Western emperor Majorian and was successful in defending Sicily against the Vandals. Subsequently he was courted by the Eastern emperor Leo. In the great imperial expedition against the Vandals in 468 Marcellinus was entrusted with command of the Western army, was successful in Sardinia then moved to Sicily, where he was killed in treacherous circumstances in August 468 (F. Vind. Pr., 601 [IX 305]; Cass., 1285 [XI 158]), as M. reports. He may have been made *patricius* by the emperor Anthemius to counterbalance the influence of Ricimer (proposed in *PLRE* 2: 709; cf. O'Flynn, 1983, 117–18, 189, n. 59). His paganism is well attested (Bury, 1923, 336). There is no reason to believe that this general was related in any way to the chronicler (as suggested by Holder-Egger, 1877, 49–50). The name was a common one and there is no hint of any relationship, or the sort of eulogistic treatment that relationship might inspire.

469 Denzic, the Latinised form of Dengizich (*PLRE* 2: 354–5), was one of the sons of Attila, king of the Huns, and after his father's death he settled in the Balkans while still retaining control over some of the Huns' subject tribes. In 466/7 he threatened war on the Romans if treaty negotiations with him and his brother Ernach (*PLRE* 2: 400–1) broke down, which they did. He then bypassed the Roman envoys sent to him and dealt directly with the emperor Leo who acceded to the Huns' request for land and cash (Priscus, fr. 46 [352–3]). Then followed battles with the Goths (Priscus, fr. 49 [356–9]), and finally we hear of Denzic being slain by the general Anagast (*PLRE* 2: 75–6) and the display of his head at CP. Normally these events are dated to 469 on the evidence of M. (e.g. Maenchen-Helfen, 1973, 168) but this is probably incorrect. The Chron. Pasch., which used a local CP source common to M., clearly dates this rare imperial victory (McCormick, 1986, 60 with Whitby/Whitby, 1989, 90, n. 294) to the consulship of Anthemius (468), and this is easily reconcilable with M.'s dating when one recalls that M. uses both indictions and consulships; that is, M. included this account of the demise of Denzic in 469 because it took place in the 7th indiction beginning 1 September 468. It is therefore likely that Denzic's death and the parade of his head in CP happened after 1 September and before 31 December 468. Beyond this point the direct parallels between M. and the Chron. Pasch. cease, which is probably to be explained by the latter's preference for the chronicle of Malalas as a source for the subsequent period. Mommsen had printed the parallel text of the Chronicon Paschale from 395 to this year.

470 Gennadius, patriarch of CP, wrote several commentaries including one on *Daniel*, but only fragments of them survive. Although he wrote other polemical works, none is preserved and there are no extant sermons at all. This entry derives from Genn., 91 but there is no evident reason why it should be placed in 470 (cf. Pintus, 1984, 809).

471 Except for arranging a truce with the Huns (s.v. **441.1**) this is the only occasion on which M. mentions the powerful general Aspar (*PLRE* 2: 164–9), who dominated the imperial court in the 450s and 460s. Aspar's position had become increasingly insecure under Leo, especially since the emperor began to show strong support for the Isaurians led by Zeno. The animosity between the emperor and his general reached a climax in 471 when, as M. notes, Aspar was killed by the palace eunuchs (on imperial orders) along with his sons Ardaburius and Patricius (Jo. Mal., 14.40 [371.10–13]; Cass., 1291 [XI 158]; Vict. Tonn., 471 [XI 188]; Chron. Pasch., 596.17–23; Theoph., AM 5964 [117.25–118.2]; Jord., *Rom.* 338; *Get.* 239). M. stresses their Arianism.

472.1 The eruption of Mt Vesuvius on 6 November 472 was a devastating event which reverberated all around the Mediterranean. Curiously enough there is no contemporary Western account of any detail; all the extant sources, including M., are of Eastern provenance: Jo. Mal., 14.43 (372.6); Chron. Pasch., 598.10–14; Theod Anag., *Epit.* 398 (111.14–6); Theoph., A.M. 5966 (119.29–33); Proc., *Wars* 6.4.27. The eruption is incorrectly dated by Seeck, 1919, 418 and 425 to 6 November 473. The propitiatory supplication ritual which was celebrated in CP on the eruption was repeated every year thereafter on 6 November and became a permanent part of the liturgical calendar (*Typ.*, I.90–92; Janin, 1966, 75).

472.2 The Western emperor Anthemius became entangled in a civil war with his *magister militum* and son-in-law Ricimer and was besieged in Rome (O'Flynn, 1983, 121–2). The forces of Ricimer were bolstered by the arrival of the *magister militum* for Gaul, Gundobad, and some of Anthemius' demoralised troops switched allegiance. On 11 July 472 Anthemius was killed in Rome, but by Gundobad and not (as M. states) by Ricimer himself (F. Vind. Pr., 606 [IX 306]; Cass., 1293 [XI 158]; Chron. Gall. 511., [IX 664]). Following the extinction of Anthemius the next Western emperor was the aristocratic Fl. Olybrius (*PLRE* 2: 796–8), one of the survivors of the family of Valentinian. Olybrius had evidently been sent to the West by the emperor Leo, probably to act as an intermediary between Anthemius and Ricimer but possibly with some hope of becoming emperor himself (Jo. Mal., 14.45 [373.13–374.1]; Vict. Tonn., 473.6 [XI 188]). In any event he was proclaimed emperor by Ricimer in April 472 but was not recognised in the East. He reigned for only seven months, as M. records, dying of natural causes (dropsy) on 2 November 472 (F. Vind. Pr., 609 [IX 306]) just a few days before the eruption of Vesuvius. Ricimer actually had predeceased him in late August.

472.3 There is no corroborative evidence for this earthquake.

473.1 For almost five months after the death of Olybrius in November 472 there was no emperor in the West and Leo ruled the entire empire from CP. The *comes domesticorum* who must have maintained the palace at Ravenna in working order throughout these months, a certain Glycerius (*PLRE* 2: 514), was himself proclaimed emperor with the support of Gundobad on 3 March 473 (F. Vind. Pr., 611 [IX 306]; Cass., 1295 [XI 158]). He was not recognised by Leo in the East, an attitude reflected by M. in his comment on the election of Glycerius and his designation of him as Caesar.

473.2 There does not appear to be any other evidence for this riot in CP, nor does it appear to be related to a riot involving Isaurians which occurred in 469/70 (Jo. Ant., fr. 206.1 [*FHG* 4, 616]). The numerous Isaurians in the capital had long been unpopular. Since the sedition is located in the hippodrome it may have been connected with an official race day when the emperor presided but was more a national protest than a regular conflict between the Blues and Greens (Cameron, 1973, 233). There is no need to assume that M.'s report is misdated and should be connected with the flight of Zeno from CP in 475 (Stein, 1949, 591, n. 68; cf. Seeck, 1919, 425–6).

474.1 In October 473, therefore in the 12th indiction in M.'s reckoning, the emperor Leo proclaimed his six-year old grandson and namesake Leo (*PLRE* 2: 664–5) junior emperor or Caesar (Theod. Anag., 398 [111.13]; Jo. Mal., 14.46 [375.19–20]; Jord., *Rom.* 339 [date: Seeck, 1919, 425–6]). At some subsequent stage the young Leo was elevated to the rank of Augustus [on Leo's death or deathbed?] before the elder Leo died of dysentery at the age of 73 on 18 January 474. On 9 February the young boy had his father Zeno proclaimed emperor (Vict. Tonn., 474.2 [XI 188]) and they ruled jointly until late November 474 (Jo. Mal., 14.47 [376.10–2]; cf. Theoph., AM 5966 [120.1–8]; Theod. Anag., 400 [112.12–3]; Jord., *Rom.* 340; cf. Seeck, 1919, 421). M. does not mention the death of Leo II. What is of special interest to the chronicler, however, is the calculation of the reign-length for Leo I. As M. calculates, Leo ruled for a total of 17 years and 6 months. Since Leo ruled in fact from 7 February 457 to 18 January 474 the period amounted to 16 years 11 months and 11 days. Yet M. includes in his calculation the months of Leo II's reign before the death of Leo I, that is, October 473 to 18 January 474, a total of three months. This brings the combined total to 17 years and 4 months and that may be what M. wrote. Still the text is not unsound at this point and the 17 years 6 months may well be M.'s calculation. If so it would appear that he was somehow reckoning in whole months. Chronographers were frequently confronted with chronological problems in correctly calculating and synchronising the reign of emperors and there was always a danger of adding together the lengths of synchronous reigns. It seems that at the time M. was writing in the sixth century there was some uncertainty and argument about the reigns of Leo I, Leo II and Zeno. Malalas, for example, spent part of a digression explaining to his audience the pitfall of adding reigns together, with particular reference to the reign of Zeno (Jo. Mal., 18.8 [429.1–9], cf. 15.6 [380.18–20]).

474.2 Glycerius was overthrown in mid-474 by Nepos (*PLRE* 2: 777–8), nephew of the Dalmatian general Marcellinus (*PLRE* 2: 708–10) and his successor as *magister militum*. Nepos was in command of a contingent sent with the support of the Eastern court (Leo II and Zeno) to oust Glycerius. He was apparently taken to Rome's port of Ostia and put on board a ship for Salona in Dalmatia, where he was consecrated bishop of the town (Anon.Val., 7.36; F. Vind. Pr., 613 [IX 306]; Auct. Haun. Ord. Post., 474.3 [IX 307]; Jord., *Get*. 239; Evag., 2.16; Jo. Ant., fr. 209.2 [*FHG* 4, 618]; Jord., *Rom*. 338). Bury, 1923, 405 thought that Glycerius was consecrated bishop at Portus and that he may never have reached Salona. Nepos was proclaimed emperor on 19 (or 24) June 474 (Anon. Val., 7.36; Jo. Ant., fr. 209.2 [*FHG* 4, 618]; F. Vind. Pr., 614 [IX 306]; Auct. Haun. ord. post., 474.4 [IX 307]). He did not die until some time after 480. Again one notes M.'s consistent labelling of Glycerius as Caesar (followed by Jord., *Rom*. 338).

475.1 Having been raised to the purple the previous year, Zeno was apprised of the plot of his mother-in-law Verina (*PLRE* 2: 1156) and her brother Basiliscus (*PLRE* 2: 212–4) and took the precaution of fleeing to Isauria (*v. Dan. Styl*., 69; Anon. Val., 9.41; Jo. Mal., 15.2–3 [377.5–12]), whereupon Basiliscus assumed the throne.

475.2 Nepos (*PLRE* 2: 777–8) had become emperor in June 474, not this year, and had reigned until he took flight from Ravenna in fear of the *magister militum* Orestes (*PLRE* 2: 810–811) on 28 August 475 and went to Salona, the same place of exile as Nepos' own predecessor Glycerius (F. Vind. Pr., 616 [IX 308]; Anon. Val., 7.36; Jord., *Get*. 241). After that Orestes created his son Romulus (*PLRE* 2: 949–50) as emperor on 31 October 475 (F. Vind. Pr., 617 [IX 308]; Auct. Haun. ord. pr., 475.2 [IX 309]). He is better known as the 'young emperor' (Augustulus).

476.1 Basiliscus, brother of the empress Verina, assumed the throne when the emperor Zeno fled the imperial city. He attempted to support the monophysite cause by issuing an edict revoking the decrees of the Council of Chalcedon. This action stirred up strong opposition in CP and is evident in the tone of M.'s description. Meanwhile, the exiled emperor Zeno marshalled his forces and marched back to CP. On his approach, Basiliscus' general Armatus joined with Zeno. On Zeno's return Basiliscus and his family were captured and despatched under guard to Limnae in Cappadocia, where they were starved to death (Jo. Mal., 15.5 [379–80]; Vict. Tonn., 475.4 [XI 189]; Theoph., AM 5967 [120.26–121.30]; Theod. Anag., 401–2 [112.15–113.16]; Jord., *Rom*. 341 with Croke, 1983b). M. indicates his contempt for Basiliscus, on account of his religious policy, by labelling him simply as an 'usurper'.

476.2 This is probably the best-known and most quoted entry in the chronicle because it is the earliest precise statement of the view that the Western Roman empire had terminated in 476. It has been argued that this viewpoint reflects that of the senatorial aristocracy of Rome and Italy lamenting the loss of their way of life under the Gothic regime (Wes, 1967), whereas in fact it reflects the perspective of CP and the East, as does most of M.'s information on Italy and the West (Croke, 1983a). Odovacer, who on 23 August 476 became the king of a variety of tribes serving in the Roman army in Italy (and not 'king of the Goths' as M. states here and at 489), had apparently occupied Rome (if M. is to be taken literally here). Not long after (on 28 August) Odovacer entered Ravenna and killed Orestes before deposing his young son Romulus from the throne (Cass., 1303 [XI 158–9]; F. Vind. Pr., 620 [IX 310]; Auct. Haun. ordo pr., 476.3–4 [IX 309–11]; Jord., *Rom.* 344; *Get.* 242–3). Romulus was not dispensed with himself but was allowed to live on as a private citizen at the Campanian fortress of Lucullanum (castle of Lucullus) (Anon. Val., 8.38; Jord., *Rom.* 345). M. records Octavian Augustus as first emperor but calculates the '709th year from the foundation of the city' from 44 BC (the death of Julius Caesar) or possibly from August 43 (Augustus' first consulship), which is the usual Byzantine form of reckoning Roman imperial dates. Even so, equating 476 with the '522nd' year is slightly inaccurate.

477 M.'s consular heading ('sine consulibus') indicates that he does not wish to record the consulship of Basiliscus and Armatus in this year (cf. Bagnall et al., 1987, 477).

The *comes* Brachila (*PLRE* 2: 241), about whom nothing else is known, was killed by Odovacer on 11 July 477 for opposing him in some way (F. Vind. Pr., 622 [IX 310], Auct. Haun. ord. pr., 477 [IX 311]; Auct. Haun. ord. post., 477 [IX 311]; Jord., *Get.* 243), perhaps because of the king's refusal to nominate an emperor in the West (*PLRE* 2: 241).

478 Theodolus was a Nestorian pupil of Theodore of Mopsuestia (Ensslin, *RE* 10 [1934], 1976–8 s.v. Theodulus 28). M. has extracted this entry from Genn., 92,who dated his death to before the end of the third year of Zeno's reign (cf. Pintus, 1984, 809).

479.1 Sabinianus (*PLRE* 2: 967) was made *magister militum per Illyricum* in 479 at Edessa in Macedonia Prima (Malchus, fr. 20 [442–3]). Clearly he was highly regarded by M. as an administrator and disciplinarian, which probably reflects his reputation in Illyricum, M.'s home territory. There is no other evidence for his treatment of the senate and the census. M. is probably suggesting here that Sabinianus instigated a new census in Illyricum which provided the basis for reconstituting the membership and authority of local city councils. The councils had been seriously affected by the disruptions caused by the successive invasions of Roman territory throughout the fifth century.

479.2 Sabinianus' 'shrewdness' may be attributed to the fact that he disrupted negotiations between the Goths' king Theodoric Valamer (*PLRE* 2: 1077–84) and the Roman envoy Adamantius (*PLRE* 2: 6–7), first by declining to swear protection for the Gothic hostages and then by attacking the Goths (and capturing their baggage train) before negotiations had been concluded. Thereupon Sabinianus returned to Lychnidus and wrote to advise the emperor Zeno to revoke any agreement with the Goths. Theodoric desisted from attacking Greece while Sabinianus was in charge there. Details in Malchus, fr. 20

(434–451) with Wolfram, 1988, 274–6 and Heather, 1991, 292–8. Theodoric reached Dyrrachium (Pasch. Camp., 478 [IX 310]).

480.1 This was one of the most protracted and destructive of the earthquakes which struck CP (Jo. Mal., 15.1 [385.3–8]) and it should probably be dated to September 479. The most complete account is contained in the so-called 'Great Chronographer' (most accessible in Whitby/Whitby, 1989, 194): numerous houses, churches and porticoes collapsed, burying many people beneath. In the Forum of Constantine the orb on Constantine's statue fell down, while in the Forum Tauri the statue of Theodosius was toppled from its column, as recorded by M. (Janin, 1964, 67; Müller-Wiener, 1977, 262); enormous tidal waves engulfed some of the city and parts of the walls around the Golden Gate were also damaged. M. is the only extant source to single out the Troad porticoes as being damaged by the quake (overlooked in Janin, 1964, 93). In M.'s description of this earthquake there are two dating problems, both of which are explicable: (1) the *year* : although the quake is usually dated to 478 (after Stein, 1949, 787) there is reason to assign it to 479. Theophanes dates it to 478 (= A.M. 5970 [125.29–126.5]) although his chronology is confused. The attempt to link the quake with the return of Illus and Pamprepius from Isauria, thereby producing a date of 478 (Stein, 1949, 787), is very tenuous (cf. Brooks, 1911, 476). Although M. includes it under the consulship of 480 he may be dating the event by indiction (as in **465**, **468**, **469**) in which case his date should be read as 'September 479'; (2) the *day* date: September 24 may be correct (cf. Chron. Pasch., 605: 'September 26'). It is possible, however, that it is an error for 25 September, although 'vii' for 'viii' is a perfectly explicable scribal error. Each year on 25 September the Byzantines celebrated a liturgical procession in memory of an earthquake (*SEC*, 77.45–55; 79.49–54; *Typ*. I.44–8), but of the tremors of 437 rather than this more damaging quake. Over time the details of the 437 quake merged with that of the 479 one. M. may therefore have confused the quakes of 437 and 479. M.'s notice is overlooked in Downey, 1955, 597.

480.2 The deposed emperor Nepos had lived and ruled in Dalmatia since fleeing from Orestes in 475, and was apparently plotting to extend his authority in Dalmatia when he was struck down by two of his associates Ovida (*PLRE* 2: 815) and Viator (*PLRE* 2: 1158) on 9 May 480 (F. Vind. Pr., 626 [IX 310]); Anon. Val., 7.36; Auct. Haun. ordo pr., 480 [IX 311]; Auct. Haun. ord. post., 480 [IX 311]).

481.1 Theodoric Strabo (*PLRE* 2: 1073–6), as head of a large contingent of Gothic warriors, had long been a powerful influence in imperial politics. He had sought in the early 470s to emulate the position of Aspar but the emperor Leo had confined his ambition to a generalship. On Leo's death in 474 he supported then deserted Basiliscus. As emperor, Zeno adopted a hostile stance towards Theodoric Strabo, although he did make him *magister militum* briefly in 479. Theodoric responded by supporting Zeno's enemies where possible and by devastating Roman territory (Wolfram, 1988, 268–76). In 481, the only occasion M. mentions him, Theodoric Strabo marched his troops to the vicinity of CP — to Anaplous or Sosthenion on the Bosporus shore. With his progress arrested, Strabo returned to Illyricum. M. describes how Strabo was thrown from his horse and fatally injured when he fell on an exposed spear (cf. Theoph., AM 5970 [126.10–19]). This happened at a place called Stabulum Diomedis, near Philippi on the Via Egnatia (Heather, 1991, 295–6). News of Strabo's death was a cause of great rejoicing at CP (Jord., *Rom.* 346).

481.2 Sabinianus, the *magister militum per Illyricum* so admired by M. (s.a. **479.1, 2**), was murdered through some ruse and on the orders of the emperor Zeno (Jo. Ant., fr. 213 [*FHG* 4, 620]). M. clearly did not approve of the murder of Sabinianus and regarded his passing as a severe loss for the Romans. M.'s judgment on Sabinianus' potential to rejuvenate the empire springs from the impact of Sabinianus in his native territory of Illyricum. Perhaps M. had seen him as a potential emperor.

482.1 Pope Felix (13 March 483–1 March 492) took a special interest in Eastern affairs, opposing the Henotikon of the emperor Zeno and the appointment of Peter Mongus as patriarch of Alexandria (Vict. Tonn., 485 [XI 190]). The Roman synod convened by Felix excommunicated the patriarch of CP Acacius, thus instigating what became known as the 'Acacian schism' (*ibid.*, 486–7 [XI 190–1]). Felix resisted the requests of the emperor and patriarch of CP to abandon his insistence on removing Acacius' name from the diptychs. M.'s date is out by one year because he counted the papal reign lengths in whole years (cf. **382.3**).

482.2 Following the death of Sabinianus Theodoric, called 'Valamer' after his uncle (*PLRE* 2: 1077), had once again felt confident about launching an attack on Roman territory. It was perhaps from Edessa that Theodoric launched his raids into Macedonia I and II ('both Macedonias') and Thessaly, including the attack on Larissa, metropolis of Thessaly (Jo. Ant., fr. 213 [*FHG* 4, 620]; Mich. Syr., 9.6). He was challenged by the Roman generals John the Scythian (*PLRE* 2: 602–3) and Moschianus (*PLRE* 2: 766). It is not clear which of the two replaced Sabinianus as *magister militum per Illyricum*. Larissa was later rebuilt by Justinian (Proc., *Aed.* 4.3.9–10).

483 As a result of the violent attack on Thessaly the previous year the emperor Zeno agreed to the terms being sought by Theodoric (cf. Wolfram, 1988, 277). M. is the sole evidence for this settlement, whereby Theodoric was made *magister militum praesentalis* and designated *consul* for the following year (484) — followed by Jord., *Rom.* 348 and *Get.* 289. The Goths moved back to their previous base at Novae on the Danube, which would be the logical place for exerting control over 'part of Dacia Ripensis and Lower Moesia' as specified by M., whose reaction — 'almost pacified by the bounties of Zeno' — may suggest he considered Theodoric somewhat arrogant and ungrateful.

484.1 Illus (*PLRE* 2: 586–90) was an Isaurian and originally a close supporter of Zeno but he had changed sides on several occasions. As *magister officiorum* he survived an assassination attempt in the hippodrome in 481 but lost an ear in the fracas

(Josh. Styl., 13; Jo. Mal., 15.13 [387.13–16]; Theoph., AM 5972 [127.13–128.12]; Jord., *Rom.* 351). When he was returned to health Illus was made *magister militum per Orientem* and proceeded to his headquarters in Antioch in 482. Annoyed by the emperor's harassment of his family, Illus openly rebelled in 484. When the *magister militum per Thracias* Leontius (*PLRE* 2: 670–1) was sent against Illus he had the empress Verina released from prison at Tarsus in order to proclaim Leontius emperor on 19 July (Jo. Mal., 15.13 [388.18–20]; Theoph., AM 5974 [129.10–21]; Theod. Anag., 437 [121.24–122.10]); cf. *PLRE* 2: 589).

484.2 On 7 February 484 the Vandal king Huneric (*PLRE* 2: 572–73) issued a decree ordering the persecution of Catholics in the kingdom by transferring their churches and church property to the Vandals (Vict. Vit., *Hist. Pers.* 3.2). Another decree on 25 February gave Catholics until 1 June to convert to Arianism or risk serious hardships (Courtois, 1955, 297–9). This persecution was particularly sudden and violent, and resulted in the exile of a significant number of bishops, as M. indicates. It also had a profound effect on the residents of CP, who witnessed refugees from the persecution with their tongues cut out. These refugees provided a stark reminder of the persecution as long as they lived (Proc., *Wars* 2.8.4; Evag., 4.14; Zach. Rhet., 8.1). The person referred to by M. was probably the deacon Reparatus (Vict. Vit., 3.6.30). M. presumably records this event not only because of his personal testimony but also because it had become the subject of an annual liturgical commemoration at CP on 8 December, which may be the date of the arrival in CP of the first refugees from the persecution (*SEC*, 287.28–289.36 with Lackner, 1972, 192–202).

485 Longinus (*PLRE* 2: 689–90) was the younger brother of Zeno. He had been imprisoned in Isauria by Illus in 475 (Theoph., AM 5975 [129.23–4]) and had remained under guard until he was released and returned to CP ten years later (for the date: Brooks, 1893, 217, n. 50). On his return he was made *magister militum praesentalis* and designated consul for the following year (486).

486 This entry on John of Antioch's theological treatises is copied directly from Genn., 91 (Pintus, 1984, 810).

487 After being summoned back from Isauria, where he had been sent by Zeno against Illus, Theodoric returned to the Goths at Novae. Again he was soon threatening Roman territory and in 487 marched on the imperial capital itself (Proc.,*Wars* 5.1.9; Jo. Mal., 15.9 [383.12–13]; Theoph., AM 5977 [130.32–131.14]; Mich. Syr., 9.6), or at least to Melantias which was situated 18 miles from the city and was the last staging post before the capital (Mango, 1985, 32, n. 55). To persuade him to withdraw from CP and return to Novae Zeno offered large sums of money. Once more M. shows his impatience at the arrogance of Theodoric — 'never satisfied by the favours of Zeno Augustus'.

488.1 After the proclamation of Leontius as emperor in 484 he and Illus proceeded to Antioch near where they were defeated by an imperial force loyal to Zeno and under the command of John the Scythian (*PLRE* 2: 602), who had replaced Illus as *magister militum per Orientem*. They then fled to the fort of Papyrium in Isauria, where they were besieged for four years before being captured and beheaded (Vict. Tonn., 488.2 [XI 191], cf. *PLRE* 2: 590, 671). The heads were displayed at St Conon's in Sycae and drew large crowds of onlookers (Jo. Mal., 15.14 [389.9 ff.]; Theoph., AM 5980 [132.16–18]; Theod. Anag., 438 [122.11–4]; Jord., *Rom*. 353; Jo. Ant., *De Ins*. fr. 98 with McCormick, 1986, 60).

488.2 It was probably in order to prevent a recurrence of Theodoric's invasion of the Balkan provinces that the emperor Zeno persuaded him to take his Goths to Italy and displace Odovacer (Wolfram, 1988, 278), although they were finding it increasingly difficult to feed themselves (Burns, 1984, 65). Theodoric and his Goths left Novae in the late spring of 488 and proceeded to Italy by way of Sirmium, where their progress was blocked by the Gepids whom they defeated (Jord., *Get*. 292 ff. with further details in Wolfram, 1988, 279–81). The Goths finally reached Italy in August 489.

489 On 28 August Theodoric succeeded in inflicting defeat on the forces of Odovacer at the Isonzo river and then advanced into Italy. Odovacer's forces were again defeated in September at Verona (F. Vind. Pr., 639 [IX 316]; Auct. Haun., 490 [IX 317]; Anon. Val., 11.50). The following year Odovacer laid siege to the Goths in Pavia but the siege was raised and Odovacer was soon defeated at the Addua river (Cass., 1319–21 [XI 159]). He then fled to Ravenna where he was blockaded for the next three years (Wolfram, 1988, 281–3). M. does not carry the story forward in his essentially Eastern chronicle except to note that Odovacer was later (493) treacherously prised out of Ravenna by Theodoric, who had agreed they would share power in Italy, and was put to death (Cass., 1331 [XI 1159]; Anon. Val., 11.55; F. Vind. Pr., 649 [IX 320]; Auct. Haun., 493.6 [IX 321]; Jord., *Get*. 293–4; cf. *PLRE* 2: 1082). Again here M.'s hostility towards Theodoric is evident (cf. **482.2, 487**). Odovacer was not himself 'king of the Goths' as M. consistently calls him, but from 476 ruled with the title of *rex* over the various tribes bound to him (Jo. Mal., 15.9 [383.15–384.5] with *PLRE* 2: 793).

490 As *silentiarius* or one of the thirty imperial guards, Pelagius (*PLRE* 2: 857–8) had acted as ambassador to Theodoric Strabo in 479 and by 490 was a *patricius*. He was apparently a distinguished writer responsible for a verse history of Rome from Augustus to his own day but was an outspoken critic of Zeno (Ced., I. 621). He was killed after the emperor Zeno had been advised that he would be succeeded on the throne by a *silentiarius* (Theoph., AM 5982 [134.25–135.6]; AM 5983 [135.25–33]). M. is the sole testimony for the location of his death.

491.1 Zeno died on 9 April 491, from either epilepsy or dysentery (Jo. Mal., 15.16 [391.1–3] with *PLRE* 2: 1202). M. indicates that his total for Zeno's reign includes the interlude of Basiliscus (475–6) during which Zeno took refuge in Isauria. In including the years of Basiliscus M. indicates his solution to the dilemma which chronographers faced when dealing with the reign of Zeno. Malalas, for instance, was forced to do the same (15.6 [380.18–20]). Zeno died childless and as his successor the empress Ariadne chose Anastasius (Evag., 3.29), native of Dyrrachium in Dardania. On his accession Anastasius was a tribune of the silentiaries (argued by Capizzi, 1969, 66–8 on the basis of Zach. Rhet.) and he was crowned by the patriarch Euphemius on 11 April 491 (Jo. Mal., 16.1 [392.4–5]; Theoph., AM 5983 [136.16–22]; Theod. Anag., 446 [125.25–126.13]; described in Const. Porph., *de caer*. 1.92). A month later he married Ariadne.

491.2 This fracas is probably that described by John of Antioch (fr. 214b [*FHG* 5, 29–30]) which was occasioned by the antagonism of the people at the restriction of theatrical shows by the City Prefect Julian (*PLRE* 2: 639), as Bury (1923, 432) thought. The riot broke out when the people clamoured for Julian's overthrow at hippodrome games presided over by the emperor. Anastasius set his soldiers on the crowd who then set fire to the hippodrome and tore down his newly erected statues. This riot became the pretext for the exile of Zeno's brother Longinus and other Isaurians (cf. Capizzi, 1969, 95–7). M. gives the impression of significant destruction. John of Antioch's description does seem to belong to 491 rather than 493 (Brooks, 1893, 231–4; contra Cameron, 1973, 233).

492 For M. the only event worth recording for this year was the outbreak of war with the Isaurians. On the death of the Isaurian emperor Zeno his brother Longinus (*PLRE* 2: 689–90) expected to become emperor and he was grievously offended when Zeno's widow preferred Anastasius. It appears that Longinus thereupon rebelled and was ordained priest and expelled by Anastasius to the Thebaid, where he starved to death seven years later (Jo. Ant., fr. 214b [*FHG* 5, 29-30]; Theoph., AM 5984 [137.1–7]; Zon. 14.3.40); two other Isaurians, Longinus of Kardala (*PLRE* 2: 688) *magister officiorum* and Athenodorus (*PLRE* 2: 178–9), were driven out of CP at the same time. Before long the new emperor's treatment of the Isaurians led to outbreak of revolt in Isauria under Lilingis (Jord., *Rom*. 355 with *PLRE* 2: 683), the governor of Isauria. The Isaurian forces of Longinus, Athenodorus and Lilingis were concentrated at Cotiaium in Phrygia, where they engaged the imperial troops but were defeated and put to flight into the mountains of Isauria (Jo. Mal., 16.3 [393.12–394.7]; Theod. Anag., 449 [126.21–4]). Lilingis, who was killed, was 'slow on foot' because he was lame (details in Brooks, 1893, 234–5). As M. notes, the war dragged on for another six years until 498 (s.v. **497.2–3** and **498.2** with Capizzi, 1969, 98–9).

493.1 This is the second outbreak of civil violence at CP reported by M. for the reign of Anastasius and there appears to be no other notice of the riot. Evidently civil opposition to Anastasius continued to foment at CP. The oft-cited reference to Jo. Ant., fr. 214b belongs, however, to 491 (contra Cameron, 1973, 233, n. 9) rather than 493.

493.2 The Bulgars had first appeared in the Balkans in c. 480 when the emperor Zeno used them against the Ostrogoths, who were then threatening that region (s.a. **480**). In 493 they had launched an invasion of Illyricum and Thrace (Zonaras s.a. 493 [III, 137.11–13]) in which the *magister militum per Thracias* Julian (*PLRE* 2: 639) was killed at an unknown location. There is no other evidence for its being a night battle between the Romans and the Bulgars.

494.1 M.'s strong negative attitude towards Anastasius stems from the emperor's religious policy (see also **495, 511, 512, 513, 514, 515, 516**). Although he may have given an undertaking on his accession to support the Chalcedonian view of Christology or at least the compromise view represented by Zeno's Henotikon, Anastasius soon demonstrated open support for the monophysites and antagonism towards the orthodox. It is suggested that he took such a stance out of political necessity rather than personal conviction (Charanis, 1939, 41–2, 54–5). In particular he clashed with the patriarch of CP, Euphemius. It was Euphemius who had extracted from Anastasius on his accession a guarantee of protection for the orthodox (Vict. Tonn., 491.1–2 [XI 191–2]) and this concession appears to have been resented by the emperor. Further, Euphemius had demonstrated strong support for the orthodox, although he was unsuccessful in healing the rift with the papacy over the acknowledgement of the patriarch Acacius. M. would appear to date the emperor's stand against the orthodox and Euphemius from this year, 494. If that is so, then a motivating factor in his attitude may have been the failure to make a settlement with the Pope and the patriarch's avowed support for the Isaurians who were dragging the emperor into a protracted military operation (Charanis, 1939, 55). M.'s reference to 'civil war' (*intestina proelia*) probably denotes the protest in the streets of CP as the people marched and yelled abusive slogans against Anastasius for his treatment of Euphemius (Theod. Anag., 446 [126.12–15]; Theoph., AM 5987 [139.6–20]).

494.2 There appears to be no other evidence for this earthquake in Phrygia.

494.3 Pope Gelasius (consecrated 1 March 492) was one of the most able and powerful of the late antique pontiffs, best known for his formulation of the division of power between the ecclesiastical and imperial realms. Like his predecessor Felix, Gelasius persisted in taking a hard line against the emperor and the patriarch of CP, Euphemius, with respect to the recognition of Acacius. At the same time he enjoyed the confidence of Theodoric, the Ostrogothic king of Italy. Gelasius, who was the first pope to claim the title of 'Vicar of Christ', ruled the church until 21 November 496 (Kelly, 1986, 47–9).

495 The patriarch of CP Euphemius had incurred the wrath of the emperor in 494 (s.a.) but retained the support of his people. Anastasius was therefore obliged to have him deposed canonically. M. refers to the fact that in November 495 the emperor called a synod at CP which convicted the patriarch on a charge of 'Nestorianism', and thereafter he was exiled to Euchaita, which led to riots in the hippodrome at CP (Jo. Mal., 16.11 [400.2–3]; Theod. Anag., 455 [128.14–20]; Theoph., AM 5988 [140.7–15] with Charanis, 1939, 56; Stein, 1949, 166–7). In his place was installed Macedonius, the treasurer of the Great Church of CP.

496.1 There is no other reference to this donative. Zach. Rhet. 7.8 (172) says that Anastasius was accustomed to give donatives every five years (presumably each *quinquennalia*) in exchange for an oath not to harbour treachery against the empire. This will have been the first of such occasions, at the end of his fifth year (Burgess, 1988, 85).

496.2 Emperors had long been the recipients of what were regarded as exotic animals from the East (cf. s.a. **448**). On this occasion the elephant and giraffes were sent from India (presumably the kingdom of Axum) and were seen by Timothy of Gaza (*PLRE* 2: 1121) passing through Gaza on their way to CP. The reference to the playwright Plautus (c. 2 BC) is to his *Casinum*, line 846. Whether *lucabum* is what M. actually wrote must remain uncertain for when this entry is quoted in the eighth century by Vergil of Salzburg (writing under the name of 'Aethicus Ister'), the author of a pseudo-geographical work *Liber monstrorum de diversis generibus*, he writes 'quem Plautus poeta ludens lucam bovem nominavit', that is, his manuscript of M. read 'lucam bovem', unless he consciously altered *lucabum* from his own knowledge of Plautus (see Laistner, 1957, 177 and 185).

497.1 This is the only record of this eclipse. It was a nearly-complete solar eclipse which occurred at CP and in Illyricum on 18 April (Newton, 1972, 541–2).

497.2 The Isaurian war apparently finished officially in this year (cf. Brooks, 1893, 236–7) after several years of indecisive activity in the mountain recesses, as the Isaurians held out against the Roman forces led by John the Hunchback (*PLRE* 2: 617-18) and John the Scythian (*PLRE* 2: 602-3; Brooks, 1893, 234–5).

497.3 Athenodorus, who had continued to command the Isaurians since 492, was captured as M. records (Theod. Anag., 449 [126.27–127.14]; Vict. Tonn., 495.1 [XI 192]; Theoph., AM 5987 [139.1–6], 5988 [139.31–3], Joh. Mal. 16.3 [393.24] = fr. 37 (*de ins.*, 167). M. is the only source for the display of Athenodorus' head at Tarsus where it was exposed to decay (cf. Brooks, 1893, 235).

498.1 Pope Anastasius II (consecrated 24 November 496) took a more conciliatory approach to the Acacian problem which attracted the emperor Anastasius into recognising Theodoric as ruler in Italy, apparently on the understanding that the pope would accept the Henotikon of Zeno. Unfortunately Pope Anastasius died (19 November 498) before a final settlement could be reached with the emperor (Kelly, 1986, 49–50).

498.2 Longinus of Selinus (*PLRE* 2: 688) had been involved throughout the war in relaying supplies to the rebels in the mountains until 498. With the war now officially completed, he was captured at Isaurian Antioch and transported to CP where he formed part of the elaborate victory spectacle (McCormick, 1986, 61). Subsequently he was moved to Nicaea where he was tortured and killed (Evag., 3.35; Jo. Mal., 16.3 [394.2–6] = fr. 37; Theoph., AM 5987 [139.1–6], 5988 [139.33–140.1]. M. is the only source to mention Longinus' captor Priscus (*PLRE* 2: 906), who must have been one of the subordinate commanders in the Isaurian war (cf. Brooks, 1893, 236). In not actually mentioning his death M. demonstrates his concentration on the victory parade involving the Isaurian captives. He may well have witnessed this occasion himself.

498.3 This is one of the most difficult and discussed entries in the chronicle. What M. appears to be referring to is a significant and controversial coinage reform. The root of the difficulty over its interpretation lies in the obscurity of the text, as printed by Mommsen. The version preferred here substitutes 'terunciani' for 'terentiani'. This reading was initially proposed by Scaliger in 1606 and discounted by Mommsen. Melville-Jones (1991), however, shows that 'teruncianos' is preferable and makes sense of the passsage. A *teruncius* (lit. 'of three ounces') was originally a fortieth of a *denarius*, and what M. is reporting is Anastasius' reform which involved striking these new copper coins at forty to the pound (i.e. 324 grammes or at 8.1 grammes each). So *terunciani* is a designation for 'fortieth'. In effect this reform was a necessary standardisation of the rate of exchange, although it was not welcomed by those who were taking advantage of the lack of stability in the ratio of copper to gold coins. This probably explains M.'s comment on the negative reaction of the populace to the emperor's reform (Blake, 1942, 84–97; Metcalf, 1969, 13).

499.1 This Roman expedition against the Bulgars was a major one. The Bulgars had remained quiet since the invasion in 493 (s.a.) but by 499 they were evidently raiding Thrace and Illyricum once more. The Roman forces were utterly overwhelmed, not least by the Bulgars' piercing battle songs (Zon., III, 140.15–141.4] with Croke, 1980, 189). The expedition was led by Aristus (*PLRE* 2: 147), *magister militum per Illyricum*, and included the four *comites rei militaris* mentioned only by M. Since M. is our primary source of information on this expedition (Jord., *Rom.* 356 apparently being based on M.) it may reflect his personal interest as an Illyrian; and it may even be an eye-witness account.

499.2 There appears to be no other evidence for this quake unless it is that mentioned in Chron. ad 846 (166.36–167.4) at 'Nicopolis'.

500.1 Pope Symmachus (consecrated 22 November 498) was dogged by controversy from the beginning of his papacy. The predominantly senatorial supporters of the conciliatory policy of his predecessor Pope Anastasius consecrated Laurentius as pope on the same day as Symmachus, and a protracted conflict ensued. The following year king Theodoric intervened and declared Symmachus the legitimate pope but he transferred his allegiance to Laurentius in 502 after Symmachus incurred his displeasure. Only in 506 was Theodoric persuaded to throw his support behind Symmachus once more. The pope's tough stand against the emperor Anastasius made him unpopular at court but in 514, under pressure from the revolt of Vitalian, the emperor invited Symmachus to convene a synod at Heracleia designed to heal the differences between Anastasius and the supporters of Vitalian. Symmachus died as pontiff on 19 July 514 (Kelly, 1986, 50–1).

500.2 Paulus (*PLRE* 2: 853) was *tribunus (et notarius)* which is presumably what M. meant by 'tribunus notariorum'. This specification of a donative to the Illyrian army may reflect M.'s local knowledge. Likewise, M. may have had some connection with Paulus if he is the same person who took ransom money to the Praetorian Prefect John in 517 (s.a.). The donative may have been occasioned by the Bulgars' defeat of the Illyrian army in the previous year (cf. **499.1**).

501.1–3 M. is our main source for this disastrous factional outburst in CP and may well have been an eye-witness to the events described. The Brytae festival involved dancing and mime and was held in the theatre. In 501 the City Prefect Constantine (*PLRE* 2: 313), not Constantius, was presiding at the Brytae festival when the Greens among the audience attacked the Blues and the violence described by M. ensued (details in Bury, 1923, 437–8). M. alone reports that 3,000 perished on this occasion, many of whom were drowned when what was evidently a water tank used as part of the stage collapsed. As a result, the factions' dancing girls were banished and the Brytae festival itself abolished, which then led to a concentration of factional violence in the hippodrome (Cameron, 1973, 233, 244).

502.1 The donative to the Illyrian soldiery (**500.2**) was not sufficient to bolster their resistance if, as M. reports, the invasion of the Bulgars in 502 met with no opposition. It may be that the raid was so rapid that the Bulgars were gone before the Romans even discovered them (cf. Theoph., AM 5994 [143.26–7). 'Consueta gens' suggests the impatience and frustration of M. as an Illyrian.

502.2 Since the 440s Rome and Persia had enjoyed a period of stable peace with each other despite occasional threats of disruption. However, by the summer of 502 mounting pressures from the Persian king for defence subsidies from Anastasius continued to meet with imperial refusal, until it led to the Persians invading Roman territory and capturing Theodosiopolis (Stein, 1949, 93–4; Blockley, 1992, 88–90). Then in October the Persians laid siege to Amida (Diyarbekir), metropolis of Mesopotamia and a crucial town in Persian/Roman relations (Jo. Mal., 16.9 [398.11–12]). For three (not five, as M. says) months the Persian army under Cavades (*PLRE* 2: 273–4) laid siege to Amida and, hard-pressed by famine, was on the brink of departing in January 503 when the defenders of the city let slip their vigilance and allowed the Persians into the city (Chron. Edess., 80 [8]; Theod. Anag., 466 [134.4–5]). It appears that 80,000 of the city's inhabitants were massacred, including a large number of monks. The claim, repeated by M., that certain monks betrayed the city is likely to have been a subsequent invention (details in Harvey, 1990, 59–61).

503 In May the emperor Anastasius sent three generals, Patricius (*PLRE* 2: 840–2) *magister militum praesentalis*, Hypatius (*PLRE* 2: 577–81) *magister militum* *praesentalis* and Areobindus (*PLRE* 2: 143–4), to command the 15,000 troops previously sent (cf. Bury, 1923a, 12). Patricius and Hypatius invaded Arzanene and eventually encamped at Siphrios, nine miles from Amida (Proc., *Wars* 2.12.3), where they remained despite a request from Areobindus for reinforcements at Nisibis (Josh. Styl., 54–55). They were unsuccessful in their encounters with the Persians and this was attributed by some, including M., to their cowardice and incompetence (cf. Jo. Lyd., *de mag*. 3.53.2). Later in the year Hypatius was replaced by the *magister officiorum* Celer (Jo. Mal., 16.9 [399.8–10] with *PLRE* 2: 275–7), who by 505 arranged for the relief of Amida by payment of 1000 pounds of gold to the Persians (Zach. Rhet., 7.5), an event anticipated by M. at this point. For details: Stein, 1949, 97–100.

504 Having already indicated the outcome of the war in 505 (s.a. 503), M. reverts to describing the movements of Celer in 504. Celer had left Patricius and his army at Amida and set out to invade Persian territory. From Callinicum he moved to devastate the countryside on his way into Persia, as M. describes. After invading Arzanene he returned to Amida and opened negotiations for peace, which resulted in the extension of the terms of the 442 treaty and the reinforcement of Roman defences in the East (Blockley, 1992, 91–2). M. is our only evidence for the fact that Armonius (*PLRE* 2: 150) was sent to assist Celer with the peace negotiations. That M.'s account of the war is more or less confined to the movements of Celer may suggest that he knew and admired Celer as a fellow-Illyrian. He may in fact be the source of M.'s information in 503 and 504.

505 The background to this episode is not entirely clear (details in Bury, 1923, 459–60). It appears that by the early sixth century the Gepids had established themselves independently in Sirmium, which Theodoric felt should be subject to the Ostrogothic regime in Italy. Consequently in 504 the Gothic army under Pitzias (*PLRE* 2: 886–7) expelled the Gepids (supported now by the Bulgars) from Sirmium (Cass., 1344 [XI 160]). It was probably the Gothic occupation of Sirmium which provoked the emperor Anastasius to despatch such a large expedition into Illyricum. M., however, does not connect the 505 expedition with the Goths' occupation of Sirmium. Rather he portrays it purely as a battle against the Gepid bandit Mundo (*PLRE* 2: 767–8 with Croke, 1982, 128–9). When the Roman army of 10,000 men (including a contingent of Bulgars) and all their supply wagons moved against Mundo he called on the support of the Gothic chieftain Pitzias, who probably confronted the Bulgars while Mundo dealt with the Romans (Jord., *Get*. 300–1). Their combined forces routed the Romans at Horreum Margi and secured Sirmium for the Goths. The *consul* and *magister militum per Illyricum* Sabinianus (*PLRE* 2: 967–8) was the son of the general who two decades previously had taken such a strong stand against Theodoric and the Ostrogoths (s.a. 479, 481). The fort of Nato is otherwise unknown. M.'s poignant reaction to the defeat of the consul's army betrays his feeling for the final loss of Roman power in the region.

506 It was the *comes sacrarum largitionum* John the Paphlagonian (*PLRE* 2: 604–5) who melted down several bronze statues which Constantine had brought to CP and out of them fashioned this new statue of Anastasius (Jo. Mal., 16.13 [400.22–401.8]). The statue was placed on top of the column of Theodosius II in the Forum Tauri, the previous statue of Theodosius having been toppled in an earthquake in 479 (s.a. 480 with Janin, 1964, 81–2).

507.1 The riot at CP reported by M. was probably the same riot which is described by Jo. Mal. and Chron. Pasch. (cf. Whitby/Whitby, 1989, 100, n. 316) in which the violent behaviour of the Greens resulted in their patron Plato (*PLRE* 2: 891–2) being made City Prefect. There is, however, no reason to think Vict. Tonn., s.a. 512 (XI 195) is describing here the riots and fire of 507 rather than that of 512. It appears that while the emperor Anastasius was presiding at races in the hippodrome the Greens chanted in the usual way for him to release some of their number who had been arrested for stone-throwing. Anastasius refused and ordered his soldiers to attack them in the hippodrome. Thereupon he was pelted with stones, and in their anger the crowd set fire to a section of the hippodrome, the northern part where the Greens were sitting (Müller-Wiener, 1977, 65).

507.2 The tiers of seating and their vaulting collapsed in the fire. Other parts of the hippodrome and outside were soon alight too, while the emperor Anastasius was making a ceremonial entrance or exit in the hippodrome. Schneider, 1941, 384, n. 1 was wrong to think that M. has confused this fire with that in 498. The Grecism 'in processibus' is quite common (McCormick, 1986, 93, n. 58)

508 The background to this imperial invasion of Italy is not clear, nor is it obvious why M. should include it as the key event for this year since he obviously did not approve of it. By any standards the force sent to Italy was a large one — 200 ships and 8,000 men — and was under the direction of two palace soldiers, the count of the domestics Romanus (*PLRE* 2: 948) and the count of the *scholarii* Rufinus (*PLRE* 2: 964). Anastasius had long been disenchanted with Theodoric, king of Italy, and Pope Symmachus for their intransigence over the matter of Acacius and the invasion may have been designed to force their hand. It was probably as a result of this raid that the *conductores* of Apulia had their crops burned (Cass., *Var*. 1.16), the merchants of Sipontum were given a two-year tax immunity (*Var*., 2.38) and certain harbours required repair (*Var*., 1.25). It was probably this invasion too which led to the speedy construction of an Ostrogothic fleet (*Var*., 5.17). Once again M. displays his hostility towards Anastasius, which suggests that the raid may have been linked to Anastasius' attempts to impose his religious policy on Italy.

509.1 There is no other evidence for this fire at CP, which evidently raged along the porticoes leading from the Forum of Constantine to the statue of Perdix. This was a bronze statue near the church of St Julian, not all that far from the Forum of Constantine (Janin, 1964, 105; Müller-Wiener, 1977, 255 with Preger, 1901, 240–1 and notes).

509.2 M. is our only reference for this extraordinary dredging by machines of the Harbour of Julian at CP, apparently involving the construction of a dyke (Suidas, s.v. 'Anastasios' [Adler, 1928–38, II: 187]). Presumably this was part of a larger program undertaken by the emperor Anastasius to dredge and improve harbours, which is referred to by a contemporary panegyrist Priscian (*Pan. Anast.* vv.184–5) and by Jo. Mal. (16.21 [409.13–16]). The harbour of Julian was subsequently deepened by the emperor Justin II, who renamed it after his wife Sophia (Janin, 1964, 231–4).

510.1 The Strategion was located in the 5th Region of CP and it contained, among other things, the Tyche or Fortune of the city in the shape of a bronze statue of a woman (Janin, 1964, 431–2). The fire evidently melted one of her arms, which was quickly remade. There is no reason to assume that this fire was connected to that of the previous year (as suggested by Schneider, 1941, 384).

510.2 'Appius' is the patrician Appion (*PLRE* 2: 111–12) from a distinguished Egyptian family. He had made his career as a result of his role in provisioning the army in the war against Persia. The reason for his exile is not known; perhaps he had been conspiring against Anastasius. He was forcibly ordained at Nicaea (Theod. Anag., 482 [137.16–22]).

510.3 Constantinus (*PLRE* 2: 314) is possibly to be identified with the general who betrayed Theodosiopolis to the Persians in 502 (*PLRE* 2: 313–14, 'Constantinus 14'; contra Honigmann, 1951, 37–8) and then gained a command with the Persians, only to desert them for the Romans in 504. Anastasius then had him made a priest at Nicaea, as he had done for Appion (510.2), where he presumably remained until his elevation to the see of Laodicea not long after 512 (Honigmann, 1951, 36). Later he became a well-known monophysite, as indicated by the letter he received from Severus of Antioch (Ep. 90 = *PO* 14, 156 — not cited in *PLRE* ; cf. Devreesse, 1945, 169, n. 1).

511 Macedonius had succeeded Euphemius as patriarch in 496 (s.a.) and had retained the support of Anastasius by endorsing the Henotikon of Zeno, although this stance alienated the orthodox monks of CP (Vict. Tonn., 501 [XI 193]). It seems that by 511 the emperor had begun to move beyond the terms of the Henotikon to a more openly monophysite position and that this aroused the antagonism of the patriarch. As noted in M.'s account, Anastasius was exposed to a stream of accusations from the monophysite enemies of Macedonius, particularly in Syria and among the monks of CP (Charanis, 1939, 65–7). A riot in CP which Macedonius was accused of instigating, followed by his refusal to hand over to the emperor the original record of the Council of Chalcedon, resolved Anastasius on the patriarch's deposition in November 511 (Jo. Mal., 16.11 [400.1–3]; Theod. Anag., 487 [138.21–6]; 491 [139.21–4] with Stein, 1949, 169–70). M. singles out for mention the patriarch's refusal to hand over the records of Chalcedon. M.'s 'sancta subscriptione' therefore refers to the signatures of the bishops present at Chalcedon not (as Allen, 1981, 150, n. 26) the declaration of orthodoxy signed by Anastasius before becoming emperor (Theod. Anag., 491 [140.13–65]. Macedonius was exiled to Euchaita (*ibid.*, 492 [139.25–7]) and succeeded as patriarch by Timothy who tentatively accepted Chalcedon.

512.1 The fiery light in the sky is also referred to by John the Lydian in his treatise on portents (*de ost.*, 6) where he makes the connection between this phenomenon, an associated eclipse at CP on 29 June 512, and the outbreak of Vitalian's rebellion (with Maas, 1992, 109). The fiery light was probably an aurora (Newton, 1972, 706).

512.2 M.'s account of the riots in November 512 against Anastasius is one of the longest and most detailed descriptions in the chronicle and it is quite likely an eye-witness account. Certainly it is substantial contemporary evidence for the riot (details in Stein, 1949, 177–8). One of the traditional components of liturgical life at CP was the Trisagion ('Thrice Holy'), the acclamation 'Holy God, Holy Mighty One, Holy Immortal One'. It was a usual part of all feasts and processions throughout the city and became part of the regular liturgy (Vict. Tonn., 513 [XI 195]); it was interpreted as a prayer to the Triune God. In Antioch in the 470s there arose an alternative version with the added verse 'who was crucified for us'; that is, it was a version which sought to emphasise the crucifixion of Christ in order to diminish the doctrine of his nature defined at Chalcedon, and that is how it was interpreted. Those who advocated this version were called the Theopaschites ('God-sufferers'; *Deipassionistae*). When this version had been publicly uttered by the monophysite monks at CP in 511 a violent disturbance resulted and the emperor sought safety in the palace (Jo. Mal., 16.19 [407.21–408.8]; Theod. Anag., 508–9 [144.24–145.19]). Now, a year later, the emperor himself instructed the monophysite version of the Trisagion to be used in the churches of CP. He apparently issued his orders through the Praetorian Prefect Marinus (*PLRE* 2: 726–7) and the City Prefect Plato (*PLRE* 2: 891–2) at Hagia Sophia on Sunday 4 November. In the ensuing cacophony some shouted the orthodox Trisagion, others the four-verse version, so the orthodox were identifiable and killed or arrested on the spot.

512.3 The following day, Monday 5 November, there was a similar disturbance in the church of St Theodore. Again many were killed. On the next day the orthodox assembled in the Forum of Constantine where the route of a procession traversed the forum. M. informs us himself that this Tuesday was the anniversary of the falling of ash on CP following the eruption of Mount Vesuvius in 472, 'quo die memoria cineris dudum totam Europam tegentis aput Byzantios celebratur' (472.1). Exactly what the 'memoria cineris' (or *mneme koneos* as it was known in Greek) involved is described in a tenth-century calendar, the Typicon of St. Sophia. A liturgy was celebrated at the church of SS Peter and Paul near the Capitol. Later, setting out from Hagia Sophia in the early morning, the procession, including the emperor and patriarch, would make its station in the Forum of Constantine (*Typ.*, I.90–2; cf. Janin, 1966, 75). Therefore, on the morning of Tuesday 6 November 512 the orthodox had encamped in the Forum to await the emperor's arrival in the procession.

512.4 According to M. the crowd in the forum had collected together the keys of all the gates of the city (that is, presumably they had locked the gates) and the military standards, again presumably of the contingents stationed in the city. When the procession passed the forum the crowd shouted for Areobindus as emperor (Jo. Mal., 16.19 [407.19–21]). M. does not add that the crowd descended on the house of Areobindus to proclaim him but he had already fled.

512.5 The statues of Anastasius in the city cannot be identified. The *magister officiorum* Celer (*PLRE* 2: 275–7) and the *magister militum* Patricius (*PLRE* 2: 840–2) were sent to pacify the crowd in the forum but they were beaten back with a barrage of stones.

512.6 The crowd set fire to part of the city, including the homes of Pompeius (*PLRE* 2: 898–9) the emperor's nephew, although he was a Chalcedonian, and Marinus. Jo. Mal., 16.19 (407.10–18) has a more detailed account of what happened at the house of Marinus. Then (Thursday?) Anastasius appeared in the hippodrome before a crowd but without his crown as a sign of supplication. According to M., Anastasius promised to retract his edict and allow order to be restored but he went back on his word.

512.7 The crowd also called for the suspension of the Prefects Marinus and Plato but the emperor only sent them home. Anastasius' offer to abdicate had won over the hippodrome crowd and afterwards reprisals were launched against certain of the orthodox rioters, which only terrified the remainder into submission.

512.8 There is uncertainty about the date of the synod of Sidon, which is generally held to have taken place towards the end of 511 and was possibly convened by Philoxenos of Mabug (Honigmann, 1951, 12). It is not clear why the name 'Sidon' should be considered ridiculous.

512.9 This is M.'s only mention of Flavianus, who had become patriarch of Antioch in 498 and was a staunch supporter of the orthodox interpretation of the Henotikon of Zeno. He had endured intense opposition from the stronger advocates of monophysitism in Syria, especially Philoxenus of Mabug (Hierapolis), and had made some concessions to his opponents' view, but their demands for open rejection of the Council of Chalcedon were uncompromising (Charanis, 1939, 63–4, 72–6; de Halleux, 1963). Flavian had originally called the synod at Tyre in 512 in order to reconcile their differences but Philoxenus refused to attend. The following year, having organised a band of monks to stir up trouble, Philoxenus entered Antioch and had Flavianus deposed. M. appears to link directly the synod and the deposition although they were many months apart. There does not appear to be any other evidence for John of Paltos, on the Syrian coast (cf. Honigmann, 1951, 30). Both were exiled to Petra, where Flavianus died while John was later restored to his see. M.'s forward reference to the restoration of John under Justin indicates the *terminus post quem* for the chronicle. Either (1) M. included the reference to John in his original edition, which suggests a date of composition in 519 or shortly afterwards; or (2) it was added with the completion of the updated edition in 534.

512.10 It is most likely that the eclipse described by M. was that at CP on 29 June 512 (Jo. Lyd., *de ost.* 6 with Newton, 1972, 542; cf. 512.1).

512.11 The Heruli were evidently resettled to strengthen depopulated lands (Bury, 1923, 436, n. 1), in the vicinity of Singidunum. M. clearly did not approve of the emperor's policy in relocating them.

513 This is M.'s only mention of Severus, who became patriarch of Antioch on 6 November 512, the very day the populace at CP was taking such a strong stand against the emperor (512.2–7). M. emphasises Anastasius' support for the accession of Severus (Charanis, 1939, 76). Severus remained patriarch until he in turn was deposed on the accession of Justin in 518.

514.1 M.'s account of the rebellion of Vitalian is an important contemporary version of events reflecting the strong support of Vitalian by someone opposed to Anastasius' religious policies. Vitalian (*PLRE* 2: 1171–4) was of mixed Goth-Roman descent and came from the province of Scythia, which is what M. means by 'Scythian' (Stein, 1949, 178, n. 2 [= 179]). As *comes foederatorum* (count of the federates), he was the leader of a contingent of Bulgars, and subordinate to the *magister militum per Thraciam*, who at that time was the emperor's nephew Hypatius (*PLRE* 2: 577–81). In the preceding years resentment had slowly built up in the Balkan provinces at the increasingly hostile attitude of the emperor towards the orthodox. At the same time this region with its prefectural and ecclesiastical capital at Thessalonike strengthened its support of the papacy in standing up to the emperor. This sentiment made it easier for Vitalian to gain support for his rebellion. Although frequently dated to 513 (e.g. Bury, 1923, 448, n. 3; Stein, 1949, 180; *PLRE* 2: 1172), M. dates the instigation of Vitalian's action to 514, which must be correct since two letters from Anastasius to Pope Hormisdas sent just after the initial phase of the rebellion are dated to late 514/early 515 (Charanis, 1939, 81, n. 7). Vitalian as *comes foederatorum* took offence at the action of the court in reducing the official supplies of the federates. Very quickly, in three days according to M., he was able to gather together a substantial force (M.'s sixty thousand is probably about right) and eventually marched as far as the Hebdomon, the military parade ground seven miles outside CP. There his large army stretched out in a single line all the way across the peninsula and marched towards the capital, up to the city's Golden Gate. As far as M. is concerned the rebellion is religiously inspired in that he faithfully reports Vitalian's claim to be moving in support of the deposed patriarch Macedonius, who was possibly his cousin. M. does not mention that the emperor sent Patricius (*PLRE* 2: 840–2) to open negotiations with Vitalian, only that the negotiations were completed by Theodorus (*PLRE* 2: 1095) and that after eight days Vitalian withdrew. M.'s comment on the treachery of Anastasius indicates the emperor's failure to keep the conditions of the settlement, although it is not known what these were (probably a rapprochement with the pope in Rome).

514.2 Odessus was the headquarters of the *magister militum per Thracias*. At the outbreak of the rebellion the emperor's nephew Hypatius was the general stationed at Odessus but he was replaced after the settlement with Anastasius by Cyril (*PLRE* 2: 335). Cyril's instructions were apparently to kill Vitalian but the count of the federates anticipated this. After several indecisive encounters Cyril withdrew to Odessus, whereupon Vitalian infiltrated the city and the general's house, and had him murdered (s.a. 514.3).

514.3 M., who may possibly have known the Illyrian Cyril, is clearly contemptuous of the general and his morals, and this probably reflects the viewpoint of Vitalian and his supporters. By this action Vitalian openly proclaimed himself an enemy of the emperor, as M. notes, and he was soon declared as such at CP.

515.1 Hormisdas (consecrated 20 July 514) was an associate of Pope Symmachus and followed his predecessor's hard-line approach in the matter of Acacius. Although Anastasius originally made compromising overtures to Hormisdas, the pope insisted on nothing less than imperial support for Chalcedon and the Tome of Pope Leo, and successive legations to CP returned without success. Anastasius refused to accept the papal conditions for settling the schism but after his death in 518 the orthodox emperor Justin I was quick to negotiate a reconciliation on Hormisdas' terms. Subsequently he was required to ensure its efficacy against the growing support at CP for the Theopaschite formula 'one of the Trinity suffered in the flesh'. He died on 6 August 523 (Kelly, 1986, 52–4). M. will therefore have added the length of his reign in the second edition of his chronicle in 534.

515.2 For a second time Vitalian now threateningly approached the imperial capital and made his base at Sosthenium, where there was an imperial palace and a chapel of the archangel Michael (Jo.Mal., 16.16 [403]). He was promising peace in exchange for the emperor's support for Chalcedon (Vict.Tonn., 514 [XI 195]). M. fails to mention that the *magister militum praesentalis* Hypatius was now sent against Vitalian, together with Alathar (*PLRE* 2: 49–50) the new *magister militum per Thracias*, but was defeated and captured.

515.3 The unnamed senators sent to placate Vitalian at Sosthenium handed over to him the balance of the ransom for the captured general Hypatius of 900 pounds of gold, 1100 pounds already having been confiscated from the earlier delegation intercepted at Sozopolis. That delegation included Uranius (*PLRE* 2: 1173) the *cancellarius* of the *magister officiorum* Celer.

515.4 As part of the agreement entered into between Anastasius and Vitalian the count of the federates was made *magister militum per Thracias* to succeed Alathar and he presumably then moved to Odessus. Meanwhile the emperor's nephew Hypatius, who was still being held at nearby Acrae where he had been captured, was sent back to CP. M. does not mention the main features of the settlement, namely the undertaking of the emperor to restore the deposed bishops and to arrange for a synod to be held at Heracleia to restore unity with the pope. For the victory celebrations at CP: McCormick, 1986, 62–3; Cameron, 1973, 125–30.

515.5 The Huns mentioned by M. were the Sabirs from the Caucasus, nearby the Caspian (Proc., *Wars* 2.29; 8.4.3–11), who played a vital role in Roman-Persian relations. They pillaged across Armenia, Cappadocia, Galatia and Pontus (Vict. Tonn., 515.1 [XI 195]. Anastasius fortified the larger Cappadocian villages and sent a three-year tax remission for afflicted provinces (Jo. Mal., 16.17 [406.9–18]; Theoph., AM 6008 [161. 28–30]; with Bury, 1923, 434, n. 5 and Capizzi, 1969, 209–10). Their presence caused alarm in Antioch where the patriarch Severus interpreted the invasion as divine punishment (*Hymns*, 263–4 [*PO* 7.299–300]).

515.6 The emperor's wife Ariadne died, aged mid-60s, in this year (Vict. Tonn., 515.2 [XI 195]; Zach. Rhet., 7.13; Theoph., AM 6008 [162.13–18]). She had been the sole Byzantine empress for over 40 years, having also been the wife of Anastasius' predecessor, Zeno.

516.1 Again Anastasius failed to keep his promises to Vitalian who took up arms once more. M. avoids mentioning Vitalian's third march on CP and his decisive defeat at the hands of Marinus the Syrian in a naval engagement in the Golden Horn (Jo. Mal., 16.16 [404–6]). Instead he mentions only his replacement as *magister militum per Thracias* by Rufinus (*PLRE* 2: 954–7).

516.2 Elias, bishop of Jerusalem since 494 had always been opposed to Anastasius' religious policy and in doing so had drawn support from the majority of the Palestinian monks (Theod. Anag., 473 [135.25–9]). In particular he continued to refuse to recognise Severus as patriarch of Antioch despite vigorous attempts to influence him (Stein, 1949, 176). By July 516 the emperor felt confident enough to initiate his deposition by force. He was overthrown by Olympus (*PLRE* 2: 804), *dux* of Palestine (*v. Sab*. 56), and exiled to Aila where he died. M.'s interest in Elias stems from his position as an opponent of Anastasius.

516.3 As a result of the rejection by Pope Felix of the Henotikon drawn up by Acacius, patriarch of CP, in 482 a schism (known as the Acacian schism) opened up between the emperor and the pope (cf. **482.1**). As the Acacian schism progressed the mainly Latin-speaking Danubian and Balkan provinces became more and more estranged from the imperial court and eventually sought a rapprochement with the pope, who was only too keen to encourage them. In 512 Pope Symmachus urged the bishops of Illyricum, Dardania and Dacia to declare their allegiance to Rome. It was against this background that the rebellion of Vitalian in 514 drew its strong local support and demonstrated to the emperor the intense opposition in those provinces to his support for the monophysites (Stein, 1949, 182–4). M. is our only evidence for the summoning of the Illyrian bishops to CP in 516 after Vitalian's rebellion had finally been crushed. Presumably Anastasius hoped by his request to secure the support of the bishops for his policy or to work out some sort of compromise with them. Of the five bishops, two died soon after in CP and two were sent home 'through fear of the Catholic Illyrian soldiery'. This obscure phrase may be a reference to another potential rebellion by troops in the regions of Serdica and Pautalia if the bishops were detained any longer. Laurence remained in CP disputing with the emperor, having been cured of an affliction in the church of Cosmas and Damian. M.'s final comment presumably means that Laurence died before 519 when the chronicle was written.

517 This invasion by what M. calls the 'Getae' probably involved the Slavs, who had begun to launch attacks through Roman territory (cf. Stein, 1949, 106, n. 1; Vasiliev, 1950, 308–9 and Croke, 1980, 190–1). This particular raid, for which M. is our only source, was clearly devastating in the regions affected and made a deep impression on M. himself, to judge from his resorting to Jeremiah 6.22, 'Behold a people cometh from the north country and a great nation shall be stirred up from the innermost parts of the earth'. Jeremiah continues by prophesying that the northern invaders will come on horseback, be armed with bows and spears and that their voices will sound like the crashing of waves (6.23), which is doubtlesss what brought Jeremiah to mind when the Slavs were reported. Of special interest is M.'s report of the emperor's contribution to securing the release of Roman captives by sending ransom money through the *tribunus et notarius* Paul (*PLRE* 2: 853) to John the Praetorian Prefect of Illyricum (*PLRE* 2: 608). Evidently it was something for which the Illyrian M. had special knowledge. Perhaps he had been somehow involved in the transaction itself. Paul is perhaps the same person who was responsible for delivering the donative to the Illyrian army in 500 (s.a). It may be that Jordanes' notice of the defeat of the emperor's nephew Pompeius by barbarians at Adrianople (*Rom.*, 356) belongs to this time (cf. Stein, 1949, 106).

518.1 M.'s account of this quake is unique and, by the standards of the chronicle, considerably detailed and lengthy. This suggests special interest on the author's part, probably because it affected his own home region. It is possible that his detailed description is his own eye-witness account; but more likely that it is based on an official report prepared for the imperial court since it resembles other such reports. The precise date of the quake is not known, but it must have been while the Slavs were still making it unsafe for local inhabitants to return home, even to the provincial capital. Some idea of the damage can be gleaned from the violent quake which struck the very same region in 1963.

518.2 At the age of 88 Anastasius died on 9 July 518 (references in *PLRE* 2: 79). M. does not elaborate on his death, although it was evidently unexpected despite his advanced age (Capizzi, 1969, 262–3).

[**518.3** Although contained in Mommsen's edition of the chronicle, this entry was not originally part of the chronicle. Rather it belonged to another of M.'s works, long since lost, namely his four books *de temporum qualitatibus et positionibus locorum*, and was inserted in the St Omer manuscript of the chronicle because it derived from the same author (explained in Croke, 1984). Dara was a village built into a powerful fortress following the Persian war of Anastasius (details in Croke/Crow, 1983 and Whitby, 1986). M. begins his account by locating the city sixty miles south of Amida and 15 miles west of Nisibis. Having determined the site, Anastasius bought out the villagers (Zach. Rhet., 7.6) and work commenced immediately. In charge of day to day operations was Calliopius (*PLRE* 2: with Croke, 1984, 86–8) who had previously been involved in the war as a commissariat officer. M. then describes the measuring out and construction of the walls before explaining how a stream known as Cordissus flowed through the city and was protected by the walls. M.'s evidence is unique in (1) noting that Dara was given the privilege of retaining its original name for use alongside the official Anastasiopolis; and (2) describing the 'Herculean tower', evidently an enormous lookout, constructed on the western wall. Construction of the city was completed in 508 (Chron. ad 724, 115.30).]

519.1 At this point M. begins the updated version of his chronicle. Instead of continuing immediately from where he left off in 518, he begins with a new consular and indictional heading, just as the Chronicon Paschale was later to do (Whitby/Whitby, 1989, 104, n. 327). This then means that he inserts the accession of Justin a year too late. Strictly speaking the heading to introduce the new year should come between **519.2** and **519.3**. Justin succeeded to the throne the day after Anastasius' death, on 10 July 518 (Theod. Anag., 524 [151.25–9]; other references in *PLRE* 2: 650). M.'s claim that Justin was 'elected by the senate' (reinforced in Const. Porph., *de caer*. 1.93) may be an attempt to stress the legitimacy of his transition to power because he had been accused of betraying the trust of the powerful chamberlain Amantius (*PLRE* 2: 67–8) in order to secure the throne for himself. M. records in his preface only Justin the Eastern consul, thereby suggesting that there was no recognised Western one (Burgess, 1989, 156, n. 5). The two versions printed by Mommsen represent the original chronicle as contained in T and a version contained in the St Omer manuscript, which is a summary made to save the space lost by the inclusion of the entry on Dara in S (Croke, 1984).

519.2 The circumstances surrounding the accession of Justin were rather controversial (Bury, 1923a; Stein, 1949, 219–20; Vasiliev, 1950, 68 ff.), although ignored by M. In this account of the aftermath he paints the picture of the emperor defending himself against a treacherous conspiracy, hatched by the close courtiers of Anastasius and designed to maintain a monophysite ascendancy in religious policy. The eunuch bedchamberlain Amantius (*PLRE* 2: 67–8) wielded great power at the court of Anastasius and on the emperor's death had procured the services of Justin as a means of having his domestic Theocritus raised to the purple (Jo. Mal., 17.2 [410–1]). When Justin used the money to secure his own election, Amantius was clearly in an insecure position. About ten days later he was captured and put to death along with his fellow *cubicularius* Andreas (*PLRE* 2: 88). Both were regarded as monophysites opposed to Justin's religious policy of establishing orthodoxy. Misahel (*PLRE* 2: 763–4) and Ardabur (*PLRE* 2:137) were also monophysites and bedchamberlains. Their involvement in the opposition to Justin was apparently lesser than that of Amantius and Andreas, to judge from their lesser punishment. Misahel later returned to CP. Theocritus (*PLRE* 2: 1065), rather than acquire the throne, suffered the same fate as his master and M. appears to have approved wholeheartedly. M. (followed by Jord., *Rom.* 360) is the main source for the manner of Theocritus' death. M.'s description of the conspirators as 'Manichaean' (a standard accusation) may well be accurate.

519.3 Having spent the years since his defeat in 516 somewhere in the Balkans, Vitalian (*PLRE* 2: 1171–176) was welcomed back to CP after the accession of the orthodox emperor Justin and was made *magister militum praesentalis* (Jo. Mal., 17.5 [411]; Vict. Tonn., 522 [XI 196]; Jord., *Rom.* 361). M. alone tells us that the appointment was made just seven days after returning to the imperial capital. M. suggests, further, that Vitalian owed his appointment to the generosity of Justin. Perhaps a guarantee of Vitalian's support had helped Justin's election.

520 Vitalian had been made consul for 520. In July of that year he was struck down in the palace (Jo. Mal., 17.8 [412]; Jord., *Rom.* 361) along with his *notarius* Paulus (*PLRE* 2: 853) and his *domesticus* Celerianus (*PLRE* 2: 278) and subsequently discredited (cf. Cameron, 1982, 93–4; Stein, 1949, 230). Although it was believed that the emperor's nephew, the general Justinian, was instrumental in these murders (Vict. Tonn., 520.3 [XI 197]), M. naturally makes no mention of the accusation. That he includes Vitalian's murder at all may suggest that Justinian could not be implicated. Since Justinian was himself made *magister militum praesentalis* in the same year, it was perhaps as a replacement for Vitalian (Vict. Tonn., 520 [XI 196]).

521 The consulship was a prized office still in the sixth century. At the time of this consulship Justinian (*PLRE* 2: 645–8) was *magister militum praesentalis* and his lavish inauguration was designed to win over the populace and perhaps overshadow rumours of his complicity in the murder of Vitalian. He was later to ensure that no other dignitary or general (as he then was) could emulate his generosity and reap the political benefits of the consulate. The amount spent by Justinian was lavish by Eastern standards, but not for a Western consul, which is why M. specifies 'of Eastern consuls' (Bagnall et al., 1987, 9–10 with n. 62). M.'s account, the only extant description, seems to suggest that the behaviour of the crowd resulted in the consul closing proceedings before the final race (cf. Vasiliev, 1950, 376).

522 M. apparently found nothing worth reporting for this year and none of the subsequent scribes was tempted to fill the gap from another source. The gap probably means M. was in a hurry at this point. On the other hand, since he was employed by Justinian at precisely this time, he may have chosen deliberately to report nothing for the year as a matter of discretion.

523 Mounting frustration at the unchecked violence of the Blue and Green factions led to the appointment of a former *comes Orientis* Theodotus as City Prefect (*PLRE* 2: 1104–5) in 520. Although active in checking the violent activities of the Blues in particular, he became over-zealous and put to death a distinguished man Theodosius (*PLRE* 2: 1102), which alienated Justinian. Theodotus was soon stripped of his position and exiled to Jerusalem (Stein, 1949, 239–40). M. is here describing Theodotus' effective measures in 523. For the date see Vasiliev, 1950, 117 and *PLRE* 2:1105 against Bury, 1923a, 22. M. obviously approved of the crackdown on violence although, perhaps in deference to Justinian, he makes no mention of Theodotus' particular role in these events. These developments occurred at precisely the time that M. was in the employ of Justinian, so he may have been closely involved in them himself.

524 M. is our only source of information for this oil shortage, which must have been quite serious. The government was an important purchaser of olive oil for free distribution to the people and supplies were always carefully controlled. That a shortage of oil was a dangerous situation was demonstrated by the revolt a few years previously in Alexandria (details in Vasiliev, 1950, 374).

525 This was the first ever papal visit to CP. The visit of a pope to the imperial capital was naturally an event of importance to an Illyrian such as M. because of the relationship of the pope to the Illyrian dioceses. John had been sent by Theodoric, ruler of Italy, to plead for security for the Arians in Italy in the face of Justin's renewed persecution of heretics (Stein, 1949, 260–1). Pope John's reception in CP was tremendous. He was given priority in liturgies including at the Easter liturgy, which was celebrated in Latin, in St Sophia, at which both M. and Justinian would have been present (details in Vasiliev, 1950, 212–21). M.'s testimony has sometimes been used to argue for Easter 525 (Stein, 1949, 795), but it is clear that these events took place at Easter 526. M. probably dates the trip to 525 because that is when the pope set out from Rome.

526 This earthquake which struck Antioch on 29 May and which would have been announced soon after at CP was probably one of the most devastating natural disasters of late antiquity killing an estimated 250,000 people (details in Jo. Mal., 17.16–7 [419.22]; Chron. Edess., 108 [Guidi, 1903, 101]; Chron. ad 724, 108–10; with Downey, 1961, 521–5 and Vasiliev, 1950, 345–9). Of special note was that the earthquake killed the patriarch Euphrasius, who was struck by a column (Chron. Edess. 109, [Guidi, 1903, 101]). News of the disaster created an impact in the imperial capital with the emperor Justin appearing in the hippodrome without his crown as a mark of respect. The imperial court contributed significantly to the cost of reconstruction, which made inroads into the treasury. As with earthquakes at CP, this disaster continued to be commemorated annually throughout the East (cf. *menologia* in *PO* 10.33; 41).

527 Justinian was created *nobilissimus* some time before 525 when he was elevated to the rank of Caesar (Vict. Tonn., 525 (XI 197), cf. Vasiliev, 1950, 95, n. 70 and Stein, 1949, 240). On 1 April 527 he was made co-emperor with his uncle Justin (*PLRE* 2: 647). Justin died on 1 August (sources in *PLRE* 2: 650), exactly four months after the promotion of Justinian, as M. says, and was buried with his wife in the convent of St Euphemia (Grierson, 1962, 45). M.'s dating by years 'from the foundation of the city' suggests a local CP source for these events, although he may well have taken some part in them himself.

528 To judge from the way it is recorded by other sources, this consulship of Justinian (his first as emperor) was one of the most memorable, even more spectacular than that in 521. Justinian spent more money on his consulship than any other emperor, according to the Chron. Pasch. (617; cf. Jo. Mal., 14.23 [426] and Theoph., AM 6020 [174.16–18]). His use of the consulship as a vehicle of imperial munificence and influence was deliberate and eventually his fear of others doing the same led to the demise of the office itself (Bagnall et al., 1987, 10–12). M., however, does not dwell on the consulship but rather on the refurbishment of the *kathisma* (Janin, 1964, 188–9) in the hippodrome, for which he is the only source. The modifications were apparently designed to improve the view from the royal box and perhaps to make it less accessible. The new seating for senators was probably in a special portico along the bottom rows (Bury, 1923, 83). Again (cf. 527), the calculation of years 'from the foundation of the city' implies a local source.

529 By contrast with his information on Illyricum, M. has little to offer on the developing war with the Persians except to claim some ownership of it — 'this expedition of ours'. The war had actually commenced in 527 as a result of Persian anger at the king of the Lazi being won over by the Romans (Stein, 1949, 267–73; Bury, 1923a, 79–81). The previous year (528) the Persians had successfully defeated the Romans and decimated their leadership (Jo. Mal., 18.4 [427], 26 [441.2]). The 529 expedition referred to by M. was that under the direction of the newly appointed *magister militum per Orientem* Belisarius (*PLRE* 3: 184–5), whom M. nowhere mentions in the chronicle. M. covers the whole war in a single entry.

530 In 529 Mundo (*PLRE* 2: 767–8 and 3: 903–5 with Croke, 1982, 125–35) was appointed to replace Ascum (*PLRE* 3: 136) as *magister militum per Illyricum* in the aftermath of the Romans defeat by the Bulgars in that year (Jo. Mal., 18.46 [450.19–451.9]; Theoph., AM 6032 (218.31–219.8). In the same year Mundo was sent against the Getae (Slavs) — 'Goths' according to M. — in Illyricum and was immediately successful, as M. explains. In the following year ('deinde his consulibus'), that is, in 530, he marched against the Bulgars in Thrace and defeated them. He even managed to capture the king of the Bulgars and have him paraded in the victory procession in the hippodrome at CP (Jo. Mal., 18.46 [451.13]; Theoph., AM 6032 [219.10–14]). This reversal in Roman fortunes was then commemorated by the City Prefect Eustathius in a dedication to him (Croke, 1980, 193–4 and McCormick, 1986, 64–5). M.'s notice of

Mundo's activities is important because he may have known him at this stage (cf. Croke, 1982, 132). In 534 Mundo was a key court figure well-known for his role in suppressing the Nika riot two years before. Certainly M. is complimentary towards Mundo's audacity and effective military leadership, in contrast to his appearance in the original edition of the chronicle as the vanquisher of Sabinianus, one of M.'s heroes (s.a. 505).

531 The Code of Justinian was not promulgated in 531; the first edition was released on 7 April 529 and a revised version on 16 November 534 (Honoré, 1978, 46, 57, 212). The publication of the Code was a signifcant enough landmark in Roman legal and political life to warrant notice in the chronicles (e.g. Jo. Mal., 18.38 [448.6]; Chron. Pasch., 619.8–10). The original purpose of the Code was to produce a single volume of law which combined the Gregorian, Hermogenian and Theodosian codes and eliminated all contradictions and uncertainty. This task was undertaken by a team of ten officials and commenced only in 528. Why M. records it under this year cannot be explained except to say that he must have been relying on his own fallible memory, unless there was some special (otherwise unrecorded) supplementary distribution or publication of the Code in 531.

532 M.'s account of the so-called 'Nika' riot (details in Bury, 1923a, 39–48; Stein, 1949, 449–55; Whitby/Whitby, 1989, 114–27) is an important contemporary, probably eye-witness, account to be set beside those of Procopius (*Wars* 1.24), John Malalas (18.71 [473–7]) followed by Chronicon Paschale (cf. Whitby/Whitby, 1989, 112) and others. What is especially striking about M.'s perspective is the way he gives priority to the role of the nephews of Anastasius in fomenting a political rebellion. This has been construed by Bury as 'an interpretation of the revolt which Justinian and the court wished or feigned to believe — namely that it was not a genuine expression of popular feeling but merely due to the machinations of Hypatius and his friends' (1897, 93; cf. 1923a, 39, n. 2).

The riot began on the evening of Tuesday, 13 January 532, when the crowd leaving the hippodrome after the monthly races to celebrate the Ides were disappointed at the lack of response from Justinian to their request for clemency on behalf of two previous rioters whose execution had been bungled. The Blues and Greens combined to attack the praetorium of the City Prefect Eudaemon (*PLRE* 3:455), who was responsible for protecting the prisoners. In their anger they fired the praetorium and proceeded to burn the senate house and Hagia Sophia. The next day (Wednesday, 14 January) the opposition of the rioters widened to include the quaestor Tribonian (*PLRE* 3:1335–9), the Praetorian Prefect John (*PLRE* 3: 627–35) and the City Prefect Eudaemon. There was obvious disenchantment with the judicial and civic administration at CP, which resulted in the instant replacement of Tribonian, John and Eudaemon. Such decisive action was not sufficient, however, to satisfy the opponents of the imperial regime. They were looking for a new emperor and moved to the house of Probus (*PLRE* 2: 912–3), the nephew of Anastasius, only to find he was not there to receive their call to the throne. Further opposition on the next day (Thursday, 15 January) resulted in forceful retaliation by Belisarius and his soldiers in the Augustaeum. There was continued rioting and firing on Friday 16 and Saturday 17 before, at dusk, two other nephews of Anastasius, Hypatius (*PLRE* 2: 577–81) and Pompeius (*PLRE* 2: 898–9), who were being protected within the palace, were dismissed. Early the following day (Sunday 18), following the crowd's rejection of Justinian's amnesty oath, they found themselves in the hippodrome after Hypatius had been crowned emperor by popular consent.

M. dates the outbreak of unrest to Tuesday, 13 January and says the riot lasted for five days, which is inadvertently inaccurate since it lasted for six days (cf. Bury, 1897, 107–8), and he gives the clear impression that throughout this period the imperial authority was powerless ('sine certo interrege'). During this time M. would appear to include the attempt to proclaim Probus as emperor on Wednesday 14, since he implicates Probus in the conspiracy. He goes on to describe how Hypatius was proclaimed emperor in the forum (of Constantine) and how he and Pompeius attempted to occupy the palace but were captured in the process and 'on the order of our most holy emperor' were chained and killed. M. fails to mention how Hypatius and Pompeius occupied the imperial box in the hippodrome and were captured there, nor does he mention the fact that their corpses were thrown into the Bosporus on Monday 19. M. does confirm the carnage in the hippodrome on Sunday 18, when Belisarius, Mundo and the soldiery killed around 30,000 during the day, and the aftermath in which those suspected of colluding with the nephews of Anastasius were immediately proscribed (Proc., *Wars* 1.24.56–7; Chron. Pasch., 628). M. concentrates on the violence and precariousness of these days but casts the whole episode as a conspiracy by the nephews of Anastasius (on behalf of the senatorial aristocracy) and its suppression as a victory over usurpers ('tyranni'). This strictly personal and political interpretation may reflect not only the version of events propagated by the emperor in which the suppression of the revolt was paraded as a victory (McCormick, 1986, 65); it may also represent the actual language of Justinian's victory announcement proclaimed to the empire (cf. Jo. Mal., 18.71 [476]; Jord., *Rom.* 364 with Scott, 1981, 17–18). As M. notes, the church of Hagia Sophia, destroyed during the riot, was immediately redesigned and rebuilt (Proc., *Aed.* 1.1.20–3).

533 M. is not here interested in the progress of the war, having summarised it in 529. Rather he reports only the peace settlement which was drawn up by Rufinus (*PLRE* 2: 954–6) and Hermogenes (*PLRE* 3: 590–3) and eventually ratified in September 532, after a long and drawn-out series of negotiations (Bury, 1923a, 87–8). One of the terms of the treaty, alluded to by M., was that the Persian king and the Roman emperor agreed to assist each other militarily whenever the need arose (Jo. Mal., 18.76 [477]). As so often, M. has placed the events described in the correct indiction but wrong consulship (cf. Jord., *Rom.* 365).

534 M.'s chronicle ends with the celebration in CP of the imperial victory in Africa (cf. Jo. Mal., 18.81 (478–9); Vict. Tonn., 534.1–2 [XI 198]; Jord., *Rom.* 366, *Get.* 171–2; McCormick, 1986, 65–6). The expedition of Belisarius set out for Africa from CP in 533 and by the end of the year had succeeded in capturing Carthage and the Vandal king Gelimer, so that the ninety-six year Vandal occupation of the city (439–534) was brought to an end (cf. 439.3). This momentous event was publicised by the imperial court as the restoration of Africa's liberty and as the restoration of the province to the empire by the will of Almighty God. This sentiment is stated specifically in the preface to Justinian's textbook of Roman law, the *Institutes*, dated 21 November 533 (*Const. imp. maiest.* [Krüger, 1929, XIII]) and in a law of 13 April 534 (*CJ* 1.27.1), and is reflected precisely by M. The African victory was celebrated in traditional style in the hippodrome with the emperor wearing the *loros* (Jo. Lyd., *de mag.*, 2.2). It was Justinian's triumph, not that of his general Belisarius (never mentioned by M.) who processed from his house to the hippodrome where he led the parade paying homage to the emperor (McCormick, 1986, 125–9). The triumph, no doubt witnessed by M., was later portrayed in mosaic in the Chalke of the imperial palace with Justinian and Theodora surrounded by the senate (Proc., *Aed.* 1.10.16–7) — perhaps with M. among the depicted senators — and at Justinian's death the scene was embroidered on his funeral vestment. The continuation of the chronicle by M. from 519 to 534 is best construed as his contribution to the celebration of Justinian's African triumph. M.'s conclusion is that the empire is now in a more advantageous position than it had enjoyed for some considerable time.

CONTINUATION OF MARCELLINUS

(534) Theodahad (*PLRE* 2: 1067–8) had become king of the Goths in 534 in succession to the youthful Athalaric, son of Amalasuintha the daughter of Theodoric. Originally he had amassed his wealth from his landholdings, especially in Tuscany, and was never thought by the Goths to be a particularly suitable leader for a warrior nation. Although he had guaranteed the safety of Amalasuintha before she had secured the kingship for him, Theodahad had her arrested and sent to the small island of Marna in lake Bolsena where she was killed (Wolfram, 1988, 338–9). Cont. blames Theodahad directly for the queen's murder (cf. Jord., *Get.* 306) although he was not responsible. Rather it was the result of vengeance on the part of those whose relatives had been liquidated by Amalasuintha. In vindicating the justice of Justinian's reaction to the demise of Amalasuintha Cont. follows the Byzantine view as recorded by Procopius (*Wars* 5.4.30).

535.1 Cont. begins with the positivist view that Justinian was following a systematic military program by automatically turning to Italy once Africa had been reclaimed. Belisarius as consul was entrusted with the expedition (Proc., *Wars* 5.5.1–4, cf. Jord., *Get.*, 307). The expedition reached landfall at Catina, which they easily won, then Syracuse where the Gothic garrison under Sinderith surrendered (Jord., *Rom.* 369, *Get.* 308) and the remainder of the strongholds of Sicily (Proc., *Wars* 5.5.12), the only difficult assignment (not mentioned by Cont.) being the capture of Panormus (Palermo). Belisarius and his army marched victorious into Syracuse on 31 December 535, where he laid down his consulship (Proc., *Wars* 5.5.19; cf. Mar. Av., 535 [XI 235]).

Cont. then proceeds to explain that while at Syracuse (early 536) Belisarius received word of a revolt in Africa against the commander there, Solomon (*PLRE* 3: 1172). Unfortunately, however, Cont. predates the revolt and its aftermath by one year, apparently including it under 535 through linking it to Belisarius' arrival in Syracuse. The Roman troops who had remained in Africa after conquering the Vandals were aggrieved at being denied access to Vandal land, although they had married the wives of the previous owners of the land (Proc., *Wars* 14.4.9), and at the government's hostility to their Arian beliefs (4.14.13–7). It was therefore arranged to kill Solomon on Easter Sunday (23 March) 536. Apprised of the plot he fled with the historian Procopius, who embarked for Syracuse and invited Belisarius to return to restore order and morale (4.14.41). Belisarius arrived in Carthage, admonished the troops (4.14.9–12) and proceeded to Membresa, where he engaged and defeated Stotzas (*PLRE* 3: 1199–200), the leader of the rebellion (4.14.13–44; Jord., *Rom.* 369). Cont. does not name Stotzas except as the 'terrible tyrant'. After reorganising the troops in Africa Belisarius was compelled to return to Sicily (4.14.49). There does not seem to be any specific evidence for Belisarius' punishment of African troops. It was only after Belisarius' departure that Stotzas killed the Roman generals Cyril (*PLRE* 3: 371–2), Marcellus (*PLRE* 3: 814) and Pharas, the Heruls' leader (*PLRE* 3: 1015–6; Proc., *Wars* 4.15.59; Jord., *Rom.* 369 with Bury, 1923, 142–4). Cont. is mistaken in implying that Solomon remained in Africa and was only replaced after further problems with his troops on his departure. Belisarius put Theodore the Cappadocian (*PLRE* 3: 1247–8) and Ildiger (*PLRE* 3: 615–16) in charge of the troops (cf. Diehl, 1896, 81, n. 4).

535.2 Pope Agapitus, who occupied the see of Peter for less than a year (13 May 535–22 April 536), was requested by Theodahad to go to CP in order to placate Justinian over the murder of Amalasuintha and to secure the withdrawal of imperial forces from Italy (Stein, 1949, 342–3). The date of his arrival (20 February 536) in CP shows that this event is in the wrong year, the date given in Lib. Pont. being a duplicate of Agapitus' death date (22 April). Perhaps Cont. meant the date of departure from Rome.

535.3 Tzitta or Sittas (*PLRE* 3: 1160–3), the patrician, was married to the sister of the empress Theodora and had distinguished himself as a commander in the East with Belisarius. There is no other evidence for this defeat of the Bulgars in Moesia at Iatrus, the late Roman fortress-town destroyed by the Huns in 442 and later rebuilt on a smaller scale.

535.4 Epiphanius, patriarch of CP, died on 5 June, well before Pope Agapitus arrived in the capital the following year (cf. **535.2**). He was replaced by the monophysite Anthimus, who had been translated from Trebizond (Jo. Mal., 18.83 [479]; Theoph., AM 6028 [217.1–4]; cf. Friend, 1972, 270–1). From the start Agapitus would have nothing to do with Anthimus, insisting that his translation to CP was uncanonical since a bishop could not be transferred from one see to another (Lib. Pont. with Stein, 1949, 381).

536.1 Evremud or Ebrimuth (*PLRE* 3: 433–4) was married to Theodenathe, the daughter of Theodahad, and was apparently based at Rhegium to guard the province of Bruttium. He surrendered there along with all his supporters and in return was made a 'patrician' at CP. Nothing is known of him after that. Ebrimuth's surrender must have been around June 536 (Bury, 1923a, 175; Stein, 1949, 346) when Belisarius finally crossed to Italy (Jord., *Get.* 309). Cont. is wrong to imply that Evremud fled to Belisarius in Sicily, although he may have made overtures to the Romans before Belisarius actually crossed to Italy.

536.2 When Justinian heard of the failure of his generals to capture Stotzas after Belisarius had returned to Sicily, he replaced Solomon (towards the end of 536) with his own cousin, the patrician Germanus (*PLRE* 2: 505–7), who had previously distinguished himself fighting against the Antae in the Balkans in 527. Solomon returned to CP. Cont., to judge from his 'likewise', pairs Ebrimuth and Solomon as generals who put themselves at odds with their armies.

536.3 From Rhegium Belisarius' army marched through Campania to reach Naples (Proc., *Wars* 5.8.5), around late October/early November 536. After a long siege Naples was finally captured but Belisarius took care to minimise any indiscriminate pillaging by his troops (Jord., *Rom.* 370 with Bury, 1923a, 125–7; Stein, 1949, 346).

536.4 After Pope Agapitus had failed to deter the Roman expedition from Italy, Theodahad had sought through embassies to conclude an agreement with Justinian whereby he would surrender part of Italy to the emperor (Proc., *Wars* 5.6.14–27), but after a Gothic victory at Salona he changed his mind (5.7.11–25). Nonetheless the Gothic warlords remained dissatisfied and resolved to replace Theodahad with the more experienced and bellicose Vitigis (*PLRE* 3: 1382–6). In November (Bury, 1923a, 177, n. 3), he was duly proclaimed by the Goths as their king near Regata, in the extensive plains used by the Goths to graze their horses (5.11.1 with Stein, 1949, 347; Wolfram, 1988, 342–3). This area was, as Cont. records, known as the 'Barbarican plains' (cf. Jord., *Rom.* 371).

536.5 After his proclamation Vitigis moved to Rome and Theodahad fled to Ravenna. Theodahad had appointed Silverius to the see of Peter on 8 June 536, having received news of Agapitus' death at CP on 22 April. Theodora had hoped to arrange for Agapitus' successor but was out-manoeuvered.

536.6 Theodahad was overtaken at Quintus, presumably a station five miles from Ravenna. Cont. is wrong to imply that Vitigis himself killed Theodahad. Instead he allowed the Gothic king to be pursued and killed by Optaris, who held a grudge against Theodahad (Proc., *Wars* 5.11.6–9; Jord., *Rom.* 372). Vitigis then moved to acquire Theodahad's considerable resources at Orvieto and later claimed it was fortunate that Theodahad was able to die at the hands of his kinsmen (Proc., *Wars* 5.29.6).

536.7 When he reached Ravenna Vitigis married Theodoric's niece, Matasuentha (*PLRE* 3: 851–2), thereby cementing his links with the noble Amal family. Cont. echoes the view of both Procopius (*Wars* 5.11.27) and Jordanes (*Rom.* 373; cf. *Get.* 311) in ascribing the wedding to duress rather than pure love. Vitigis apparently divorced his former wife (Jord., *Rom.* 373).

536.8 Belisarius took the Via Latina from Naples to Rome and entered it in December 536 through the Appian Gate, while the Gothic garrison had retreated through the Pincian Gate to Ravenna, except for Londaris, who was despatched to CP (Proc., *Wars* 5.14.12–15 with Bury, 1923a, 180; Wolfram, 1988, 344).

536.9 After arriving in Africa, Germanus (*PLRE* 2: 505–7) was successful in taking the fight to Stotzas and his forces, initially by winning back some of the rebels to the imperial cause with impunity (Proc., *Wars* 4.16.5–7; Jord., *Get.* 310 with Diehl, 1896, 83–4). Cont. offers no details, however.

536.10 Pope Agapitus arrived in CP in February 536. Having failed to dissuade Justinian from sending his forces against the Goths, he was preoccupied then with challenging the position of Anthimus as patriarch and testing his orthodoxy. He refused to meet him at CP and soon secured his deposition (12 March). Justinian was persuaded to summon Anthimus and have him confess the two natures in Christ. Anthimus' refusal to do so caused the emperor to exile him and replace him on 13 March with Menas (Vict. Tonn., 540 [XI 199]). Agapitus died next month (22 April). Cont. makes no suggestion of Anthimus' monophysism, his connections with Severus and his promotion by Theodora. Her attempts to have him restored, by trying to influence papal elections, came to nothing (Bury, 1923a, 378–80). Cont. places the initiative for Anthimus' banishment with Agapitus not Justinian.

536.11 Despite several attempts to amend this passage, it is correct as it stands. The Saracen chiefs were probably from the the tribe of Kinda, which had strong links with CP by the 530s, reflected in their status as 'phylarchs' or leaders of tribes federated to the Roman empire. The Saracen phylarchs Ka^{c}b, or Chabus (*PLRE* 3: 279), and Yazid, or Hezidus (*PLRE* 3: 596), were forced to seek pasture in the Roman province of Euphratesia when turned away from the territory of the Lakhmid tribe, affiliated to Persia, by Al Mundhir (*PLRE* 2: 41–3). Batzas (*PLRE* 3: 179), the dux of Euphratesia, coped with this influx peaceably. The drought in Mesopotamia may have been part of a wider climatic disaster in that year, possibly traceable to a severe volcanic eruption in the southern hemisphere. The winter was severe with much snow and birds perishing (Zach. Rhet., 10.1 [298]).

537.1 Vitigis arrived with his army before Rome on 21 February. Procopius reports (*Wars* 5.25.13) that Pope Silverius, who had been the controversial choice of Theodahad on 8 June 536, was accused of treasonable dealings with Vitigis and was expelled from the city by Belisarius and replaced as pope by Vigilius on 29 March 537. This accusation may only have been a fabrication, however, for it seems that the empress Theodora harboured resentment against Pope Silverius for refusing to restore Anthimus as patriarch of CP. She then bribed Vigilius, who had apparently come to CP as Agapitus' deacon (and remained as *apocrisarius*), to have himself elected Pope, whereupon he would restore Anthimus. Belisarius and Antonina, under direction from Theodora, accused

Silverius of passing incriminating letters to Vitigis and stripped him of the see on 11 March 537 (Lib. Pont). Cont. gives the official line that Belisarius had to remove Silverius.

537.2 By the time Belisarius asked the emperor Justinian for reinforcements by letter (quoted, perhaps accurately, in Proc., *Wars* 5.24.1–17) he had undergone a series of skirmishes with the Goths camped outside Rome, culminating in a major battle. Martin (*PLRE* 3: 839–48) and Valerian (*PLRE* 3: 1355–61) were then directed to Italy (5.26.18–21) and arrived in July (5.27.1–3). Not only did Vitigis not slacken off the siege but he launched many unsuccessful attacks (5.27.15–23) before a successful one (5.29.1 ff.).

537.3 In the spring the armies of Germanus and Stotzas finally clashed at Scalae Veteres (Collas Vatari) and the rebels were put to flight (Proc., *Wars* 4.17.4). Another rebellion against Germanus was forcefully extinguished (Diehl, 1896, 84–6).

537.4 John Cottistis (*PLRE* 3: 639–40), a soldier stationed at Dara, took control of the city, occupying the palace of the dux of Mesopotamia who was normally stationed there. After four days the palace was infiltrated and John met his end (Proc., *Wars* 1.26.5–12). He was presumably the person referred to in the broken part of Zach. Rhet., 10.1 (299) — not cited in *PLRE* — who describes how John plotted a rising at Dara in the summer of that year.

537.5 Following its destruction during the Nika riot in January 532, construction of a new church of Hagia Sophia soon commenced. Cont. records its dedication on 27 December (Jo. Mal., 18.86 [479]; Theoph., AM 6030 [217.21–2])

538.1 In November 537, the army under John (*PLRE* 3: 652–61) landed at Hydruntum and marched into Campania by the coast road to reach Ostia, where they met Belisarius: Conon and Paulus (*PLRE* 3: 976) with 3000 Isaurians were sent to Naples, while Batzas (*PLRE* 3: 179) and Rema (*PLRE* 3: 1082) were sent separately and linked up under John's command at Ostia. Cont. is mistaken in saying John's army embarked at Portus Romanus which was then held by the Goths (Proc., *Wars* 6.7.1), although they relinquished it soon after (6.7.16). The truce was indeed for three months, as Cont. says, and was concluded at Rome (6.7.13).

538.2 Belisarius used the opportunity of the peace to travel through Campania securing food supplies for the city of Rome. On his return he was confronted with an attempted assassination by Constantine (*PLRE* 3: 341–2), who had antagonised Belisarius and Antonina by refusing to yield up some precious daggers he had stolen. He was eventually killed by Belisarius in trying to uncover the truth of the accusation (Proc., *Wars* 6.8).

538.3 John occupied Portus on the departure of the Goths (cf. **538.1**) and from there advanced to Alba where he wintered (Proc., *Wars* 6.7.25–34). On orders from Belisarius he attacked the Goths in Samnium and Picenum, capturing Aternum where he defeated Tremo (*PLRE* 3: 1335) the local garrison commander. From there he advanced to Ortona and eventually to Rimini (6.10.3–19.8).

538.4 When the three-month peace had expired and John had reached Rimini, Vitigis decided to abandon the siege of Rome and burn his camps there (Proc., *Wars* 6.10.12). He crossed the Appenines and laid siege to Rimini (6.11.1–2; 12.1–25).

538.5 The eunuch Narses (*PLRE* 3: 912–28) had been sent with a large army to Rome by Justinian (Jo. Mal., 18.88 [480]). He met up with Belisarius and his army at Fermum (Proc., *Wars* 6.16.1), whereupon they marched towards Rimini. Vitigis then abandoned the siege of Rimini for the safety of Ravenna.

538.6 Oraio (Vraias: *PLRE* 3: 1392–3) was the nephew of Vitigis and he was sent to besiege the Roman generals at Milan, Mundilas (*PLRE* 3: 901–3) and Paul (*PLRE* 3: 976–7). The siege lasted nine months, which severely oppressed the city (Proc., *Wars* 6.12.36–41; Stein, 1949, 355, n. 1).

538.7 In mid-December Belisarius laid siege to Urbinum (Proc., *Wars* 6.19.1–17) but Narses held back his support and withdrew to Rimini (6.19.8–10) for the winter, where he heard the news of Belisarius' capture of Urbinum and Urbs Vetus (6.20.3 ff.).

539.1 Narses had continued to disagree with Belisarius' approach to the war in Italy and was recalled to CP by Justinian (Proc., *Wars* 6.22.4). There is no hint in Cont. of any rivalry between the two senior generals.

539.2 Auximum was subject to a protracted seven-month siege (April–October 539) before being starved into submission by Belisarius' army (Proc., *Wars* 6.27). As for Faesulae, Belisarius originally planned its capture (6.23.1), but the siege was carried out by Cyprian and Justin (6.23.2, 24.18, 25.19) and the city eventually surrendered (6.27.25–7).

539.3 After a long siege the Romans who had occupied Milan could survive no longer and surrendered. The capture of Milan actually predates the sieges of Auximum and Faesulae (above **539.2**). When the city was captured the walls were razed and all the males in the city (estimated at 300,000) were taken off to captivity (Proc., *Wars* 6.21.39). There is no other evidence for the transporting of the Roman generals Paulus and Mundilas to Ravenna. Razing the walls was part of a wider strategy (cf. Burns, 1984, 210).

539.4 The invasion of North Italy by Theudebert (*PLRE* 3: 1228–30) had a dramatic impact on events until his army was afflicted by plague (Proc., *Wars* 6.25; Mar.

Av., 539 [XI 236]). Cont. is the only source to indicate the capture of Genoa. It was the decimation of his own army which compelled Theudibert into a settlement with Belisarius (cf. Jord., *Rom*. 375).

539.5 Germanus (*PLRE* 2: 505–7) had been *magister militum* in Africa since 536 and had been successful in suppressing the rebellion of Stotzas (cf. 536.9, 537.3). After two years of peace he was now summoned by the emperor back to the imperial capital and replaced by Solomon (*PLRE* 3: 1167–77) as head of a new expedition (Proc., *Wars* 4.19.1 with Diehl, 1896, 87–8).

539.6 Calluc (*PLRE* 3: 266) was probably the *magister militum per Illyricum* at the time he fought successfully against the Gepids, then located in the vicinity of Sirmium and Singidunum. This was evidently a famous battle at the time (cf. Jord., *Rom*. 387), although no other details are known.

540.1 In March 540 the peace with Persia was broken by a Persian invasion of Roman territory in which several cities were destroyed (Jord., *Rom*. 376; Mar. Av., 540.1 [XI 236]). Germanus was sent to Antioch with three hundred men and his son Justin who was consul at the time (Proc., *Wars* 2.6.9 ff.; Jo. Mal., 18.87 [480]; Chron. ad 724 [112.19–24]; Chron. ad 846 [174.8–12]). It was unusual, as Cont. implies, for the consul to take the field in his year although there was the recent example of Belisarius in 535.

540.2 After a brief siege the Persians captured Antioch, the most important and wealthiest city in the East, in June (Jo. Mal., 18.87 [480]). Its inhabitants were abducted to Persia.

540.3 Belisarius had been lured by the offer of the throne of Italy but had remained loyal to the emperor and eventually was successful in wearing down the Goths in Ravenna, which he entered in May 540 (Proc., *Wars* 6.29; Jo. Mal., 18.88 [480]; Jord., *Rom*. 375 and *Get*. 313 sees it as a great achievement). Then he was summoned back to CP by Marcellus (*PLRE* 3: 814–6), probably a *comes consistorianus*. Cont. makes nothing of the victory celebration which was a private one for senators only and with no special rewards for Belisarius (McCormick, 1986, 66).

540.4 Solomon had been successful in Africa (details in *PLRE* 3: 1174–5). Confident in his troops, and having learned from previous battles in Africa, Solomon successfully encountered the Moors under Iaudas (*PLRE* 3: 610–11) and defeated them by the river Abigas. He followed up his victory with an attack on their base in the Aures (Proc., *Wars* 4.19–20 with Diehl, 1896, 89–93).

540.5 When the Transpadane Goths heard of the capture of their king they turned to Vitigis' nephew Vraias (Proc., *Wars* 6.30), but he turned down the offer, suggesting instead Ildibadus (*PLRE* 3: 614–15), who was then in charge of the strong garrison at Verona (6.29.41) from where he was summoned and elected king (cf. Jord., *Rom*. 378). When Ildibadus was elected as king his predecessor Vitigis had not yet been taken to CP by Belisarius who was still in Italy.

540.6 Ildibadus' first encounter was at Placentia with Bessas (*PLRE* 2: 226–9), the experienced Roman general, now patrician and stationed at Ravenna; Cont. is the only evidence for this. Constantianus (*PLRE* 3: 334–6), not 'Constantine', had been stationed in Dalmatia and was sent to Ravenna to replace Belisarius (Proc., *Wars* 6.30.2). Although M. calls Bessas a 'patrician' here and at 542.3, he may only have acquired the title in 544 (Stein, 1949, 566, n. 2).

541.1 Since the Persian war was dragging on, Germanus returned to CP early in 541 and Belisarius was sent to the East (Proc., *Wars* 2.14.18; Jord., *Rom*. 377).

541.2 Ildibadus was slain at a banquet (around May) by a Gepid named Velas who held a grudge against him (Proc., *Wars* 7.1.47–9, 2.4.8.10), although the Rugian strong-man Erarichus (*PLRE* 3: 447–8) may have had something to do with it (cf. 7.2.10). The Rugians then proclaimed Erarichus as king and the Goths accepted him though not a Goth himself (Proc., *Wars* 7.2.1–5; Jord., *Rom*. 379).

541.3 After returning to Africa in 539 Solomon had succeeded in suppressing the raids of the Moors (cf. **540.4**). In 543, however, a dispute between the Roman general Sergius (*PLRE* 3: 1124–8), nephew of Solomon and *dux* of Tripolitania, and the Leuathae near Leptis Magna spilt over into a further dispute between Antalas (*PLRE 3* : 81–7) and Solomon. The combined Moorish forces mounted a formidable threat to the Romans and in a battle at Tebessa, six days from Carthage, they were defeated. Subsequently there was again dissension among the Roman troops and some of Solomon's loyal Moors defected. This led to him losing the battle at Cillium in Byzacena after which Solomon's horse stumbled and he was soon set upon by the Moors and slain (Proc., *Wars* 4.21.28; Vict. Tonn., 543 [XI 201] with Diehl, 1896, 340–3). Sergius was then appointed by Justinian to succeed Solomon as *magister militum* (4.22.1), that is, with control of both the military and civil government. It was not a happy choice (details in Diehl, 1896, 344–5). Cont. has considerably telescoped these events, which occurred not in 541 but in spring 544 (Diehl, 1896, 342–3; Stein, 1949, 548).

542.1 The Romans had decided to concentrate their efforts at Verona and an army of 12,000 men under the generals Constantianus and Alexander marched there (Proc., *Wars* 7.3.3–4). An advance party secured entrance to Verona through bribing a guard (cf. Cont. 'secretly') and drove out the Gothic garrison (7.3.6–14). When the Goths realised that the main army had halted due to squabbling over the spoils (7.3.15–18) — as Cont. notes — they returned and drove out the Romans (7.3.19–22), who retreated to Faventia (Faenza). The Goths' 'hideouts' were in the rocky outcrop overlooking the city (7.3.14). This occurred after, not before, the death of Erarichus (542.2), probably in the spring (Bury, 1923a, 230, n. 1).

542.2 After gaining the kingship Erarichus sought to agree to Justinian's terms for Vitigis, namely that the Goths should withdraw to the north of the Po. Envoys were sent to CP and put to the emperor the more radical proposal for the surrender of all of Italy and its kingship in exchange for the Roman patriciate (Proc., *Wars* 7.2.15–17). Meanwhile Erarichus was treacherously killed, although the precise circumstances are not known (7.2.18; Jord., *Rom.* 379), except that the Gothic chieftains preferred a more bellicose leader and looked to Totila (*PLRE* 3: 1328–32), the young nephew of Ildibadus (7.2.7–13). Erarichus had reigned for only five months (7.2.6) and died in 541, not 542. Cont. has placed his death in the following year as part of an introduction to the increasing devastation caused by Totila, which the author (or rather his source; cf. Jord., *Rom.* 379) laments.

Totila's first success was at Faventia (Jord., *Rom.* 379). There he crossed the Po with the bulk of his army of 5000 and marched towards the Romans (Proc., *Wars* 7.4.19–30). In the ensuing battle the turning point seems to have been the appearance behind the Romans of 300 Goths who had crossed the river further upstream and come around behind the Roman lines (7.4.19, 31). All the Roman standards were captured in this disastrous defeat and, as Cont. notes, the generals sought refuge in various strongholds (7.4.32). Subsequently, Totila did capture Caesena and Petra Pertusa (7.6.1), as well as Urbinum and Mons Feretris (Montefeltro), for which Cont. is the only source. However, that was after the victory at Mugellum (Mugello), which is the next entry in Cont. who has here reversed the order of events.

542.3 Soon after the victory at Faventia (above 542.1) Totila sent an army to besiege Florence, whose general Justin (*PLRE* 3: 748–9) called for reinforcements from Ravenna, whereupon the Goths retreated into the valley at Mugellum (Proc. 5.7.2–7). In the ensuing skirmishes the indecisive Roman forces were again defeated and the generals put to flight (5.7.8–18). Cont. is the only source to mention the wounding of the veteran general Bessas. Procopius reports (7.5.1) that the Gothic forces were under the command of Rudericus (*PLRE* 3: 1096–7; Cont.: Ruderit), Vliaris (*PLRE* 3: 1388–9; Cont.: Viliarid) and Bleda (*PLRE* 3: 233).

543.1 Totila advanced from Mugellum across the Tiber and into Campania. He quickly won Beneventum and then decided to besiege Naples and sent a contingent to capture Cumae (Proc., *Wars* 7.6.1–4). Cont. does not mention the surrender of Naples in March/April 543 and the razing of its walls (7.7.19–20; 8.10) except under the next year, a year too late. There is no other evidence to confirm Cont.'s statement that the Goths began their siege of Tibur in 543 which led to its surrender the following year (s.a. 544.1). Totila was able to cajole his army by both gifts and blandishments (Jord., *Rom.* 379).

543.2 The severe bubonic plague began in Egypt and reached CP in the spring of 542 and later ravaged Antioch and Syria. By 543 it had reached Illyricum and passed to Italy. It made a deep impact on the Roman world, to judge from the comments of contemporaries such as Procopius and John Malalas (Jo. Mal., 18.92 [482] with Allen, 1979, 5–20).

543.3 In this year the ongoing war with Persia saw the Romans choosing to take advantage of Chosroes' misfortunes by invading Persarmenia, but they were themselves defeated by the Persians at the fortress of Anglon (Proc., *Wars* 2.24). In Africa Sergius was subdued by the Moors under Antalas (*PLRE* 3: 86–7) and the rebels of Stotzas who joined up after the defeat and death of Solomon. These events should be dated to 544 after the death of Solomon. Cont. confuses events of 544 in Byzacium with those of 543 in Tripolitania (Stein, 1949, 549, n. 1).

544.1 Again the chronology of Cont. is confused. The siege of Firmum (Fermo) and Asculum (Ascoli) did not commence until late in 544 after Belisarius had again taken charge in Italy (Proc., *Wars* 7.11.39), while Naples had been captured the previous year. Tibur was captured by the Goths after a dispute between the Isaurians guarding the gates and the other guards who opened the city to the Goths who killed all the inhabitants and razed the walls (7.10.19–23; 24.32–33).

544.2 Following the collapse of resistance in Naples Totila's army advanced to Rome (c. April 544) and mounted a blockade against the city. At that time the garrison in the city was commanded by John the nephew of Vitalian (Proc., *Wars* 7.6.8; 9.20), though he returned to CP and was replaced by Bessas.

544.3 John the Cappadocian (*PLRE* 3: 627–35) had been Praetorian Prefect. His authority and influence antagonised the empress Theodora, who contrived his downfall. He was exiled to Antinoe in Egypt in August 541, not 544 (Stein, 1949, 483 with n. 1 and Excursus A). Cont. alone records the confiscation of his house to Belisarius, which may have occurred in 544, thereby explaining the insertion of this entry in this year.

545.1 After a long siege the Goths succeeded in capturing Firmum and Asculum (Proc., *Wars* 7.12.12). Cont. is the only evidence for the subsequent cruelty of Totila's forces to the inhabitants of the captured cities, but it is quite likely, given the similar treatment accorded the citizens of Tibur (7.10.22).

545.2 Stotzas' rebellion against Sergius resulted in raids over a wide area. Meanwhile Sergius was feuding with his *magister peditum* John, son of Sisinniolus. The Moors and Stotzas pillaged to Hadrumetum, where John killed Stotzas but in the flight was intercepted and killed himself (2.24.9–14; Cor., *Ioh.* 4.382; Jord., *Rom.* 384), apparently by his unnamed armour-bearer (Cont.).

545.3 Cont. has post-dated by a year the return of Belisarius to Italy, which took place in the summer of 544. It was when Justinian was apprised of the capture of Otranto and the beginning of the siege of Rome that he invited Belisarius to resume the command in Italy (Proc., *Wars* 7.9.23; Jord., *Rom.* 380). Belisarius had been summoned from the East in 542 as a result of suspicion and envy on the part of the empress Theodora, but was back in favour by 544. Bessas (*PLRE* 2: 226–9) was put in charge of the defence of Rome (7.11.37) and John, nephew of Vitalian, sent off to Justinian with a request for reinforcements (7.12.1–10).

545.4 The Roman garrison defending Auximum, the capital of Picenum, was reinforced by 1000 soldiers under three of Belisarius' bodyguards — Thurimuth, Ricilas and Sabinianus (Proc., *Wars* 7.11.19–20). However, the Romans decided it was preferable to abandon the city and fled by night towards Ariminum (Rimini), but were intercepted by the Goths and lost two hundred men in the attack (7.11.26–31). The Goths then advanced through Tuscany and pressured Spoletium into surrender (7.12.12–16), then they laid siege to Assisi, which surrendered too (7.12.12,18) but they were unsuccessful in their attempt on Perusia (7.12.18–20). Cont. is the only evidence for the capture of Clusium.

546.1 Pope Vigilius was not summoned by the emperor, as Cont. puts it, but was abducted by imperial agents while celebrating mass in Saint Cecilia's on 22 November 545. He was taken to Catania in Sicily, where he was involved in organising the supply of provisions for Rome (Proc., *Wars* 7.15.9). He had incurred the ire of Justinian by refusing to subscribe to the 'Three Chapters' edict. He later moved to CP (547) with the promise to support Justinian.

546.2 Cont. here introduces a general overview statement of the extent of Totila's Italian occupation. He had long since held Lucania and Bruttium and had won Naples in 543. Now, however, he laid siege to Rome in earnest in 545, although Cont. does not elaborate on the siege which continued through the year (Proc., *Wars* 7.13.1, 15.7,16.7).

546.3 Ariobindus (*PLRE* 3: 107–9) and his army arrived in Africa in 545 and had engaged Stotzas. Sergius failed to co-operate with Ariobindus and in autumn 545 (not 546) was summoned to CP, whereupon Ariobindus took over as commander (Proc., *Wars* 4.24.16 with Stein, 1949, 553, n. 1). Cont. gives the impression that Ariobindus only recently married Praejecta (Stein, 1949, 551, n. 1).

546.4 The general Constantianus (*PLRE* 3: 333–4), together with the rhetor Sergius (*PLRE* 3: 1124), was sent by Justinian to negotiate peace with the Persians in 543 but was unsuccessful. The following year they made contact with the Persian court at Seleucia–Ctesiphon and in spring 545 finalised the peace. Constantianus was successful in negotiating a five year truce (545–550) with Chosroes (Jord., *Rom.* 377; Proc., *Wars* 2.28.2–11). Cont. has placed the peace a year too late.

547.1 There is no corroborative evidence for this statement that the bishop of Assisi named Aventius was sent as an envoy to CP. It is therefore probably based on local knowledge.

547.2 This entry is apparently misplaced. John advanced to Italy with his army late in 545 (Proc., *Wars* 7.13.20–1 with Bury, 1923a, 235).

547.3 Belisarius had left Ravenna late in 545 for Dyrrachium, where he awaited the arrival early in 546 of John in order to mount a continued attack on Rome. John, however, considered it necessary first to occupy Italy before moving to Rome. Belisarius sailed to Portus (putting in at Otranto) and eventually reached Rome (Proc., *Wars* 7.13.19). John, meanwhile, occupied Calabria (7.18.6–7). These events do not belong in 547 and there is no other evidence for Cont.'s statement that Belisarius sailed by way of Sicily.

547.4 Pope Vigilius arrived in CP on 24 Jan 547 (Proc., *Wars* 7.16.1, cf. Jo. Mal., 18.97 [482]; Mar. Av., 547.1 [XI 236]) and was solemnly received by the emperor and accompanied to Hagia Sophia by a crowd singing psalms.

547.5 The Romans had been hard pressed by the Gothic siege although there were not many inhabitants left in the city to defend the extensive ramparts. Then Belisarius' attempt to relieve the city failed. The Goths actually entered Rome on 17 December 546, not 547. Again, here is a case where Cont. has placed the event in the correct indiction but in the wrong consulship, because the whole entry is linked to Belisarius' reoccupation of Rome in February 547. In the end the Isaurian guards were let down the walls at night and made contact with the Gothic army (Jord., *Rom.* 382). Totila did indeed have part of the walls knocked down (Proc., *Wars* 7.22.7; 24.3) but probably not as much as one-third of them (Hodgkin, 1889, 566), and he allowed his troops to plunder the city before they were restrained by a reluctance to despoil such a great capital (cf. Mar. Av., 547.2 [XI 236]). Several aristocrats who had resisted to the end were rounded up and interned somewhere in Campania. Rome then lay empty and desolate for the first time in its history and was reoccupied by Belisarius who moved in from Portus in the following February (Proc., *Wars* 7.24.8–26; Mar. Av., 547.3 [XI 236]) to the annoyance of Totila who was then obliged to move against the city once more (7.24.10–31). The occupation of Rome was reported at CP (Jo. Mal., 18.97 [483])

547.6 This entry provides a summary account of events in Africa leading up to the arrival there of John Troglita in the autumn of 546 (Stein, 1949, 555, n. 2). Praejecta (*PLRE* 3: 1048–9), to whom Ariobindus was married, was the niece (not the granddaughter) of Justinian, which is an odd mistake for a contemporary to make. Ariobindus had been killed by Guntharic (*PLRE* 3: 574–6) in March 546 during a banquet organised, as Cont. notes, by John Stotzas the Younger (Vict. Tonn., 546.2 [XI 201]). In May 546 Guntharic himself met his end at the hands of Artabanes (*PLRE* 3: 125–30), while John Stotzas (*PLRE* 3: 643–4) was captured and transported to CP where he was put to death (Jord., *Rom.* 354). Soon after, Artabanes was recalled and replaced by John Troglita (*PLRE* 3: 644–9) in 546. It is Praejecta's return to CP which anchors the event in 547.

548.1 While Belisarius was engaged in refortifying Rome John, nephew of Vitalian, was continuing in his strategy to take control of southern Italy. At one stage he evidently encountered the Goths guarding the Roman prisoners in Campania and managed to arrange the escape of some of the senators' wives, as confirmed by Procopius (*Wars* 7.26.1–13). It was apparently in Lucania that he was later set upon by Totila and his army (7.26.17–23), although Cont. is the only evidence for the treachery of the Bulgars. They were probably guarding John's camp at night and were enticed from their duty by the Goths.

548.2 Verus (*PLRE* 3: 1570–1) was sent as *magister militum* to Italy in 547 with three hundred Heruli to support Belisarius but was attacked by Totila and escaped in Campania, where he apparently worked in conjunction with John (Proc., *Wars* 7.26.6–9). Valerian (*PLRE* 3: 1355–61) was also sent by Justinian to bolster the effort in Italy (7.30.1–2).

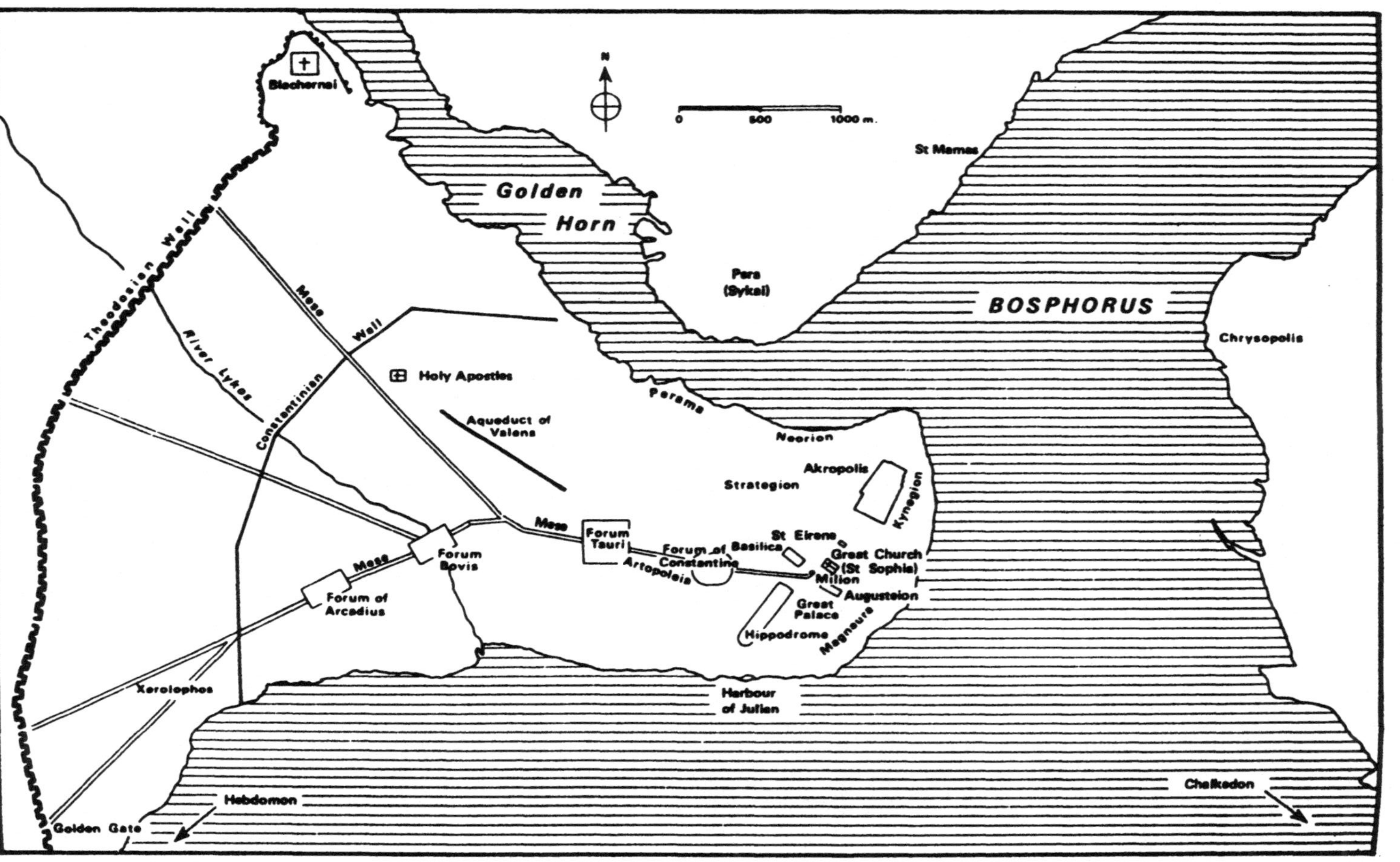

Sketch map of Constantinople in the sixth century

INDEX